CRIME, POLICY, AND CRIMINAL BEHAVIOR IN AMERICA

CRIME, POLICY, AND CRIMINAL BEHAVIOR IN AMERICA

James G. Houston

Criminology Studies
Volume 13

The Edwin Mellen Press
Lewiston•Queenston•Lampeter

Library of Congress Cataloging-in-Publication Data

Houston, James, 1943-
   Crime, policy, and criminal behavior in America / James G. Houston.
     p. cm. -- (Criminology studies ; v. 13)
   Includes bibliographical references and index.
   ISBN 0-7734-7661-X
   1. Criminal justice, Administration of--United States. 2. Crime--United States. I. Title.
II. Series.

HV9950 .H68 2000
364.973--dc21

00-058244

This is volume 13 in the continuing series
Criminology Studies
Volume 13 ISBN 0-7734-7661-X
CrS Series ISBN 0-7734-8583-X

A CIP catalog record for this book is available from the British Library.

Copyright © 2001 James G. Houston

All rights reserved. For information contact

The Edwin Mellen Press
Box 450
Lewiston, New York
USA 14092-0450

The Edwin Mellen Press
Box 67
Queenston, Ontario
CANADA L0S 1L0

The Edwin Mellen Press, Ltd.
Lampeter, Ceredigion, Wales
UNITED KINGDOM SA48 8LT

Printed in the United States of America

Dedicated to

Dr. Lloyd M. Braithwaite
teacher and friend

Table of Contents

List of Illustrations

Foreword

The spine of criminologist James Houston's timely and interesting book, "Crime, Policy, and Criminal Behavior in America" is found in his comment, "The criminal justice system is a loose confederation of independently funded, managed, and operated agencies that often have trouble talking to each other. The system is composed of law enforcement, courts, and corrections and each of these can be broken up into federal, state, and local units." In addition to these factors Houston deals cogently with the cost of crime and the causal context of "why they do it." In a clear, precise and effective literary style Houston takes the reader, both professional and average citizen, through this maze of American crime.

On the economics and the cost of crime, Houston delineates the fact that too many low-level criminals are incarcerated, and this mounts up to an enormous price tag for American society. About this issue, he comments, "The costs of crime are staggering, more precisely the costs of a continued policy of imprisoning every petty criminal, drug user, and loser who happens to make a bad decision is going to break the bank... In short, we all pay out of pocket because of the crime rate." Beyond the monetary element Houston appropriately refers to the significant social cost of fear in the general populace. The fear element affects business, the fear of citizens to leave their homes at night in certain cities of the country, and a generalized belief that we have somehow degenerated into a nation of barbarians."

Houston clarifies the complexity of America's criminal justice system, which mystifies most citizens who see individuals who appear innocent go to prison, and individuals like O.J. Simpson appear to beat the rap. He correctly points out that citizens are often confused and even angered by court decisions that seem to fly in the face of justice. He defends the court system by stating that "Many politicians and columnists have made political gain by reviling the courts and decisions that are meted out to convicted criminals. However, with few exceptions, the sentences handed down at the time of sentencing are sound and thoughtful and the sentencing judge has made every effort to take into consideration the needs of the community and the offender." He clarifies many issues involved in the judicial system by presenting in detail the process of the American judicial system from law enforcement to corrections.

Houston's analysis of the police role in the administration of justice is effectively presented. He refers to the police as, "the most visible component of the system and the one agency available twenty-four hours a day to respond to calls for help. To say that the job of the police officer is a difficult one is an understatement." Moreover, he analyzes how a major facet of police work is to prevent crime, and a fact, little noted by the public, is that an important job of the police officer is that of peacekeeping by maintaining law and order in our society. The important police role of responsibly investigating crimes is also analyzed in some detail.

James Houston is a recognized and a highly regarded expert on corrections, in part, based on his research, articles and books on prisons and corrections. A centerpiece of this book is Houston's comprehensive analysis of the correctional system and its role in controlling the overall crime problem. He points out that "the American corrections system is a varied and complex enterprise designed to handle the many responses to crime available to the courts. The corrections system is responsible for investigations, community programs, institutions, and post institutional programs. Corrections can be defined as the programs, facilities, and organizations responsible for the supervision, care, custody, and control of people who have been accused or convicted of a criminal offense. As a consequence, this includes jails, probation, prisons, minimum custody camps, boot camps, half way houses and restitution centers, and parole agencies." In his extensive analysis of all of these approaches, he goes into detail on the issue of whether corrections should be "humane confinement or rehabilitation." In many respects, he points out that the managers of the system have not yet determined the proper direction of the American corrections approach on this issue.

Jeffrey Dahmer, Ted Bundy, and John Wayne Gacey, America's premier serial murderer; the killings of students on high school campuses around the country; child murders including the Jon Benet Ramsey murder, and other complex homicides intrigue the public, and pose the difficult question about killers and other criminals, "Why do they do it?" Houston provides some provocative answers in this book in his analysis of the causal context of crime. In part, he answers the most controversial types of crimes as follows: "Even the most reasonable of us are sometimes unable to keep a lid on our emotions or despair. But we can explain a certain amount of crime and certain kinds of crime based upon scientific research." In this most informative book Houston cogently presents a brief discussion of the theories of crime causation developed by important criminologists in the field.

Anyone, and this includes every criminologist and average citizen, can benefit from reading this compelling analysis of the American crime problem. The reward that accrues to the reader from this important book is a clearer understanding of the American crime problem, and how it can be resolved to the benefit of our society.

Lewis Yablonsky, Ph.D.
Emeritus Professor of Criminology, California State University

Dr. Yablonsky is the author of 17 books including: GANGSTERS, CRIMINOLOGY and JUVENILE DELINQUENCY: INTO THE 21ST CENTURY

Preface

This book is the product of a good deal of encouragement and grew out of frustration with the amount of misinformation about crime put forward by political candidates over the last fifteen years. In addition, the media, in it's press to increase readership or viewership, is forced to focus on crime giving rise to a crisis mentality. The reality is that the crime "problem" is not as severe as we are led to believe, rather, selected areas of the nation have a severe problem. On a daily basis we are confronted with murder, robbery, and random violence that make it appear that we have lost control of our nation and our lives. Yet the majority of us manage to go to work, raise our family, and be involved in community activities without witnessing much in the way of crime. There is no question that crime is a major concern to the citizens of this nation, and there is no question that certain areas of certain cities are under siege. This book is an attempt to acquaint the reader with the facts and perhaps from that we can be more effective in our attempts to alleviate the problem.

This book is not aimed at professionals, although I hope they take the time to read it, rather it is aimed at the average citizen who is outraged, confused, and motivated to understand the dynamics of crime and the criminal justice system. I have attempted to put what we know about crime and criminal justice in an easily understandable format so the reader can begin to understand that the crime issue is so complex that we cannot spend our resources on panaceas such as building more prisons. Certainly we need prisons, but if we continue to put people into prisons that should be placed elsewhere, we will not have adequate bed space for the violent individual that must be locked up.

It is my hope that the average person who reads this book will gain a greater understanding of the dynamics of crime and criminal behavior. Out of this understanding, I hope the reader will then take time to pressure his or her elected representative to be truthful when speaking about crime and to start the search for effective measures to fight crime that are free of ideological considerations. The recent years are encouraging; crime is down, the economy is strong and anyone who wants a job, has one, and finally we as a people seem hopeful and have a positive view of our future. One thing is certain however, things will change and we must be prepared for the future, including a sensible approach to the issue of crime.

James Houston

Acknowledgments

Crime is multi-faceted and so intertwined with our economy, culture, and law that we cannot begin to understand the total picture until we have a basic understanding of several disciplines. Many people have an understanding of various parts of that picture and I did not hesitate to take advantage of their good nature and willingness to help. I cannot thank all the people who encouraged me and contributed in some way to this text. However, I can thank those who come immediately to mind and I apologize to anyone I have left out. The omission is entirely mine.

A special thanks to Rosemary Gido, Marty Shockey, Bob Weinberg, Ken Mullen, and John Norton for reading all, or portions, of the text and for offering their helpful suggestions. I tried to take their ideas into consideration and any faults are mine and not theirs. I also grateful to Andy Swift for his good humor, his counsel and ability to call my attention to faulty logic and for reading portions of the text as well. Lori Fletcher, my former research assistant at Appalachian State University was a great help in tracking down many details for which I have little patience. In addition, I want to thank Phil Yerington, Peter McGinty and David Kalinich for their encouragement and assistance.

J.H.

Chapter 1

Crime in America

Introduction

For some time we have witnessed the making of a tragedy in that the American public has become convinced that we are in the throes of a desperate fight against crime. The nightly news programs carry stories of murder, desperation, and violence that instills a fear of strangers and suspicion of our neighbors. At election time those seeking political office often feed those fears further and attempt to outdo each other in the rush to get tough on crime and criminals.

Facts about crime are ignored by many public officials as they seek election or re-election to public office. In addition, many public figures foster contempt for the criminal justice system by hyping nonexistent loopholes. Vitriolic attacks on the Constitution and the people who work in the system also breeds animosity and contempt for the people who place their lives on the line to preserve the safety of the community.

The truth is, we have witnessed a steady decline in criminal victimizations since 1973. However, we have witnessed in the last few years an increase in violent crime among youth and among many alienated, angry citizens in our over crowded cities. In addition, spectacular and heinous crimes such as the murders at Columbine High School have grabbed our attention and raised our fears. These types of crimes are quickly seized upon by the media and politicians as examples of life in America, much to our detriment. The result has been a deep suspicion of the criminal justice system and skepticism about the safety of life in America.

Our impression is that crime is rising and getting more violent every week. We are the world's greatest democracy and it seems as if we have lost control of our streets. We have poured billions of dollars into police, prisons, and the courts and we are told that only recently have we gained a handle on crime. However, those attempting to take credit for the recently recognized decline in crime is quite lengthy. For example, prosecutors point out that a tough stance on prosecutions is responsible for the decline in crime. Legislators point out that get tough legislation and more prisons are responsible and policing experts claim that the increased use of community policing is responsible for the decline in crime. However, perhaps the decline in crime can be attributed to the aging of the baby boom.

Whatever the reason for the decline in crime, we are forced to ask how much of what we hear from the media and those seeking elective office coincides with reality? The truth is, not much. There are two different ideologies in the United States on the issue of crime. One confesses to a conservative ideology and the other a liberal ideology. Samuel Walker (1994) asserts that both subscribe to a theology that is based upon certain canons of faith and facts do not alter that faith. Further, according to Walker, crime control programs of neither right or left have successfully confronted the problem of crime.

How much crime is there in the United States? What is the criminal justice system and how does it work? What are the true costs of crime? These are important questions to the average taxpayer and they deserve answers. This book attempts to answer those questions and to explain the workings of the criminal justice system.

Myths of Crime

It is difficult to believe that we aren't being over run by predators. From Atlanta we read that four men, ages 19, 24, 31, and 32 stole a jeep and while driving it on the Interstate, fired four shots at a motor home. The driver and his 12 year old son were seriously wounded. No explanation was given for the wounding of the man and his son.

In New York City, Queen Latifah, the popular and well known rap star, was accosted by two young men who stole her car and shot her male companion in the stomach for no reason. Ironically, Queen Latifah is well known for her denunciation of violence and the lyrics of her music condemning the acceptance and use of violence by youth.

A continent away in Los Angeles, violence has become so over-whelming that two emergency room surgeons developed a program that attempts to take some of the glamour out of violence. They give a presentation to ninth graders that includes slides of mutilated bodies that arrive in the emergency room. They hope that the impact of blood, mutilation, and bullet wounds cause them to think twice before condoning the use of violence or using violence themselves to settle a score.

Violence is also no stranger to those who live in the heartland. During August, 1993, a 17 year old Davenport, Iowa high school senior was murdered for the keys to her car. The perpetrators where members of a notorious Chicago street gang, the Vice Lords. What shocked the region, and the nation, is that those who carried out the crime were white boys. The recruiting efforts of the large super-gangs includes young people from all races and has led to a number of similarly tragic incidents. Violence also visits those who need the most protection. In Kansas City a young boy was dragged to his death by a car-jacker after he became entangled in his seatbelt. Fortunately the perpetrator was captured by two citizens who demonstrated remarkable self restraint and held him for police.

Part of the problem is that we live in a society dominated by information. Unfortunately, television is the major tool for the dissemination of information and it relies on short, snappy one-liners that are short on analysis. These one-liners are known as "sound bytes" and fit into the thirty minutes usually allowed for the evening news, less commercials. The print media is also guilty of giving a skewed image of what is happening in one's local area. Due to the need to grab readership, the rule of thumb is to lead with stories that appeal to human interest. The result is that the media is able to construct a sense of crisis, a belief that a problem is at hand and must be dealt with immediately. Soon, however, the issue plays out and the journalists all begin to look around for another "problem" to be dealt with.

Abadinsky and Winfree (1992) point out that science and journalism differ a great deal. Science demands that the subject be approached cautiously and the scientist is enjoined to follow certain procedures in order to be assured that cautious and restrained conclusions are reached. Journalists, on the other hand are not bound by the canons of scholarly research and the overriding concern of the journalist is to produce exciting copy that may or may not be the result of painstaking investigation. As a result, truth and fact are often trampled in the pursuit of getting a byline and to boost sales. The result has been that the media is responsible for forming much of what the general public knows about crime and the criminal justice system. The tendency of the media to feature "celebrity cases" causes us to view such occurrences as the norm, rather than aberrations in the total picture. In other words, myths are accepted as gospel in spite of the facts.

The construction of certain myths, according to Kappeler, Blumberg, and Potter, serve at least three purposes:

* Myths tend to organize our views of crime, criminals, and the proper operation of the criminal justice system. This framework helps us identify certain social issues as crime-related and help us form opinions that allow us to apply ready made solutions to complex problems.

* Myths support and maintain established views on crime. The reinforcement of established views of crime and what to do about it prevents us from defining the issues accurately, explore new solutions, or search for alternatives to existing socially constructed labels and crime control practices.

* Myths tend to provide the necessary information for the construction of a social reality of crime. Kappeler, Blumberg, and Potter point out that, "Myths of crime become a convenient mortar to fill gaps in knowledge and to provide answers to questions social science either cannot answer or has failed to address."

* Crime myths provide an outlet for emotionalism and channel emotions into action. They allow for interpretation of general social emotions and sentiment and direct those emotions to designated targets.

Fortunately most of us are not that intimately acquainted with crime. We go about our daily business, raise our families, attend church, synagogue or mosque and hold jobs without having to deal with the kind of problems the Los Angeles physicians are trying to treat. On the other hand, too many of our citizens cower in their homes each night because of crime and related gang activity in their building or neighborhood. What we must do is learn where the problems are, the true scope of the problem, insist on action by our elected officials, and become involved ourselves in efforts to do something about crime in the United States.

Moving Through the System

The criminal justice system is a loose confederation of independently funded, managed, and operated agencies that often have trouble talking to each other. The system is composed of law enforcement, courts, and corrections and each of these can be broken up into federal, state, and local units.

There are several factors that affect the structure of criminal justice including: federalism, that is the balance of power between state and federal government; separation of powers, with which the founding fathers meant to divide power among the three branches of government; and the concept of judicial review, which gives the judiciary the authority to determine the constitutionality of the other two branches of government. The result is that federal, state, and local criminal justice agencies are largely autonomous and any constitutional changes that affect this careful balance of power should be made only after careful consideration.

We begin with a brief description of the criminal justice system and then move on to important points in criminal justice, including how much crime there really is in the United States. The remainder of the chapters in this book discuss each component of the criminal justice system in some detail. Finally, the last chapter provides a framework that will enable the reader to be able to distinguish rhetoric from truth and some suggestions on how to work in the system for effective change are offered.

Television gives a false impression of the way the criminal justice system works. To begin, popular television crime fiction only needs sixty minutes, less commercials, to solve a case, bring the perpetrator to trial, and get him or her off to prison. In real life, it takes a great deal of time to build a case and prosecute it.

Law violators move through the criminal justice system in a less than orderly fashion. From television and the newspapers we gain the notion that the criminal justice system allows each and every citizen full access to the full menu of services such as we see on a **Perry Mason** episode. The O.J. Simpson trial is an excellent example of a celebrity case. The media put on full display the ideal operation of the criminal courts, however that image is far removed from reality for all but a small minority of American citizens.

Figure 1.1
Crime Commission's Model of the Criminal Justice System

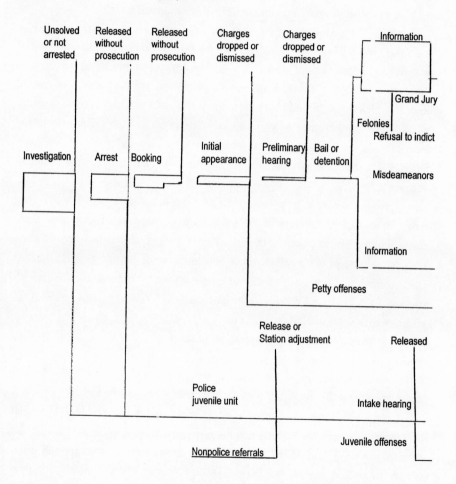

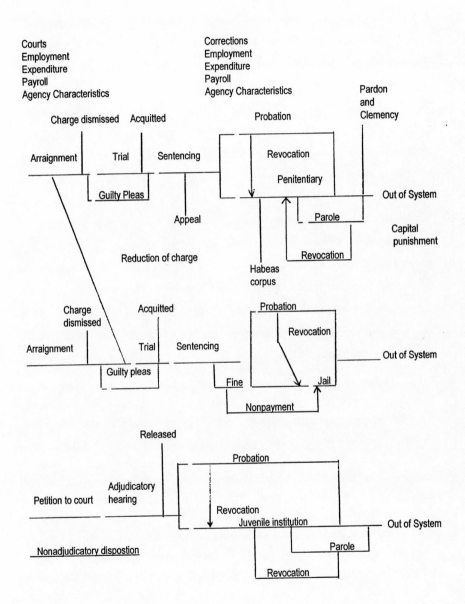

Worry about crime is nothing new. The 1960's were a turbulent time and President Lyndon B. Johnson wanted to do something about it. He appointed a special commission known as **The President's Crime Commission** in 1964. The Commission was made up of the most knowledgeable authorities of the time. Men and women representing colleges and universities, police departments, departments of correction, probation, law, and organized labor. They spent a great deal of time attempting to show how a suspected criminal moved through the system from arrest to final determination. To do that they devised an elegant and detailed model that depicted the criminal marching into the system at one end and marching out of the system reformed and ready to rejoin the community at the other. However, human beings are much more complex than that and today we think that model (Figure 1.1) is a little too naive. However, the people who devised that model were marinated in an attitude that caused them to believe that whatever they wished to happen, would happen. They had overcome the depression, won against the axis powers in WWII and put a man in space. They believed that a dollop of pressure in one place would result in something happening elsewhere.

The above diagram emphasizes criminal justice as a *system*. That is, what goes on in one part of the system affects the rest of the system. It's like hurting our foot. We limp around thinking the foot will get well and soon the knee begins to hurt. Soon after that our back begins to hurt and after that we begin to get a headache. All because we hurt our foot and ignored the injury. The criminal justice system is like that, and the above chart shows how the criminal moves through the system, ideally at least. If the system is overloaded at one point, the rest of the system soon feels the stress.

While the diagram above illustrates how we want the system to work, it works quite differently in reality. Professor Samuel Walker describes what he calls the "Wedding Cake Model" as developed by Lawrence Friedman and Robert V. Percival. Walker states that the Crime Commission Model portrays the criminal justice system as a single model and that this is misleading. In fact, there are fifty-one systems (fifty states and one federal system) and each of these is divided into several informal layers. They make up what Walker calls the **Wedding Cake Model** of criminal justice. In this model there are four layers made up of: the top layer which is composed of celebrated cases such as the O.J. Simpson case; the second layer is made up of serious felonies such as robbery assault and so on, in the third layer we find the less serious felonies such as burglary and the fourth layer is made up of misdemeanors.

The top layer-celebrity cases. These are the cases that usually make the papers and television. O.J. Simpson, Susan Smith, Jeffery Dahmer, John Hinkley, and Klaus Von Bulow. These cases are the drama that the media lives for. Into our living rooms come a steady parade of actors and the process assures us that the defendants constitutional rights are carefully guarded. We learn quite a bit about evidence, investigations, admissibility of evidence, witnesses, cross examination, redress, and so on. Somehow after seeing, or reading of the proceedings, we are reassured that we are safer and that the system somehow works.

The above cases, and others like them, are different from the majority of cases that come before the Court. They involve famous people, or terrible crimes, or critical constitutional issues. But, they are different in another way, they involve the full criminal court process and usually involve appeals. Secondly, celebrity cases receive a lot of publicity and as a consequence, heavily shape our perception of the legal process.

The Second and Third layers-Felonies. According to Walker, prosecutors routinely classify cases on the basis of three factors;
1. the seriousness of the crime.
2. the prior record of the suspect.
3. the relationship between the suspect and the offender.

In actuality the prosecutor must ask, "How much is this case worth?" They and the police classify cases into those that are "heavy" and "lightweight" by looking at such factors as seriousness of the offense, use of a weapon, prior record of the defendant, injuries incurred by the victim, and whether or not the defendant and victim were strangers.

Walker's analysis of second layer offenses brings him to the conclusion that the criminal justice system is very tough on crime, "Suspects are very likely to be prosecuted on the top charge, convicted, and given a relatively severe sentence (usually prison)." Once in prison, it is now difficult for the convict to be released early because parole has often been abolished or where there is the opportunity for parole, guidelines have been severely tightened.

According to Walker, the third layer in the Wedding Cake Model is entirely different from layers one and two. Less serious cases are routinely dismissed, offenders are allowed to plead guilty to less serious offenses, and if convicted, they are often placed on probation. More on this topic later, but to an extent this makes some sense if we are going to keep our prisons available for the more serious and violent offenders. These distinctions are not out of line with the rest of society. We all make them and a number of research efforts have indicated that citizens want the serious offender locked up but we are willing to allow a measure of leniency towards the less serious offender.

The Third Layer-Misdemeanors. Have you ever been in traffic court? Perhaps you have a friend or a son or daughter appeared in court on a charge of driving under the influence. If your offspring subjected you to this humiliation, you looked on as the Bailiff called the names of all the defendants, they marched up to the front of the court room to stand before the Judge. Soon all twenty or so defendants had made the trek and the Judge looked down upon them and advised them of their rights, told them what the charges were and advised them that he would ask each one individually if they pled guilty or innocent. If they pled innocent, they would have to see the clerk and a date for trial would be set. "Guilty," "guilty," "guilty," each defendant intones in turn. "I find you guilty of the charge of Driving under the Influence. I fine you $50.00 and place you on informal probation for six months, pay the clerk on your way out the door" states His Honor.
"Next."

So it is in the world of Traffic Court and misdemeanors. It may seem that lessons learned while watching Perry Mason are all wrong. Not really. According to Walker, the world of the courts that handle the misdemeanors is a "world unto itself." The caseload is staggering and court staff barely have time to handle the cases, let alone worry about the fine points of law. In addition, most defendants are interested in getting in and out with minimal trouble.

Index crimes, that is the crimes that the F.B.I consider the most serious: Criminal Homicide, Forcible Rape, Robbery, Aggravated Assault, Burglary, Larceny/Theft, Motor Vehicle Theft, and Arson make up only about 20 per cent of all offenses. In 1998, according to the F.B.I., there were 14.5 million arrests, out of which nearly 2.4 million were for the serious crimes just mentioned. The remainder, (12,5051,900) were for what are called Part II Crimes, that is "less serious" crimes; that means the misdemeanor courts handled a large number of the 12 million suspects. Regardless of whether or not the case went to trial, the individual had to be arraigned and the prosecutor and his or her staff needed to determine whether or not sufficient evidence was available for prosecution.

The volume of crimes coming before the misdemeanor courts demands that no one get too excited about due process and at least one study showed that most defendants did not have a jury trial and at least half did not have an attorney (Feeley, 1979). One feels that most defendants are just glad to get the process over with. That is just the point according to Feeley, the process is the punishment. This brings us to:

> *Proposition #1: The courts are doing an excellent job with the tools they presently have. We must devote adequate resources for them to effectively prosecute offenders.*

Figure 1.2

Types of Crimes

Part I Crimes

Murder and nonnegligent manslaughter
Robbery
Burglary
Motor Vehicle Theft

Forcible Rape
Aggravated Assault
Larceny-Theft
Arson

Part II Crimes

Forgery and Counterfeiting
Fraud
Embezzlement
Stolen property: Buying, Receiving, Possessing
Vandalism
Weapons: Carrying, Possessing, etc.
Prostitution and Commercialized Vice
Sex offenses (except rape and prostitution)
Drug Abuse Violations

Gambling
Offenses Against Family and Children
Driving Under the Influence
Liquor Laws
Drunkeness
Disorderly Conduct
Vagrancy
All Other Offenses Except Traffic
Curfew and Loitering
Runaways

Discretion and the Law

The field of criminal justice is probably the most discretionary field of work to be found. Discretion, that is the ability of the individual police officer, probation officer, judge, prosecutor, and so on have wide latitude to determine what they will enforce and who they will enforce the law upon, is a big part of the job. It is difficult to change this without affecting the ability of the individual to effectively perform their job. For example, the police officer on patrol may have the choice between confronting a street walker and patrolling an area where there have been a number of violent incidents. True, the two often go together, but the point is that the officer has a choice.

Probation officers also make choices. In these times of heavy drug usage, they can, and often do, violate a probationer for a first time positive urine sample for use of a drug when no other "crime" has been committed. However, the probation officer, may believe that arresting and placing the probationer in jail pending a revocation hearing will do no good in light of the fact that he may lose his job, thereby making it necessary for the family to apply for whatever relief is available. He or she may then apply another sanction, such as being placed on intensive probation and "suggesting" that he or she volunteer for a few hours of service at a homeless shelter.

Counselors in work release centers also can make choices. For example, several years ago an inmate in a mid-western work release center had served four and one half years for second degree burglary. Prior to his mandatory release he was transferred to the work release center in order to find employment, accrue a savings account, and begin to aid in the support of his wife and two children who were on welfare while he was in prison. He was doing well and had advanced to the level where he could have a week-end pass to stay with his family. With only nine weeks to go before discharge, he had a fight with his wife while on pass. He failed to return on time and was AWOL for nearly ten hours. Legally the staff of the work release center could have revoked his status, along with earned good time, and returned him to prison for nearly six months. They didn't return him to prison because they believed that the community, and the man's family, would not be well served. Instead, he was allowed to continue to work, but all privileges were revoked and he was required to attend family counseling with his wife. He has since then been fully employed, remained married, and stable.

There is a natural tension between the law and the discretion of law enforcement authorities to act upon the law. On the one hand, the law is very specific, on the other hand, the task of enforcing the law is quite subjective. Therefore, we need to keep in mind certain "facts" of criminal justice:

1. The law does not enforce itself.

2. It is impossible for law enforcement officials to refer to a book of rules which they mechanically apply to a particular situation.

3. The processes of criminal justice requires that cooperation, resolution of differences, and negotiation take precedence over confrontation.

4. There is a mixture of formal proceedings and discretionary proceedings in criminal justice.

5. Personal opinion does not enter into the job of law enforcement or corrections. The law commands and we must obey.

6. There are several reasons for discretion:
   a. not enough resources.
   b. too many laws.
   c. vague laws.

7. Selective law enforcement forces officials to choose among alternatives.

Crime: An Epidemic or Just Newsworthy

Worry about crime is nothing new. The ancient Romans felt that criminals were about to take over. Historically we see a pendulum like swing from fear of government to fear of crime. For example, Rome went from one extreme to another. In England there was a swing from great royal authority to lawlessness and back again.

From 1066 to about 1200 A.D. English Kings enjoyed great power, but in 1215 the Magna Carta was signed. That document returned some power to the nobles and there followed a period of lawlessness for about two centuries. Then Henry the VII and his son Henry VIII tightened things up and there was a period of obedience to law. The process has been repeated over and over since then.

In America things have been no different. Colonial America was based on a farming economy and we remained that way until around the Civil War. However, industrialization and immigration fundamentally changed the face of the United States as it moved from a farming economy to a manufacturing economy. The census of 1920 showed for the first time that more people lived in the city than lived on the farm

From the 1920's through the 1950's there was a relatively tough stance on crime. The due process revolution of the 1960's, led by the Supreme Court, saw a great many decisions that expanded individual rights, not because the Court was necessarily interested in forcing change in policy, but perhaps because the states had abdicated their responsibility to its citizens. The police for example relied on confessions as the major tool to solve crimes, the Bill of Rights was trampled in searches and police stops and state courts did nothing.

Many see the 1960s as a time when the stance on crime became somewhat lenient. However, the late 1960's and early 1970's was a period of social upheaval. A great many social changes came about, in part from the change in our cities, the civil rights movement, the war in Vietnam, the sexual revolution, the "discovery" of drugs as a recreational outlet, and of course the baby boom coming of age resulting in an overwhelming number of people demanding jobs and services.

The baby boom was responsible for an increase in crime simply because there are more of them than any other single age group and it was the baby boom that demonstrated and went to jail for crimes of civil disorder in the late 1960's and early 1970's. It was then that the term **Law and Order** began to creep into our everyday language. However, crime comes in many forms. Many people, usually to the left of the political spectrum, point out that white collar crime is the most costly and reprehensible of crimes for it preys on unsuspecting victims while the perpetrators continue their lives as pillars of the community. On the other hand, many of those to the right of the political spectrum, point out that street crime is the most serious because of it's social and financial cost, to say nothing of the fear and suspicion that is engendered. Actually, both sides have a point and there is no need to argue the finer points, although unarguably it is street crime that is the main concern to most citizens.

James Q. Wilson (1985), a respected criminologist and political scientist, points out that "Predatory crime does not merely victimize individuals, it impedes and, in the extreme case, prevents the formation and maintenance of community."

That we are concerned about predatory crime is natural, for as Wilson says, it "prevents the formation and maintenance of community." How many neighborhoods do we read about in the papers and see on nightly television news that appear to be having a difficult time maintaining a sense of community? We all mourn the destruction of the mechanisms of social control and the turmoil many normal people have in simply going about their daily business.

The truth is, even during a period of affluence such as the late 1990s, there are many areas in our inner cities where social control has broken down. There are places in our nation where despair, hopelessness and chronic poverty are the norm and where young people have no positive role models to emulate. In spite of an unemployment rate hovering around 3% - 4% in 2000, there are still pockets of unemployment where there are few possibilities on the horizon for many individuals. That crime flourishes in these areas is not surprising for that has always been the case. People who commit crimes, regardless of their circumstances should pay the price, but we must keep in mind that many people simply have not had the opportunity to learn law abiding behavior. This is discussed at more length later.

On the other hand, we as a nation have not sunken into chaos and disorder, but stories in the media have had their effect and sometimes the fear that is engendered has tragic consequences. For example, not long ago a man mistakenly shot a young exchange student who came to the wrong address seeking a Halloween party and in another instance, the father of a young girl shot a small daughter hiding in a closet playing a prank. Both are instances of people being fearful of crime and who reacted without much thought. Contrary to the professional doomsayers, the media, and many politicians, we are not in the midst of a crime wave that threatens to undermine the foundations of our civilization.

How Crime Statistics Are Collected

We cannot really determine how much crime exists in our society. However, from a high of 14,872,900 offenses known to the police in 1991 we have seen a drop in crime to 12,975,634 known offenses in 1998. This amounts to a substantial drop in crime by any measure. Still our prisons are over crowded and we still justify the terrible expense of sending so many lawbreakers to prison. Unfortunately, in the process of talking about crime and it's prevalence over the past several years, we have successfully convinced ourselves that the United

States is an unsafe place in which to live. In the process we have marketed ourselves abroad as a nation of barbarians.

If we are to regain a sense of balance and faith in ourselves as a people, we need to gain an understanding of crime statistics in order not to be swayed by "lies, half lies, and damn lies." To begin we need to recognize that crime statistics are notoriously unreliable. For example, how many of us have had the wheels stolen from our car and we did not report it to the police? In many instances the same is true for rape, many burglaries, and so on. In general, the crime of murder and car theft are just about the most accurate statistics.

Crime statistics are gathered in three ways. The first is the Federal Bureau of Investigation's **Uniform Crime Report**. This report is the compilation of statistics from nearly all police agencies in the United States and represents about 98% of the U.S. population. The second set of data is the **National Crime Victimization Survey** and is gathered by the Bureau of Census. It reports only victimizations, many of which are not reported to the police, in contrast to the **Uniform Crime Report** which is reported crime. The third way is through self report studies, usually by college professors for one reason or another.

Abadinsky and Winfree report that all three ways of gathering statistics have problems. The **Uniform Crime Report (UCR)** collects only reported crime. That is, crimes unknown to the police are not entered into the total. The **UCR** is also subject to political manipulation. For example, if a Mayor is running for reelection, he or she may not allow the Chief of Police to enter some of the known crimes for fear it may affect his or her chance for reelection. There are also some problems with recording practices. Let us say a man has been beaten, robbed and his car stolen. The *Hierarchy Rule* requires that the offenses be classified and the most serious be recorded and the rest ignored. This rule applies to all offenses except arson. Still there are strengths: the data are easily accessible, we have nationwide data that covers approximately 98% of the population, and we can compare statistics over time because the statistics have been collected since 1930.

The National Crime Victimization Survey (NCVS) began in 1973 under the auspices of the Law Enforcement Assistance Administration. The survey is now conducted by the Bureau of Census and collects limited information from 59,000 households across the nation. These households are constantly replaced after being surveyed every six months for three years. According to Abadinsky and Winfree (1992), "In a normal year Census Bureau workers conduct two interviews each with 100,000 people aged 12 and older." There are some strengths associated with the **NCVS** and it allows for comparisons with the **UCR**. The **NCVS** is not subject to political manipulation, and because of the questions and approach we can examine the psycho-social effects of victimization of crime and a lot of information about a limited number of crimes. There are also weaknesses, for example the survey only questions persons aged 12 years and older, crime against tourists and the homeless are not considered, and it is costly.

Self report studies are the third way of gathering crime statistics. Usually they are in the form of anonymous surveys and confidential interviews. The shortcomings include the fact that respondents may tend to minimize criminal involvement and self-report studies have been applied to a limited population. Nevertheless, self-report studies do give criminologists a look at crime in a specific group and allows them to draw some conclusions.

In the world of journalism, self report studies seldom are mentioned. Usually the **Uniform Crime Report** is most often cited as the authoritative source of crime statistics. However, the public is given a limited amount of information about crime because only the **UCR** is cited. On the other hand, data from the **NCVS** is used if the reporter or other person has a vested interest in illustrating how effective a particular program is.

The Extent of Crime

As pointed out earlier, the FBI Crime Index is made up of eight crimes and the FBI collects data on crimes known to the police. According to Professor Don C. Gibbons (1987), a noted criminologist, these crimes are selected because they are most likely to be reported to the police when they occur. Table 1.1 shows the year, number of crimes, and the total population of the U.S. since 1979. A glance at this table shows that reported crime has increased from 12,249,500 in 1979 to 14,872,900 reported crimes in 1991, an increase of 2,623,400 reported crimes over twelve years. There then began a drop in crime to its level of 12,475,600, a drop of more than 2 million known crimes. During that period the U.S. population increased by 50 million people.

The UCR illustrates the crime rate as X crimes per 100,000 persons in order for it to be more easily understood, whether we are talking about a rural area or an urban area. In that way we can more easily grasp very large numbers. Table

18

Table 1.1 – Crime in the U.S.

Index of Crime, United States, 1979-1998

Population	Crime Index Total	Violent Crime	Property Crime	Murder and non-negligent man-slaughter	Forcible Rape	Robbery	Aggravated Assault	Burglary	Larceny/Theft	Motor Vehicle Theft
				Number of Offenses						
Population by year:										
1979-220,099,000	12,249,500	1,208,030	11,041,500	21,460	76,390	480,700	629,480	3,327,700	6,601,000	1,112,800
1980-225,349,264	13,408,300	1,344,520	12,063,700	23,040	82,990	565,840	672,650	3,795,200	7,136,900	1,131,700
1981-229,146,000	13,423,800	1,361,820	12,061,900	22,520	82,500	592,910	663,900	3,779,700	7,194,400	1,087,800
1982-231,534,000	12,974,400	1,322,390	11,652,000	21,010	78,770	553,130	669,480	3,447,100	7,142,500	1,062,400
1983-233,981,000	12,108,600	1,258,090	10,850,500	19,310	78,920	506,570	653,290	3,129,900	6,712,800	1,007,900
1984-236,158,000	11,881,800	1,273,280	10,608,500	18,690	84,230	485,010	685,350	2,984,400	6,591,900	1,032,200
1985-238,740,000	12,431,400	1,328,770	11,102,600	18,980	88,670	497,870	723,250	3,073,300	6,926,400	1,102,900
1986-241,077,000	13,211,900	1,489,170	11,722,700	20,610	91,460	542,780	834,320	3,241,400	7,257,200	1,224,100
1987-243,400,000	13,508,700	1,484,000	12,024,700	20,100	91,100	517,700	855,090	3,236,200	7,499,900	1,288,700
1988-245,807,000	13,923,100	1,566,220	12,356,900	20,680	92,490	542,970	910,090	3,218,100	7,705,900	1,432,900
1989-248,239,000	14,251,400	1,646,040	12,605,400	21,500	94,500	578,330	951,710	3,168,200	7,872,400	1,564,800
1990-248,709,873	14,475,600	1,820,130	12,655,500	23,440	102,560	639,270	1,054,860	3,073,900	7,945,700	1,635,900
1991-252,177,000	14,872,900	1,911,770	12,961,100	24,700	106,590	687,730	1,092,740	3,157,200	8,142,200	1,661,700
1992-255,082,000	14,438,200	1,932,270	12,505,900	23,760	109,060	672,480	1,126,870	2,979,900	7,915,200	1,610,800
1993-257,908,000	14,144,800	1,926,020	12,218,800	24,530	106,010	659,870	1,135,610	2,834,800	7,820,900	1,563,100
1994-260,341,000	13,989,500	1,857,670	12,131,900	23,330	102,220	618,950	1,113,180	2,712,800	7,879,800	1,539,300
1995-262,755,000	13,862,700	1,798,790	12,063,900	21,610	97,470	580,510	1,099,210	2,593,800	7,997,700	1,472,400
1996-265,284,000	13,493,900	1,688,540	11,805,300	19,650	96,250	535,590	1,037,050	2,506,400	7,904,700	1,394,200
1997-267,637,000	13,194,600	1,636,100	11,558,500	18,210	96,150	498,530	1,023,200	2,460,500	7,743,800	1,354,200
1998-270,396,000	12,475,600	1,531,040	10,944,600	16,910	93,100	446,630	974,400	2,330,00	7,373,900	1,240,800
Percent change, number of offenses:										
1998/1997	-5.4	-6.4	-5.3	-7.1	-3.2	-10.4	-4.8	-5.3	-4.8	-8.4
1998/1994	-10.8	-17.6	-9.8	-27.5	-8.9	-27.8	-12.5	-14.1	-6.4	-19.4
1998/1989	-12.5	-7.0	-13.2	-21.3	-1.5	-22.8	+2.4	-26.5	-6.3	-20.7

Table 1.1 – Crime in the U.S. (Continued)

Index of Crime, United States, 1979-1998

Rate per 100,000 Inhabitants

Year	Crime Index Total	Violent Crime	Property Crime	Murder and non-negligent man-slaughter	Forcible Rape	Robbery	Aggra-vated Assault	Burglary	Larceny/ Theft	Motor Vehicle Theft
1979	5,565.5	548.9	5,016.6	9.7	34.7	218.4	286.0	1,511.9	2,999.1	505.6
1980	5,950.0	596.6	5,353.3	10.2	36.8	251.1	298.5	1,684.1	3,167.0	502.2
1981	5,858.2	594.3	5,263.9	9.8	36.0	258.7	289.7	1,649.5	3,139.7	474.7
1982	5,603.6	571.1	5,032.5	9.1	34.0	238.9	289.2	1,488.8	3,084.8	458.8
1983	5,175.0	537.7	4,637.4	8.3	33.7	216.5	279.2	1,337.7	2,868.9	430.8
1984	5,031.3	539.2	4,492.1	7.9	35.7	205.4	290.2	1,263.7	2,791.3	437.1
1985	5,207.1	556.6	4,650.5	8.0	37.1	208.5	302.9	1,287.3	2,901.2	462.0
1986	5,480.4	617.7	4,862.6	8.6	37.9	225.1	346.1	1,344.6	3,010.3	507.8
1987	5,550.0	609.7	4,940.3	8.3	37.4	212.7	351.3	1,329.6	3,081.3	529.4
1988	5,664.2	637.2	5,027.1	8.4	37.6	220.9	370.2	1,309.2	3,134.9	582.9
1989	5,741.0	663.1	5,077.9	8.7	38.1	233.0	383.4	1,276.3	3,171.3	630.4
1990	5,820.3	731.8	5,088.5	9.4	41.2	257.0	424.1	1,235.9	3,194.8	657.8
1991	5,897.8	758.1	5,139.7	9.8	42.3	272.7	433.3	1,252.0	3,228.8	659.0
1992	5,660.2	757.5	4,902.7	9.3	42.8	263.6	441.8	1,168.2	3,103.0	631.5
1993	5,484.4	746.8	4,737.6	9.5	41.1	255.9	440.3	1,099.2	3,032.4	606.1
1994	5,373.5	713.6	4,660.0	9.0	39.3	237.7	427.6	1,042.0	3,026.7	591.3
1995	5,275.9	684.6	4,591.3	8.2	37.1	220.9	418.3	987.2	3,043.8	560.4
1996	5,086.6	636.5	4,450.1	7.4	36.3	201.9	390.9	944.8	2,979.7	525.6
1997	4,930.0	611.3	4,318.7	6.8	35.9	186.3	382.3	919.4	2,893.4	506.0
1998	4,615.5	566.4	4,049.1	6.3	34.4	165.2	360.5	862.0	2,728.1	459.0
Percent change, number of offenses:										
1998/1997	-6.4	-7.3	-6.2	-7.4	-4.2	-11.2	-5.7	-6.2	-5.7	-9.3
1998/1994	-14.1	-20.6	-13.1	-30.0	-12.5	-30.5	-15.7	-17.3	-9.9	-22.4
1998/1989	-19.6	-14.6	-20.3	-27.6	-9.7	-29.1	-6.0	-32.5	-14.0	-27.2

Source: U.S.Department of Justice. Federal Bureau of Investigation. *Crime in the United States, 1998* Uniform Crime Reports, Washington,DC

Table 1.2 – Total Arrest Trends

Offense Charged	Males Total 1990	Males Total 1999	Males Total Percent change	Males Under 18 1990	Males Under 18 1999	Males Under 18 Percent change	Females Total 1990	Females Total 1999	Females Total Percent change	Females Under 18 1990	Females Under 18 1999	Females Under 18 Percent change
Total[1]	6,092,905	5,788,285	-5.0	897,082	939,176	+4.7	1,382,203	1,629,304	+17.9	269,578	355,337	+31.8
Murder and non-negligent manslaughter	9,741	5,880	-39.6	1,397	616	-55.9	1,129	719	-36.3	81	49	-39.5
Forcible Rape	19,774	14,535	-26.5	2,814	2,450	-12.9	214	169	-21.0	57	48	-15.8
Robbery	72,993	53,465	-26.8	16,580	13,784	-16.9	6,770	6,123	-9.6	1,515	1,354	-10.7
Aggravated assault	229,471	208,264	-9.2	29,667	28,147	-5.1	33,839	50,312	+48.7	5,068	7,948	+56.8
Burglary	215,967	137,505	-36.3	72,290	47,618	-34.1	22,979	21,246	-7.5	6,778	6,229	-8.1
Larceny-theft	575,614	425,314	-26.1	178,745	135,989	-23.9	273,421	234,755	-14.1	71,384	75,632	+6.0
Motor vehicle theft	102,851	60,118	-41.5	43,600	20,908	-52.0	11,851	11,176	-5.7	5,593	4,234	-24.3
Arson	8,938	7,603	-14.9	4,070	4,341	+6.7	1,267	1,224	-3.4	406	555	+36.7
Violent Crime[2]	331,979	282,144	-15.0	50,458	44,997	-10.8	41,952	57,323	+36.6	6,722	9,399	+39.8
Property Crime[3]	903,370	630,540	-30.2	298,705	208,856	-30.1	309,518	268,401	-13.3	84,161	86,650	+3.0
Crime Index Total[4]	1,235,349	912,684	-26.1	349,163	253,853	-27.3	351,470	351,724	-7.3	90,883	96,049	+5.7

[1] Does not include suspicion
[2] Violent crimes are offenses of murder, forcible rape, robbery, and aggravated assault
[3] Property crimes are offenses of burglary, larceny-theft, motor vehicle theft, and arson
[4] Includes arson
[5] Except forcible rape and prostitution

Table 1.2 – Total Arrest Trends (Continued)

Offense Charged	Males Total 1990	Males Total 1999	Males Total Percent change	Males Under 18 1990	Males Under 18 1999	Males Under 18 Percent change	Females Total 1990	Females Total 1999	Females Total Percent change	Females Under 18 1990	Females Under 18 1999	Females Under 18 Percent change
Other assaults	457,158	517,385	+13.2	61,770	83,116	+34.6	89,614	153,361	+71.1	18,994	36,576	+92.6
Forgery & counterfeiting	32,473	34,994	+7.8	2,683	2,401	-10.5	17,930	21,819	+21.7	1,401	1,410	+0.6
Fraud	98,579	90,558	-8.1	2,993	3,298	+10.2	84,173	75,855	-9.9	1,524	1,685	+10.6
Embezzlement	4,450	4,911	+10.4	353	478	+35.4	3,258	4,781	+46.7	210	440	+109.5
Stolen property; buying, receiving, possessing	78,345	52,472	-33.0	22,266	13,467	-39.5	10,764	9,698	-9.9	2,413	2,012	-16.6
Vandalism	154,711	127,384	-17.7	64,701	56,400	-12.8	18,740	22,569	+20.4	5,982	7,681	+28.4
Weapons: carrying, Possessing, etc.	107,563	80,497	-25.2	20,850	19,356	-7.2	8,409	6,830	-18.8	1,343	1,935	+44.1
Prostitution & comm. Vice	23,158	19,655	-15.1	427	309	-27.6	36,146	239,921	-17.2	482	376	-22.0
Sex offenses[5]	54,862	47,307	-13.8	8,367	8,210	-1.9	4,492	3,521	-21.6	494	653	+32.2
Drug abuse violations	488,454	660,104	+35.1	38,005	85,226	+124.2	101,490	144,920	+42.8	5,208	15,126	+190.4
Gambling	7,537	4,069	-46.0	383	397	+3.7	1,176	650	-44.7	28	25	-10.7
Offenses against the family & children	40,193	59,130	+47.1	1,287	2,992	+132.5	7,504	16,770	+123.5	637	1,687	+164.8
Driving under the influence	893,756	629,889	-29.5	9,478	9,158	-3.4	127,997	119,565	-6.6	1,553	1,866	+20.2
Liquor laws	286,026	277,294	-3.1	58,613	60,692	+3.5	64,082	78,467	+22.4	22,021	27,304	+24.0
Drunkenness	500,375	330,902	-33.9	12,692	9,628	-24.1	54,492	47,332	-13.1	2,252	2265	+0.6
Disorderly conduct	290,239	242,822	-16.3	47,475	62,755	+32.2	67,907	75,124	+10.6	12,267	24,673	+101.1
Vagrancy	21,426	13,520	-36.9	1,949	1,053	-46.0	3,600	3,336	-7.3	367	247	-32.7
All other offenses (except traffic	1,244,366	1,580,872	+27.0	119,742	164,551	+37.4	261,843	410,738	+56.9	34,403	55,004	+59.9
Suspicion	9,150	3,144	-65.6	2,175	794	-63.5	1,592	856	-46.2	515	230	-55.3
Curfew & loitering law violations	33,890	68,927	+103.4	33,890	68,927	+103.4	12,729	30,456	+139.3	12,729	30,456	+139.3
Runaways	39,995	32,909	-17.7	39,995	32,909	-17.7	54,387	47,867	-12.0	54,387	47,867	-12.0

Source: U.S.Department of Justice. Federal Bureau of Investigation. *Crime in the United States, 1998* Uniform Crime Reports, Washington,DC

1.1 illustrates that from 1991 to 1994 (the period in which many politicians were denouncing the very large numbers of crime) the rate dipped for both violent and property crime. From 1994 to 1998 the violent crime rate dipped another 8 percent and it continues to drop. Clearly, there is a trend here, but we should put any rejoicing on hold as criminologists need time to study the data for another five years or so before drawing any solid conclusions about what the data mean.

Clearly, we have seen a drop in known offenses since 1994. The early 1980s witnessed a drop in murder and non-negligent manslaughter, but there began a rise in 1985 that continued until 1994. The murder and non-negligent manslaughter rate increased 22.7%, during that time forcible rape decreased 3.5%, robbery went up 23.3%, and so on. However, since 1994 crime has dropped again and we are compelled to ask who is committing these crimes (or better yet, who stopped doing the crime?), where are the crimes being committed, why the recent drop in crime? We know that no area of the nation is safe from crime, but a closer look is somewhat revealing. Again looking at the **UCR** statistics we see that the under 18 age group is responsible for the largest increase in crime. Between 1989 and 1998 crime by those under 18 increased by 23.9% compared to only 3.8% for those over eighteen years of age. It appears that aggravated assault has risen dramatically in the past decade while murder and nonneglegent manslaughter has dropped 21.3 percent.

The question of race invariably comes up whenever the topic of crime is discussed. Perhaps no issue has so divided our black citizens from white citizens than the issue of crime. We cannot deny that African-Americans comprise a disproportionate share of arrests and of our prison population. Why? This text is not the place to discuss a topic that would take a great deal more time and space than available here. What we can say with a good deal of certainty is that African-Americans, in terms of percentage of the population, make up a disproportionate share of the poor, urban population. With ever increasing numbers of minorities being caught in the clutches of generational poverty has also come a diminution of thoughts of ever achieving a piece of the *American Dream.*

Another point is also necessary however, poverty does not automatically cause criminality. Just because one is poor does not mean that he or she will engage in criminal behavior, but what is certain is that poverty establishes the conditions that breed crime. For example, we can assume that even the poorest of our citizens have a television set. Through that one medium alone, one is constantly bombarded with the message that material possessions determine one's innate worth. One is constantly exposed to the *American Dream* without admonitions to play by the rules. Just the opposite, one is encouraged to succeed at any cost.Stir into this into the broth of discontent irresponsible or nonexistent parents, a glorification of violence, a plentiful supply of guns and drugs for use or sale and we have a stew that has begun to cause a national heartburn.

The **UCR** indicates that if one is young, male, and African-American there is a much better chance of being arrested for a crime. In 1998 53.4% of all arrests for murder and nonnegligent manslaughter were of African-Americans, 37.4% for rape, 55.3% for robbery, and so on in a dismal litany that tells us that something is wrong. There is hope as these figures are all down 4-6%. Clearly, *the American Dream* is quickly becoming more a piece of fiction meant to pacify our young, African-American males than an attainable goal.

The question next arises, where do most of these arrests occur? A look at The arrests by state shows that 18 states account for 73.8 percent of all arrests. Most of these states are characterized by large urban areas with California, Texas, North Carolina, and New Jersey leading the list. Arrests in North Carolina, Wisconsin, Alabama, and South Carolina are not easily explained by the presence of large metropolitan centers. Clearly other factors must be at work. Table 1.4 illustrates arrests by state.

We are also interested in how much crime is committed in urban areas verses rural areas. Again the **UCR** illustrates the dimensions of the problem. Tables 1.4 and 1.5 shows the disparity in the rural/urban dichotomy as well as the crime rate per 100,000 population for the 50 states and the District of Columbia. Fifteen states account for 71.2% of urban crime.

Table 1.3
Percent Arrests by Race 1988, 1994 and 1998

	White			Black		
	1988	1994	1998	1988	1994	1998
Murder and nonneglegent Manslaughter	41.2	38.5	44.4	57.1	59.4	53.4
Forcible Rape	48.8	55.2	60.1	50.0	42.6	37.4
Robbery	33.5	36.5	42.9	64.9	61.5	55.3
Aggravated Assault	53.0	55.2	61.5	45.4	42.6	36.2
Burglary	74.0	73.5	68.3	23.6	24.0	29.4
Larceny/Theft	71.4	69.7	65.2	25.7	27.0	31.8
Motor Vehicle Theft	58.6	56.2	57.9	39.0	40.8	39.2
Arson	82.0	79.9	73.7	16.1	18.0	24.2

Source: U.S. Department of Justice. Federal Bureau of Investigation. **Crime in the United States**, 1988, 1994 and 1998: Uniform Crime Reports. Washington, D.C.

Not all of the states rated in the top 17 crime producing states appear in the urban crime statistics, Massachusetts and Louisiana appear in the top urban crime list and rural California appears to be a lot safer than rural Ohio. On the other hand, rural New York is a lot safer than rural Texas. When we compare the urban crime numbers with rural crime numbers we get a sense that most of us a are lot safer in our homes and communities than we commonly think. Some care should also be taken in reading statistics in table 1.5. The **UCR** notes that many states such as California, Maine, Arkansas, and New York actually report 100% of rural crime. However, others such as Indiana, Mississippi (only 25% in 1984 and 32.7% in 1998), Missouri, New Mexico, and South Dakota report less than 60% of areas in the state. Consequently, the **UCR** makes an estimate of how much rural (or urban) crime occurred based upon the area reported. Thus, in the states noted above, the rural crime rate is often twice as large are reported in table 1.5. This is a clear example of one weakness of the **UCR** and how incorrect statistics can provide a false picture.

Still, one lesson we can learn from tables 1.4 and 1.5 is that the "Crime wave" is not as severe as we are told by politicians and led to believe on the part of the media. If we eliminate the states of California, Texas, Florida and New York, the"crime wave" dissipates somewhat, at least in sheer volume. Certainly a crime index of 3,500.6 (1998) in a rural state such as Iowa is much too high, if we disregard violence between associates and other crimes of passion that have plagued the human race since Cain killed Able, the issue of crime begins to be more easily grasped and is not so frightening. Which leads me to point out that the probability of victimization is far less than what we perceive. The following discussion of the **National Crime Victimization Survey** sheds more light on that probability.

The **NCVS** was redesigned in time for the victimization report for 1993, in which report victimization figures went up a great deal. However, the changes included: "additional cues to help survey participants recall incidents, questions encouraging respondents to report victimizations they may not themselves define as a crime, more direct questions on rape and sexual assault, and new material to measure victimizations by non-strangers, including domestic violence" (BJS, October 30, 1994).

According to the **NCVS**, annual data "indicate that year-to-year trends continue relatively unchanged: little change in violent crime and a slight decline in property crime" (October, 1994). Thus, even though the **NCVS** does not believe rates have gone up, much of the data to follow from the NCVS is to 1992, or when 1994, 1995 or 1998 is reported, it should be kept in mind that the questionnaire was redesigned to elicit responses that the respondents "may not themselves define as crimes."

The National Crime Victimization Survey (NCVS)

We have discussed crimes reported to the police and concluded that these figures should be viewed with some skepticism as not all crime is reported. The **NCVS** is different from the **UCR** in that we cannot get information about a particular

Table 1.4 – Arrests by State, 1997

ALPHA ORDER

Rank	State	Arrests	% of USA
16	Alabama	223,057	2.1
45	Alaska	19,779	0.2
13	Arizona	275,565	2.6
20	Arkansas	191,805	1.8
1	California	1,594,841	15.1
22	Colorado	181,404	1.7
23	Connecticut	181,010	1.7
44	Delaware	23,688	0.2
NA	Florida	NA	NA
21	Georgia	187,809	1.8
35	Hawaii	70,000	0.7
34	Idaho	73,120	0.7
11	Illinois	291,338	2.8
25	Indiana	164,871	1.6
30	Iowa	98,412	0.9
NA	Kansas	NA	NA
39	Kentucky	50,844	0.5
14	Louisiana	273,715	2.6
38	Maine	53,028	0.5
10	Maryland	306,522	2.9
27	Massachusetts	158,347	1.5
6	Michigan	366,523	3.5
18	Minnesota	211,496	2.0
33	Mississippi	80,698	0.8
12	Missouri	284,954	2.7
46	Montana	10,515	0.1
31	Nebraska	96,236	0.9
37	Nevada	56,094	0.5
NA	New Hampshire	NA	NA
4	New Jersey	414,998	3.9
32	New Mexico	86,050	0.8
9	New York	360,483	3.4
3	North Carolina	520,165	4.9

RANK ORDER

Rank	State	Arrests	% of USA
1	California	1,594,841	15.1
2	Texas	1,084,247	10.3
3	North Carolina	520,165	4.9
4	New Jersey	414,998	3.9
5	Virginia	408,428	3.9
6	Michigan	366,523	3.5
7	Ohio	361,976	3.4
8	Wisconsin	363,333	3.4
9	New York	360,463	3.4
10	Maryland	306,522	2.9
11	Illinois	291,338	2.8
12	Missouri	284,954	2.7
13	Arizona	275,565	2.6
14	Louisiana	273,715	2.6
15	Washington	228,503	2.2
16	Alabama	223,057	2.1
17	South Carolina	218,788	2.1
18	Minnesota	211,496	2.0
19	Pennsylvania	202,715	1.9
20	Arkansas	191,805	1.8
21	Georgia	187,809	1.8
22	Colorado	181,404	1.7
23	Connecticut	181,010	1.7
24	Tennessee	165,603	1.6
25	Indiana	164,871	1.6
26	Oklahoma	158,837	1.5
27	Massachusetts	158,347	1.5
28	Oregon	150,369	1.4
29	Utah	102,541	1.0
30	Iowa	98,412	0.9
31	Nebraska	96,236	0.9
32	New Mexico	86,050	0.8
33	Mississippi	80,698	0.8

Table 1.4 – Arrests by State, 1997 (Continued)

Rank	State	ALPHA ORDER Arrests	% of USA		Rank	State	RANK ORDER Arrests	% of USA
42	North Dakota	28,996	0.3		34	Idaho	73,120	0.7
7	Ohio	361,976	3.4		35	Hawaii	70,000	0.7
26	Oklahoma	158,837	1.5		36	West Virginia	63,439	0.6
28	Oregon	150,369	1.4		37	Nevada	56,094	0.5
19	Pennsylvania	202,715	1.9		38	Maine	53,028	0.5
40	Rhode Island	41,223	0.4		39	Kentucky	50,844	0.5
17	South Carolina	218,788	2.1		40	Rhode Island	41,223	0.4
43	South Dakota	25,249	0.2		41	Wyoming	35,030	0.3
24	Tennessee	165,603	1.6		42	North Dakota	28,996	0.3
2	Texas	1,084,247	10.3		43	South Dakota	25,249	0.2
29	Utah	102,541	1.0		44	Delaware	23,688	0.2
NA	Vermont	NA	NA		45	Alaska	19,779	0.2
5	Virginia	408,428	3.9		46	Montana	10,515	0.1
15	Washington	228,503	2.2		NA	Florida	NA	NA
36	West Virginia	63,439	0.6		NA	Kansas	NA	NA
8	Wisconsin	361,333	3.4		NA	New Hampshire	NA	NA
41	Wyoming	35,030	0.3		NA	Vermont	NA	NA
NA	District of Columbia	NA	NA		NA	District of Columbia	NA	NA

Source: *Crime State Rankings, 1998.* Lawrence, KS:Morgan Quinto Press, 1998.

Table 1.5
Urban/Rural Crime by State 1994 and 1998

	Urban Crimes 1994	Urban Crimes 1998	Rural Crimes 1994	Rural Crimes 1998	Crime Rate per 100,000 1994	Crime Rate per 100,000 1998
CA	1,887,635	1,375,647	21,043	17,839	6,173.8	4342.8
TX	979,187	914,095	32,531	36,942	5,872.4	5111.6
FL	1,083,977	975,347	29,619	32,044	8,250.0	6886.0
NY	875,318	607,788	19,038	16,140	5,070.6	3588.5
MI	443,404	407,974	26,060	18,452	5,445.2	4682.9
OH	399,549	359,853	10,770	13,555*	4,461.4	4327.5
GA	321,809	314,067	31,716	36,617	6,010.3	5463.0
NJ	368,400	296,527	-0-	-0-	4,660.9	3654.1
PA	348,443	342,666	15,650	17,518	3,271.9	3273.0
NC	295,085	292,863	40,761	45,958	5,625.2	5322.2
WA	275,419	265,927	14,298	17,055	6,027.5	5867.4
MA	237,298	192,046	109	54	4,441.0	3475.9
MD	290,193	259,222	6,609	6,570	6,122.6	5365.7
AZ	292,699	283,336	7,249	6,176	7,924.6	6575.0
LA	238,107	218,844	14,927	15,667	6,671.1	6098.3
VA	231,881	210,391	16,018	18,589	4,047.6	3660.4
MO	233,750	217,135	15,757	8,560	5,018.8	4826.4
IN	182,374	174,987	19,576	8,740	4,592.8	4169.4
TN	197,962	203,604	8,913	14,736	5,119.8	5034.4
AL	165,960	155,347	9,009	9,327	4,903.0	4597.1
WI	156,394	-0-	16,508	-0-	3,944.4	3543.1
CO	163,062	152,962	8,842	6,213	5,318.4	4487.5
MN	156,241	150,467	17,639	17,336	4,341.0	4046.5
SC	163,101	160,534	31,372	36,324	6,000.8	5777.0
OK	134,527	120,450	11,007	11,064	5,570.1	5003.9
CN	143,330	118,460	3,521	3,399	4,548.0	3786.5
OR	147,339	141,077	14,296	14,596	6,296.4	5646.6
KS	N/A	-0-	N/A	-0-	4,893.8	4858.8
KY	87,197	-0-	19,744	-0-	3,498.6	2889.4
AR	74,732	68,283	12,615	12,761	4,798.7	4283.4
MS	57,000	46,896	4,161	6,145	4,837.1	4384.0
IA	65,905	63,759	8,918	8,204	3,654.6	3500.6
UT	84,619	95,628	4,443	4,716	5,300.9	5505.9
NM	59,031	71,067	5,231	6,391	6,187.8	6719.1
NV	89,103	84,720	5,967	5,066	6,677.4	5280.5
NE	49,520	48,419	5,550	5,897	4,440.4	4405.2
HI	60,825	47,453	15,110	16,170	6,680.5	5463.0
RI	37,949	31,702	23	36	4,119.1	3517.8
ME	18,364	17,238	6,421	5,998	3,272.7	3040.7
WV	26,240	27,694	10,552	10,441	2,528.4	2547.2
ID	17,353	19,966	8,076	7,528	4,077.0	3714.6
NH	19,357	-0-	953	-0-	2,741.0	2419.8
DE	24,444	-0-	2,942	-0-	4,147.6	5363.2
MT	N/A	-0-	N/A	-0-	5,018.8	4070.7
AK	18,662	13,364	6,049	4,991	5,708.1	4777.0
WY	7,344	6,272	2,709	2,308	4,289.7	3807.7
SD	10,921	9,583	1,693	1,775	3,102.2	2624.1
ND	10,713	10,227	2,055	1,951	2,735.9	2681.0
VT	7,179	6,850	3,664	4,038	3,250.3	3139.1

IL	N/A	-0-	N/A	-0-	N/A	4872.8
DC	63,186	46,210	-0-	-0-	11,085.3	88.35.6

* Denotes less than 75% of rural area reporting.

Source: U.S. Department of Justice. Federal Bureau of Investigation. **Crime in the United States**, 1994 and 1998: Uniform Crime Reports. Washington, D.C.

jurisdiction. Rather we get an aggregate, all statistics are lumped together in order to tell a nationwide story.

According to the **NCVS**, Americans age 12 years and older experienced approximately 31 million violent and property victimizations in 1998. This represents a decline from 35 million victimizations in 1997 and continues a downward trend that is the lowest since 1973 when there were 44 million victimizations.

Between 1993 and 1998 violent crime rates fell 27% from 50 to 37 per 1,000 persons over the age of twelve. Property crime decreased as well by 12% from 1997 to 1998 and by a whopping 32% from 1993 to 1998. According to the **NCVS**:

* Every major type of crime measured - rape or sexual assault, robbery, aggravated assault, simple assault, burglary, theft, and motor vehicle theft – decreased significantly between 1993 and 1998.

* For virtually every demographic category considered there was a significant drop. For example, violent victimization decreased between 1993 and 1998. Male victimization rates fell 39% and black violent victimization rates fell by 38%.

* Property crime rates declined across all demographic groups between 1993 and 1998; 31% for white, black, urban, and suburban households.

* About half of the violent crime victims knew the offender(s). Over 7 in 10 rape or sexual attack victims knew the attacker(s).

* In about one-fourth of victimizations a weapon was used.

* From 1993 to 1998, almost half of all victimizations were reported to the police. Females and blacks reported violent victimizations in greater percentages than males or whites.

We discussed above that the **NCVS** collects data from the victims of crime. To get that figure 59,000 households across the nation are interviewed every six months. Residents over the age of 12 are asked if they have been the victim of a crime in the last six months and, according to the **NCVS,** crime since 1973 is relatively flat. That is, from 1973-1992 the number of victimizations either went down or, as in the case of violent crimes, remained flat. Figure 1.2 shows the number of victimizations for the period in various catagories from 1993 to 1998.

Criminal victimizations fluctuated from 1973 to 1981 rising from 35,661,030 victimizations in 1973 to 41,454,180 victimizations in 1981. Since that time the number of victimizations has decreased to 31,307,000 in 1998 with about half of all victimizations reported to the police. This represents a significant decline in victimizations and hardly illustrates the crime wave many politicians claim to exist.

We must remember that the **NCVS** is a survey, that is a limited number of randomly selected households are questioned periodically and the results are extrapolated to the general population. In survey research, this is a legitimate approach if the entire population cannot be surveyed. Presidential polls use this approach, attitudes on the death penalty are determined by this approach, and a host of surveys that try to determine what is going on in our society from eating habits to our attitudes on crime and politics. Thus, as is the case for the Uniform Crime Report and self report studies, the NCVS is only one source for the scope of crime. By looking at data from all three sources, we get a more complete picture of crime.

In many instances the **NCVS** is not that far off reported crime. For example female rape, a crime that is often not reported out of fear of the trial process, because of shame, or because the victim is acquainted with the aggressor, in 1998 was only a little higher than reported instances of rape. According the **NCVS,** there were 110,000 rape victimizations in 1998 and 93,100 rapes reported to the police in 1998. However, the water is rather murky here and this is a good lesson in how reporting procedures and changes in the way statistics are collected can impact our perceptions and the recording of crime.

According to the **UCR,** the reported incidents of rape increased from 76,390 in 1979 to a high of 109, 060 in 1992 and has declined to 93,100 in 1998. That is, the rate has remained relatively stable at 34.7 per 100,000 in 1979 and 34.3 per 100,000 in 1998. On the other hand, the **NCVS** reports that the rate of rape victimization declined during that time, from 1.8 per 1,000 population in 1973 to a rate of .7 per 1,000 population in 1998. Clearly, it is easy to be confused by the numbers, however, the rate of victimization has not escalated as

Figure 1.3

Victimization Trends – 1993-1998

**Rate of violent crime
per 1,000 persons age 12 or older**

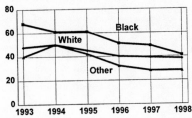

**Rate of property crime
per 1,000 households**

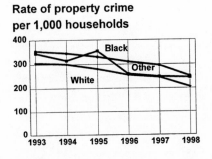

**Rate of violent crime
per 1,000 persons age 12 or older**

**Rate of property crime
per 1,000 households**

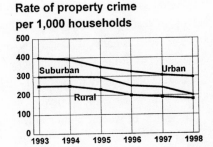

Source: Callie Marie Rennison, Ph.D. **Criminal Victimization 1998**.
Washington, D.C.:USDOJ, Bureau of Justice Statistics, July, 1999.

greatly as we fear. In this instance, the willingness of women to report the crime of rape has had an impact on the numbers of known offenses.

Crimes of violence in general have remained relatively flat since 1973. We see nightly images on the national network news of young people shooting each other and we are exposed to grieving parents of dead or seriously wounded children and we are frightened, disgusted, and moved by these images.However, according to the **NCVS**, the rate of crime has not increased as much as we are led to believe.

The age group we fear for the most, and in which the crime victimization rate has risen dramatically, are the 12-15 year old and the 16-19 year old age groups. Of the first group, 106.8 white youths between 12-15 per 1,000 population were victims of violent crime in 1995. For black youth the figures are slightly higher. In 1998, the UCR reports 1,470 arrests of youth under the age of 18 for murder/nonnegligent manslaughter, 3,769 for forcible rape, 23,400 for robbery, and 51,360 for aggravated assault. Clearly, children are both the perpetrators and the victims of violence in this country.

Clearly, the statistics are confusing and sometimes contradictory, but there has not been as much of an increase in crime as we tend to think when we factor in the increase in the U.S. population. Even when we mentally factor in crimes against children under the age of 12 and crimes against the homeless and tourists, there still is less crime than we believe. Still, the fear of crime far outweighs the probability of victimization and fear has just as a corrosive effect on our society as crime itself because it instills fear of those of a different skin color, different habits, and those who may affect a different manner of dress. In addition, fear of crime affects a sense of trust in others, that is we are mistrustful of others in our neighborhoods, towns, and cities and that further contributes to the erosion of community.

A series of Louis Harris polls reveals that overall Americans see crime as decreasing. In 1989, eighty-four percent (84%) of those polled said there was more crime than a year ago in the United States. By 1997 that percentage had declined to 64%. In 1997 forty-six percent (46%) believed that there is more crime in their immediate area; 41% of males and 51% of females believed crime is up in their area. However, 18% of males and 40% of females feel "fairly unsafe" or "very unsafe" walking in their neighborhoods. Compare these figures with 32% of males and 52% of females who felt "unsafe walking in their neighborhoods in 1992.

In looking at urban/rural differences 1997, we see that 58% of the urban respondents and 63% of suburban residents state that they believe that crime is up and 74% of rural residents believe that there is more crime. It is difficult to explain why so many small town residents feel crime is increasing, except to say that perhaps the impact of television has eroded a sense of security and the demographic changes in small towns has had its affect and they somehow feel a loss of an ideal. There has been an increase in crime in small towns, but according to the **UCR**, there has also been an increase in the population of smaller towns. The greatest increase has been in towns under 10,000 population. A critical look at the UCR reveals that the population gain in smaller towns may be responsible for any reported increase in crime and in the crime rate and is a natural corollary of the overall population growth of the United States. In addition, perhaps the increased probability of citizens to report crime to the Sheriff or local police is the result of increased fear of crime. In addition, it may be that people are now more prone to report crime rather than attempting to handle the problem themselves.

From the **NCVS** we are able to piece together a profile of the typical crime victim. The average crime victim is under 25 years of age, black, unemployed, living in a rented apartment, a high school drop-out, and with no skills.

The group with the least to fear of victimization are white females over the age of 65. It is interesting to note that white males over age 65 are less likely to be victimized than are black females over age 65. When the elderly are the victims of a crime, most likely it will be that of larceny.

Proposition #2: Authorities do not really know how much crime is committed. We can be reasonably sure that it is always higher or lower than what the storyteller relates.

Table 1.6 – Personal Crimes of Violence by Age of Victim

Personal Crimes of violence and theft: Victimization levels and rates by age of victim

Age of Victim and year	Crimes of Violence		Personal Thefts		Number of persons
	Number	Rate	Number	Rate	
12-15					
1973	928,700	55.6	2,857,600	171.2	16,692,900
1974	878,100	52.7	2,780,000	166.8	16,664,100
1975	907,000	54.6	2,630,300	158.5	16,598,400
1976	849,300	52.0	2,431,300	148.7	16,349,800
1977	901,600	56.5	2,301,600	144.2	15,963,100
1978	880,100	57.0	2,250,700	145.6	15,454,400
1979	796,400	53.4	2,116,400	141.9	14,918,300
1980	729,800	49.5	1,749,500	118.6	14,756,200
1981	853,900	58.9	1,857,400	128.1	14,505,500
1982	755,900	52.0	1,851,900	127.4	14,532,800
1983	747,570	51.3	1,833,200	125.8	14,575,580
1984	766,660	53.2	1,733,180	120.3	14,404,520
1985	768,250	54.1	1,536,740	108.3	14,189,130
1986	716,650	52.4	1,499,230	109.7	13,670,280
1987	785,890	59.3	1,452,020	112.3	13,249,170
1988	746,330	56.9	1,471,840	112.3	13,109,920
1989	834,120	62.9	1,315,960	99.3	13,256,460
1990	926,280	68.8	1,233,090	91.5	13,469,110

Table 1.6 – Personal Crimes of Violence by Age of Victim (Continued)

Personal Crimes of violence and theft: Victimization levels and rates by age of victim

Age of Victim and year	Crimes of Violence		Personal Thefts		Number of persons
	Number	Rate	Number	Rate	
16-19					
1973	975,600	61.4	2,559,500	161.1	15,890,500
1974	1,100,300	68.0	2,583,000	159.7	16,175,900
1975	1,053,600	64.4	2,653,900	162.1	16,371,000
1976	1,099,600	66.7	2,423,900	147.0	16,487,000
1977	1,118,000	67.7	2,471,700	149.8	16,505,100
1978	1,134,400	68.9	2,513,100	152.6	16,466,300
1979	1,151,700	70.2	2,397,700	146.1	16,410,500
1980	1,138,600	68.7	2,064,800	124.6	16,576,600
1981	1,093,900	67.8	2,129,600	131.9	16,140,200
1982	1,116,500	71.2	2,004,200	127.9	15,676,000
1983	982,240	64.8	1,799,110	118.7	15,155,400
1984	996,250	67.9	1,765,840	120.4	14,664,050
1985	975,880	67.2	1,774,420	122.1	14,529,590
1986	887,680	60.7	1,723,500	117.9	14,620,380
1987	1,019,520	69.4	1,796,440	122.3	14,686,760
1988	1,046,920	72.0	1,758,520	120.9	14,542,850
1989	1,049,960	73.8	1,641,950	115.3	14,235,270
1990	1,022,210	74.4	1,557,990	113.4	13,738,870

Source: *Criminal Victimization in the United States: 1973-90 Trends.* A National Crime Victimization Report Washington, D.C.: Bureau of Justice Statistics, 1992). December 1992, p. 11.

Summary

Crime is a social problem of which we must all be concerned. However, it never was as great a problem as we were led to believe and since 1994 crime has been steadily dropping. The media, to a large extent is responsible for the crisis mentality that exists in regard to crime. Is crime up? Yes, but to what extent we cannot be sure. Part of our problem in determining how much crime exists lies in our desire for figures and we look to the **UCR** and the **NCVS**. According to Biderman and Lynch:

> When the comparisons between the two series were confined to those components of each that can be identified as dealing with a common universe of events, when the same units were used for crime counts and when rates for the two series were calculated on an equivalent population base, the two indicators displayed the same directional changes...NCS-UCR differences in the magnitudes of rate changes and the general levels of crime also were greatly reduced. The trends for the two series converged rather than diverged over the period studied.

Crime may be up, but the real question is how much? Biderman and Lynch lead us to believe that the answer lies somewhere between the two indicators. It is safe to say that crime is not up as much as we are led to believe. It is also safe to say that the media will continue to feature the abnormal, the gruesome, and the heart wrenching stories that sell papers and get reporters stories on the 6:00 PM news.

The Federal Bureau of Investigation's **Uniform Crime Report** and the Bureau of Census' **National Crime Victimization Survey** each give us a different picture of crime in the United States and from the two we can piece together the real picture. It is important that we question the claims of journalists and those running for political office in order to determine what is on their agenda. Most importantly, we must not cast a vote based upon fear or suspicion.

Bibliography

Howard Abadinsky and L. Thomas Winfree, Jr. **Crime and Justice: An Introduction**, 2nd ed.. Chicago: Nelson-Hall, Inc. 1992.

A.D. Biderman and J.P. Lynch. **Understanding Crime Incidence Statistics: Why the UCR Diverges From the NCS**. New York: Springer-Verlag New York, Inc., 1991.

Bureau of Justice Statistics. **Criminal Victimization in the United States: 1973-90 Trends**. Washington, D.C.

Bureau of Justice Statistics. **Sourcebook of Criminal Justice Statistics-1993**. Washington, D.C.

_____. **Criminal Victimization 1993**. Washington, DC. May, 1995.

_____. **Questions and Answers about the Redesign**. Washington, DC. October 30, 1994.

_____. **Technical Background on the Redesigned National Crime Victimization Survey**. Washington, DC. October 30, 1994.

Corrections Compendium. CEGA Publishing. (August, 1994) Lincoln, Nebraska

Malcolm Feeley. **The Process is the Punishment**. New York: Russell Sage Foundation, 1979.

Don C. Gibbons. **Society, Crime, and Criminal Behavior**, 6th ed. (Englewood Cliffs: Prentice Hall, 1992).

Kappeler, Blumberg, and Potter. **Mythology of Crime**.

The Challenge of Crime in a Free Society. A Report by the Presidents Commission on Law Enforcement and the Administration of Justice. Washington, D.C.: U.S. Government Printing Office, 1967.

U.S. Department of Justice. Federal Bureau of Investigation. **Crime in the United States**, 1988, 1992, 1994, and 1998: Uniform Crime Reports. Washington, D.C.

Samuel Walker. **Sense and Nonsense about Crime and Drugs: A Policy Guide**, 3rd ed. Belmont, CA: Wadsworth Publishing Company, 1994.

James Q. Wilson. **Thinking About Crime** (Revised Edition). New York: Vintage Books, 1985.

Chapter 2

The Economics of Crime

Introduction

The costs of crime are staggering, more precisely the costs of a continued policy of imprisoning every petty criminal, drug user, and loser who happens to make a bad decision is going to break the bank. It is enough that as victims we must pay for the replacement of stolen items or for personal injury through insurance premiums or out of pocket. We also pay for the loss to others through higher insurance premiums or higher hospital costs because those without insurance, or the means to pay, use the emergency room for primary medical care. In short, we all pay out of pocket because of the crime rate.

There is another cost that is not calculated in monetary terms. Fear! The social cost of fear is translated into declining, or decimated, Central Business Districts, the fear of citizens to leave their homes at night in certain cities of the country, and a generalized belief that we have somehow degenerated into a nation of barbarians. The issue of how much crime exists in the United States today was covered in chapter one, but regardless of how much crime exists, we pay dearly and public policy makers and legislators do not share the true costs of present policies with the taxpayer.

Dollars and $ense

While the figures are somewhat dated, we gain a sense of loss through data from the Bureau of Justice Statistics. According to the Bureau of Justice Statistics, "Crime victims in 1992 (the latest year for which such statistics are available from the BJS on this issue) lost $17.6 billion in direct costs" (Klaus, 1994). The losses are due to theft of property, damage to property, cash losses, medical expenses, and lost pay due to the commission of a crime. Compare seventeen billion dollars to the $14.5 billion in the 2000 US Department of Education budget as discretionary funds for elementary and secondary education. Seventeen billion dollars spent on elementary and secondary education in the United States would be quite a boost to education. Nevertheless, losses due to crime amounts to a tax placed upon the American people that is put to no good use. Seventeen billion dollars represents money that could have been spent on education, medical care, highways, recreation and parks, and caring for our families.

While we lost more than $17 billion to crime in 1992, we spent more than $97 billion in 1993 on criminal justice activities. While the amount of money spent on controlling crime has steadily risen over the last 25 years, when one accounts for inflation, the amount of money lost to crime has remained relatively constant for the past 25 years. Still, to assert that we do not need to spend money on criminal justice activities is nonsense, but we need to question how that money is spent and whether or not we can get a better return.

In 1998, according to the BJS, 105,322,920 households were victimized. In many of the cases, there was no monetary loss, but there was a loss of something the victim regarded as having value. Table 2.1 illustrates the victimizations of households by various characteristics.

In 1994, Klaus found that for crimes that involved loss:

* About 12% of personal crimes and 24% of household crimes
  involved economic losses of $500 or more.

* For personal crimes, 11% of whites and 15% of blacks
  lost $500 or more. For household crimes, 23% of whites and
  25% of blacks had such losses.

* In robberies at least $250 or more was taken from the victim in
  about a fourth (26% of all victimizations). Black victims lost this amount
  in 41% of the victimizations, and white robbery victims, in 19% of the
  incidents.

Table 2.1

**Household Property
Victimizations in 1996**

Characteristics of head of household	Number of households	Total	Burglary	Motor vehicle theft	Theft
Race					
White	86,828,970	259.9	44.3	12.1	203.5
Black	12,610,740	310.0	69.3	22.2	218.5
Other	3,257,780	268.4	39.4	16.5	212.5
Ethnicity					
Hispanic	8,029,100	328.1	55.2	24.6	247.3
Non-Hispanic	94,046,690	261.2	46.4	12.5	202.3
Household income					
Under $7,500	9,169,350	282.7	74.5	11.8	196.5
$7,500 to $14,999	13,196,430	247.5	59.5	11.5	176.5
$15,000 to $24,999	15,715,240	273.1	45.9	14.1	213.1
$25,000 to $34,999	13,529,800	285.1	47.8	14.5	222.8
$35,000 to $49,999	14,894,950	287.6	39.3	16.1	232.1
$50,000 to $74,999	12,444,620	284.0	38.1	14.4	231.6
$75,000 and over	9,471,690	304.6	41.8	14.4	248.3
Region					
Northeast	20,287,590	215.2	35.5	12.0	167.8
Midwest	24,933,490	249.6	44.4	10.0	195.1
South	36,181,470	259.9	51.0	13.2	195.7
West	21,294,940	345.6	55.0	19.6	271.0
Residence					
Urban	31,501,620	334.5	64.2	20.3	250.0
Suburban	48,322,180	250.5	37.8	12.9	199.8
Rural	22,873,690	206.0	43.7	5.4	156.9
Home ownership					
Owned	66,798,710	233.7	38.9	10.7	184.1
Rented	35,898,780	327.1	62.6	18.8	245.8

Source: Kathleen Maguire and Ann L. Pastore, eds., **Sourcebook of Criminal Justice Statistics 1994.** U.S. Department of Justice, Bureau of Justice Statistics. Washington, D.C.: USGPO, 1998

---

* Lost property was not recovered in 89% of personal crimes and 85% of household crimes in 1992.

* About 31% of all victims of crimes of violence in 1992 sustained some physical injury.

Table 2.2 – Type and Value of Property Stolen and Recovered, 1998

9,947 Agencies; 1998 Estimated Population 195,957,000

Type of Property	Value of Property		Percent recovered
	Stolen	Recovered	
Total[1]	$11,324,104,000	$4,001,286,000	35.3
Currency, notes, etc.	821,281,000	35,892,000	4.4
Jewelry and precious metals	844,605,000	43,256,000	5.1
Clothing and furs	237,053,000	47,512,000	20.0
Locally stolen motor vehicles	5,520,490,000	3,580,277,000	64.9
Office equipment	439,707,000	17,479,000	4.0
Televisions, radios, stereos, etc.	818,811,000	35,818,000	4.4
Firearms	92,067,000	9,387,000	10.2
Household goods	189,383,000	10,810,000	5.7
Consumable goods	75,244,000	10,287,000	13.7
Livestock	14,725,000	1,543,000	10.5
Miscellaneous	2,270,738,000	209,025,000	9.2

[1]All totals and percentages calculated before rounding

Source: Kathleen Maguire and Ann L. Pastore, eds., *Sourcebook of Criminal Justice Statistics, 1998*. U.S. Department of Justice, Bureau of Justice Statistics. Washington, D.C.:USGPO, 1998. Complete data for 1998 were not available for states of Illinois, Kansas, Kentucky, Montana, New Hampshire, and Wisconsin; therefore, it was necessary that their crime counts be estimated.

*   In 1992, 69% of the victims who were injured had
health insurance or were eligible for public medical assistance.
Seventy percent of whites and 66% of blacks had insurance coverage
or were eligible for public medical services (Klaus, 1994).

Table 2.2 calls our attention to the property loss to Americans in 1998.
Clearly, the amounts are substantial. What needs to be remembered is that since
working class and lower class citizens are the group most victimized by criminals,
they suffer the most. The sense of being violated aside, the loss of a $200
television set may be an inconvenience to someone in the $100,000 income
bracket. For someone in the $18,000 income bracket, the replacement of a $200
television requires planning and most likely deferring the purchase of another item.

The **Uniform Crime Report,** published annually by the Federal Bureau of
Investigation, states that in 1998 total dollar losses due to property crime
(Burglary, larceny-theft, motor vehicle theft, and arson) were estimated at $15.4
billion. In 1988 loses were estimated at $14.6 billion. Thus we see a decline in
real dollars when we control for inflation over the past decade.

Table 2.3 illustrates the FBI's estimate of monetary loss due to property
crime.

Table   2.3

**Property Crimes by Year by Dollar Amount
(in billions)**

	1988	1994	1998
Burglary	$3.3	$3.6	3.1
Larceny-Theft	$3.3	$4.0	4.8
Motor Vehicle Theft	$7.0	$7.6	7.5
Arson	$1.0	1.3 (1993)	981 Million

Source: Federal Bureau of Investigation. **Crime in the United States,
1988,1994, and 1998.** Uniform Crime Reports for the United States.
(Washington, D.C.: U.S. Department of Justice, 1988,1994, and 1998).

In comparing the years 1988 to 1994 and 1998. we see very little overall increase in financial loss due to burglary, larceny-theft, motor vehicle theft, and arson even though we see a small decrease in burglary and arson loss. For Arson, there was a reported loss in excess of $7 billion dollars in 1994, but a great deal of those losses are due to the wildfires that occurred in California as well as the Los Angeles riots that occurred in 1994. Therefore, the figure for 1993 is given in light of the staggering losses in California in 1994. Still, examination of the totals fail to substantiate a crime wave, but there are other losses.

According to the National Insurance Crime Bureau (NICB), the total cost of insurance fraud may exceed $100 billion per year, that includes casualty insurance fraud in the amount of an estimated $20 billion dollars per year. To put this figure in perspective, Hurricane Andrew resulted in $17 billion dollars of damage. This amount adds approximately $200 per year in additional premiums for each household to make up for the loss to insurance companies (NICB). Insurance fraud, however, is not street crime and as a consequence, not high on the list of concerns to most Americans even though most Americans will lament the high cost of insurance.

Attempting to put a dollar amount on personal crimes is most difficult. How does one calculate the worth of a murder victim or the value of feeling free to walk about one's neighborhood? It is worthwhile to briefly mention the number of personal crimes and victimizations in order to put the issue in perspective. Just imagine that for every crime and every victim, there is a cost, such as time off from work to appear in court or the additional cost to be paid by the victim for medical care.

Personal crimes, or violent crimes, include: murder and nonnegligent manslaughter, forcible rape, robbery, and aggravated assault. According to the NCVS, there were 5,350,550 crimes of violence in 1973. By 1998 that figure had climbed to 8,412,000 showing a small increase from 32.6 victimizations per 1,000 to 37.9 victimizations per 1,000 in 1998. However, according to the FBI, in 1998 there were 1,531,044 violent offenses reported to the police.

The media is interested in sensational crimes that grab us by the throat and will not let go. Such copy and visual images sell papers and get our attention on the evening news. The power of the media is such that we learn of heinous crimes on the same day of their commission. We grieve with the parents of Polly Klass in California; we are outraged that a boy is brutally murdered by being dragged to his death by a carjacker. We identify with residents of an inner-city neighborhood who tell us on the 6:00 PM news that gangs and drugs have taken over their neighborhood. Somehow, we feel that our lives and our neighborhoods are threatened just as greatly. The statistics do not support such feelings and they certainly do not support politicians who attempt to play upon that fear.

Taxes and the Criminal Justice System

In 1993 (the last year for which we have figures) taxpayers spent more than $97 billion on criminal justice activities. This includes police protection, courts, public defense, corrections and other directly related activities. Table 2.4 illustrates the dollar amounts spent for criminal justice activities in 1993. As we can see, police protection is the largest single cost to taxpayers. However, while figures are not yet available, the increase in the prison population since 1993 has most likely pushed the cost of corrections into the stratosphere and may even exceed the cost for police services. For example, on December 31, 1992 there were 883,656 inmates in American prisons. By June of 1994 the U.S. prison population passed the 1,000,000 mark. By the end of 1997 it reached 1,197,590 inmates. At an average daily cost of approximately $35.00-$55.00 per inmate, we are talking about a lot of money.

Another cost that must be considered by the taxpayer is the cost of keeping inmates in the local jail. Jails are a fixture in every county seat in the nation and very few people give them much thought. However, on any given day there are more than 567,000 prisoners in county jails in the United States. In response to the question, "How much does it cost to keep a prisoner in jail for one day?" one receives various answers. Usually the answer will be somewhere between $25.00 to $80.00 per day. Again we are talking about a lot of money.

Jails have traditionally been neglected, under-funded, unsafe, and over-used. According to one authority jails are the central intake point for the entire criminal justice system and as a consequence play host to a wide variety of social, economic, and welfare problems (Mattick, 1974). It makes sense to take care of our jails, for if we take care of them, including allocating adequate funds for training of staff, in the long term we may save money by keeping future inmates out of the state correctional system.

There are other costs that can be avoided, but because of the short term view of many elected leaders, we often end up paying when we do not have to pay. That is the cost of class action lawsuits. The courts have been very specific

Table 2.4 – Justice System Expenditures
(Direct and Intergovernmental)

By level of government and type of activity, United States, fiscal year 1993
(Dollar amounts in thousands)

Activity	Total all governments	Federal Government	State governments	Local governments
Total justice system	$97,541,826	$18,591,000	$34,227,194	$52,561,979
Direct expenditure	97,541,826	14,429,000	30,695,903	52,416,923
Intergovernmental expenditure	X	4,162,000	3,531,291	145,056
Police protection	44,036,756	8,069,000	5,603,484	31,733,159
Direct expenditure	44,036,756	7,345,000	4,960,517	31,731,239
Intergovernmental expenditure	X	724,000	642,967	1,920
Judicial and legal	21,558,403	7,832,000	7,820,251	10,282,702
Direct expenditure	21,558,403	4,662,000	6,644,044	10,252,359
Intergovernmental expenditure	X	3,170,000	1,176,207	30,343
Corrections	31,946,667	2,690,000	20,803,459	10,546,118
Direct expenditure	31,946,667	2,422,000	19,091,342	10,433,235
Intergovernmental expenditure	X	268,000	1,712,117	112,793

Source: Kathleen Maguire and Ann L. Pastore, eds., *Sourcebook of Criminal Justice Statistics, 1994.*
U.S.Department of Justice, Bureau of Justice Statistics, Washington, D.C.:USGPO, 1994.

in demanding that jails adhere to minimum standards of cleanliness, availability of showers and other hygienic standards, exercise, and freedom from fear of other prisoners. If a lawsuit is lodged against a county and the court finds that such standards have been violated, in not too long of a period, the fines exceed the amount it would have cost to design and implement alternative programs, make improvements or even build a new jail. Therefore, requests by the local Sheriff for a new jail or for improvements should be taken seriously. He, or she, is in a position to accurately assess the probable costs to the county and should be paid heed.

Lock'em Up at any Cost?

For nearly two decades the United States has been engaged in an unprecedented prison building spree. This has occurred in spite of the fact that crime is not as high as we are led to believe. Since 1980 our prison population has nearly quadrupled from 329,821 to nearly 1.2 million in 1997. During that time we have spent billions on construction of new prisons and for additions to existing prisons. An example of how much we have spent on prison construction can be obtained by reviewing past issues of **The Corrections Compendium**. Annually **The Corrections Compendium** sends a survey to all departments of correction in the United States. Not all departments respond, but of those who do respond, we learn that from the period 1986 to 1994, a reported $30.4 billion dollars was spent on new prison construction. This appears to be a low figure, but we can get an idea of the costs of imprisonment.

The December, 1999 issue of **The Corrections Compendium** published the most recent annual survey of corrections budgets. Of those departments who responded (5 did not) they state that (after the construction frenzy of the early 90s) budget increases were obtained primarily to fund new positions. The addition of 10,347 new positions was a factor in the budget increases. However, four states did report a budget decrease. It should also be noted that in 1997, $1.3 billion was spent on community programs. That was increased to $1.5 billion for 1998. Table 2.5 illustrates the budgets of the various states.

Today we imprison more citizens than any other country in the world, even more than the former Soviet Union, South Africa, and China (Irwin and Austin, 1994). On December 31, 1997 the incarceration rate for the United States

Table 2.5

**Budgets for Departments of Corrections
1998-1999**

State	Total DOC Budget	State	Total DOC Budget
Alabama	$166,950,000	Montana	No Response
Alaska	$158,210,000	Nebraska	$116,319,673
Arizona	$535,259,800	Nevada	$259,151,610
Arkansas	$151,336,081	NH	$ 52,723,741
California	$4,114,265,000	New Jersey	$876,843,000
Colorado	$399,779,855	New Mexico	$164,105,700
Connecticut	$414,417,465	New York	$2,250,567,900
Delaware	$141,163,600	No. Carolina	$1,009,209,553
Dist of Columbia	$250,733,000	No. Dakota	$ 30,050,741
Florida	$1,739,817,408	Ohio	$1,360,432,077
Georgia	$818,797,188	Oklahoma	$385,601,641
Hawaii	$127,212,273	Oregon	$537,861,432
Idaho	$ 87,879,500	PA	$1,013,598,572
Illinois	$810,145,200	Rhode Is	$129,384,126
Indiana	$445,100,000	So. Carolina	$401,639,001
Iowa	$218,571,173	So. Dakota	$ 33,527,779
Kansas	$217,035,260	Tennessee	$435,844,900 `
Kentucky	$268,262,400	Texas	$2,084,338,005
Louisiana	$461,932,917	Utah	No Response
Maine	$ 55,664,096	Vermont	$ 65,528,000
Maryland	$476,961,647	Virginia	$704,711,148
Massachusetts	No Response	Washington	$578,711,172
Michigan	$1,441,935,000	W. Virginia	No Response
Minnesota	$162,874,215	Wisconsin	$569,053,300
Mississippi	$236,099,488	Wyoming	No Response
Missouri	$510,506,279	US Bureau of Prisons	$3,299,850,000

Source: The Corrections Compendium. Vol. XXI :12. (December, 1999).
CEGA Publishing, 3900 Industrial Avenue North, Lincoln, Nebraska.

was 445 persons per 100,000 population, up from 96.0 per 100,000 in 1973. Table 2.6 illustrates the incarceration rate from 1925 to 1997. Table 2.7 illustrates the incarceration rate by state from 1977 to 1997. Clearly, some states are making an effort to find alternatives to incarceration, while others seem intent on locking up a good portion of their population

A close inspection of Table 2.8 reveals that those states with the highest incarceration rate also have the highest crime rate. On the surface this makes sense, but if those states are locking more criminals up, shouldn't they eventually reach the point where there will be no criminals left on the street? Advocates of the "lock'em up" philosophy point to the declining crime rate as proof that tough . sentencing policies are bearing fruit. But as we shall see in later chapters, it is not as simple as that. It will take a few more years of study to determine the real reason for the decline. However, there are a number of reasons for the drop in crime, including the fact that the baby boom has aged out of its high crime prone years and there is increasing prosperity at hand with a very low unemployment rate.

It is a fact that the matter of crime causation is complicated and we as taxpayers run the danger of trivializing the causes of crime and searching for panaceas. However, the impulse to build our way out of the crime problem must be rethought. California, according to experts "seems to be opening up a new prison every week." Still there seems to be no end in sight to the numbers of California citizens who must do time in prison. For example in 1987, according to the FBI, California had a crime rate of 6,506.4 crimes per 100,000 population. By 1992 the crime rate in California had risen somewhat to 6,679 per 100,000 population. During the same period of time California added 47,427 beds to the Department ofCorrections. Surely, the addition of that many beds should have made a larger dent in the crime rate if a policy of locking them up actually works. Finally California citizens revolted and in March of 2000 passed Proposition 21 which requires that those individuals arrested for drug use (or possession of a

50

Table 2.6 – Rate per 100,000 of Sentenced Prisoners in State and Federal Institutions By Sex, United States, 1925-97

(Rate per 100,000 resident population in each group)

Year	Total	Rate	Male Number	Male Rate	Female Number	Female Rate
1925	91,669	79	88,231	149	3,438	6
1926	97,991	83	94,287	157	3,704	6
1927	109,983	91	104,983	173	4,363	7
1928	116,390	96	111,836	182	4,554	8
1929	120,496	98	115,876	187	4,620	8
1930	129,453	104	124,785	200	4,668	8
1931	137,082	110	132,638	211	4,444	7
1932	137,997	110	133,573	211	4,424	7
1933	136,810	109	132,520	209	4,290	7
1934	138,316	109	133,769	209	4,547	7
1935	144,180	113	139,278	217	4,902	8
1936	145,038	113	139,990	217	5,048	8
1937	152,741	118	147,375	227	5,366	8
1938	160,285	123	154,826	236	5,459	8
1939	179,818	137	173,143	263	6,675	10
1940	173,706	131	167,345	252	6,361	10
1941	165,439	124	159,228	239	6,211	9
1942	150,384	112	144,167	217	6,217	9
1943	137,220	103	131,054	202	6,166	9
1944	132,456	100	126,350	200	6,106	9
1945	133,649	98	127,609	193	6,040	9

Year	Total	Rate	Male Number	Male Rate	Female Number	Female Rate
1960	212,953	117	205,265	230	7,688	8
1961	220,149	119	212,268	234	7,881	8
1962	218,830	117	210,823	229	8,007	8
1963	217,283	114	209,538	225	7,745	8
1964	214,336	111	206,632	219	7,704	8
1965	210,895	108	203,327	213	7,558	8
1966	199,654	102	192,703	201	6,951	7
1967	194,896	98	188,661	195	6,235	6
1968	187,914	94	182,102	187	5,812	6
1969	196,007	97	189,413	192	6,594	6
1970	196,429	96	190,794	191	5,635	5
1971	198,061	95	191,732	189	6,329	6
1972	196,092	93	189,823	185	6,269	6
1973	204,211	96	197,523	191	6,004	6
1974	218,466	102	211,077	202	7,389	7
1975	240,593	111	231,918	220	8,675	8
1976	262,833	120	252,794	238	10,039	9
1977[a]	278,141	126	267,097	249	11,044	10
1977[b]	285,456	129	274,244	255	11,212	10
1978	294,396	132	282,813	261	11,583	10
1979	301,470	133	289,465	264	12,005	10

Table 2.6 – Rate per 100,000 of Sentenced Prisoners in State and Federal Institutions (Continued)

Year	Total Number	Rate	Male Number	Rate	Female Number	Rate
1946	140,079	99	134,075	191	6,004	8
1947	151,304	105	144,961	202	6,343	9
1948	155,977	106	149,739	205	6,238	8
1949	163,749	109	157,663	211	6,086	8
1950	166,123	109	160,309	211	5,814	8
1951	165,680	107	159,610	208	6,070	8
1952	168,233	107	161,994	208	6,239	8
1953	173,579	108	166,909	211	6,670	8
1954	182,901	112	175,907	218	6,994	8
1955	185,780	112	178,655	217	7,125	8
1956	189,565	112	182,190	218	7,375	9
1957	195,414	113	188,113	221	7,301	8
1958	205,643	117	198,208	229	7,435	8
1959	208,105	117	200,469	228	7,636	8
1980	315,974	139	303,643	275	12,331	11
1981	353,167	154	338,940	304	14,227	12
1982	394,374	171	378,045	337	16,329	14
1983	419,820	179	402,391	354	17,429	15
1984	443,398	188	424,193	370	19,205	16
1985	480,568	202	458,972	397	21,296	17
1986	522,084	217	497,540	426	24,544	20
1987	560,812	231	533,990	453	26,822	22
1988	603,732	247	573,587	482	30,145	24
1989	680,907	276	643,643	535	37,264	29
1990	739,980	297	699,416	575	40,564	32
1991	789,610	313	745,808	606	43,802	34
1992	846,277	332	799,776	642	46,501	36
1993	932,074	359	878,037	698	54,037	41
1994	1,016,691	389	956,566	753	60,125	45
1995	1,085,363	411	1,021,463	796	63,900	48
1996[c]	1,138,984	427	1,069,257	819	69,727	51
1997[d]	1,197,590	445	1,123,478	853	74,112	54

Note: See Notes, figures 6.1 and 6.4. These data represent prisoners sentenced to more than 1 year. Both custody and jurisdiction figures are shown for 1977 to facilitate year-to-year comparison. Some data have been revised by the Source and may differ from previous editions of SOURCEBOOK. For information on methodology, definitions of terms, and jurisdictional explanatory notes, see Appendix 4.

[a] Custody counts.
[b] Jurisdiction counts.
[c] Rates for 1996 and are preliminary and subject to revision.
[d] All data for 1997 are preliminary and subject to revision.

Source: Kathleen Maguire and Ann K, Pastore, eds., *Sourcebook of Criminal Justice Statistics, 1997*. U. S. Department of Justice Bureau of Justice Statistics, Washington, DC: USPGO, 1998

Table 2.7 – Rate of Sentenced Prisoners in State and Federal Institutions in 1977-1997 By State

Rate per 100,000 resident population

Region and Jurisdiction	1977	1978	1979	1980	1981	1982	1983	1984	1985	1986	1987	1988	1989	1990	1991	1992	1993	1994	1995	1996	1997
United States, total	129	135	136	139	153	170	179	188	200	216	228	244	271	292	310	330	365	389	411	427	445
Federal	13	12	10	9	10	10	11	12	14	15	16	17	19	20	22	26	28	30	32	33	35
State	116	123	126	130	144	160	167	176	187	201	211	227	253	272	287	305	322	358	379	394	410
Northeast	77	82	84	87	103	115	127	136	145	157	169	186	215	232	248	261	272	286	301	308	317
Connecticut	53	70	69	68	95	114	114	119	127	135	144	146	194	238	263	268	320	321	318	314	397
Maine	61	53	58	61	71	69	75	72	83	106	106	100	116	118	123	121	116	113	107	112	124
Massachusetts	48	49	50	56	65	77	79	84	88	92	102	109	122	132	143	161	154	174	170	302	278
New Hampshire	26	32	35	35	42	47	50	57	68	76	81	93	103	117	132	160	157	177	174	177	184
New Jersey	78	74	76	76	92	107	136	138	149	157	177	219	251	271	301	290	301	311	340	343	351
New York	108	114	120	123	145	158	172	187	195	215	229	248	285	304	320	340	354	367	378	383	386
Pennsylvania	56	65	67	68	78	88	98	109	119	128	136	149	169	183	192	207	216	235	268	286	291
Rhode Island	56	56	63	65	72	82	92	92	99	103	100	118	146	157	173	170	172	186	186	205	213
Vermont	57	76	62	67	76	84	72	74	82	81	91	98	109	117	124	151	154	168	179	137	140
Midwest	108	104	105	109	121	130	135	144	161	173	184	200	225	239	255	273	282	299	310	326	346
Illinois	95	96	95	94	113	119	135	149	161	168	171	181	211	234	247	271	294	310	317	327	342
Indiana	80	98	98	114	138	152	164	165	175	181	192	202	217	223	226	242	250	258	275	287	301
Iowa	70	70	72	86	88	93	92	97	98	98	101	107	126	139	144	160	174	192	207	222	243
Kansas	97	98	95	106	116	129	152	173	192	217	233	232	222	227	231	238	226	248	274	301	304
Michigan	151	162	163	163	165	162	159	161	196	227	259	298	340	366	388	413	414	427	429	440	442
Minnesota	44	49	51	49	49	50	52	52	56	58	60	64	71	72	78	85	92	100	105	110	113
Missouri	111	116	113	112	131	147	162	175	194	203	218	236	269	287	305	311	308	338	358	409	442
Nebraska	83	80	71	89	104	99	91	95	108	116	123	129	141	140	145	151	153	164	183	194	200
North Dakota	30	21	19	28	33	47	51	54	55	53	57	62	62	67	68	85	70	78	85	101	112
Ohio	120	122	125	125	139	160	155	174	194	209	219	243	279	289	324	347	365	387	400	413	429
South Dakota	76	74	77	88	97	109	115	127	146	160	160	143	175	187	191	208	216	236	252	281	303
Wisconsin	72	73	73	85	93	96	102	105	113	119	126	q130	138	149	157	176	166	187	201	230	283

Table 2.7 – Rate of Sentenced Prisoners in State and Federal Institutions in 1977-1997 By State (Continued)

Region and Jurisdiction	Rate per 100,000 resident population																				
	1977	1978	1979	1980	1981	1982	1983	1984	1985	1986	1987	1988	1989	1990	1991	1992	1993	1994	1995	1996	1997
South																					
Alabama	169	181	196	188	201	224	225	231	236	248	255	266	292	316	333	355	380	454	483	490	506
Arkansas	94	144	141	149	183	215	243	256	267	283	307	300	328	370	394	407	431	450	471	492	500
Delaware	111	115	132	128	143	166	179	188	195	198	227	230	261	277	317	340	327	345	361	357	392
District of Columbia	330	383	433	426	467	531	558	649	738	753	905	1078	1132	1148	1221	1287	1549	1782	1650	1609	1682
Florida	221	239	220	208	224	261	235	242	247	272	265	278	307	336	344	355	384	406	447	439	437
Georgia	224	216	224	219	220	247	259	254	251	265	282	281	300	327	342	365	387	456	470	462	472
Kentucky	106	97	105	99	114	110	127	128	133	142	147	191	222	241	262	274	274	288	311	331	372
Louisiana	152	184	190	211	216	251	290	310	308	316	346	370	396	427	462	484	522	556	578	615	672
Maryland	198	193	187	183	218	244	277	285	279	280	282	291	323	348	366	381	383	395	404	412	413
Mississippi	67	110	141	132	177	210	211	229	237	249	256	277	307	330	330	327	305	323	384	379	370
North Carolina	234	223	240	244	248	255	233	246	254	257	250	250	361	381	416	459	506	508	552	591	617
Oklahoma	129	146	147	151	169	201	212	236	250	288	296	323	361	381	473	486	488	637	515	532	536
South Carolina	239	243	237	238	251	270	276	284	294	324	344	369	416	451	330	344	386	276	677	686	309
Tennessee	127	134	151	153	171	173	187	154	149	157	156	240	257	290	311	327	346	406	410	404	717
Texas	176	189	196	210	210	237	221	226	226	228	231	230	263	279	297	327	346	406	410	404	407
Virginia	142	157	158	161	165	177	177	185	204	215	217	207	263	279	311	299	319	334	358	386	174
West Virginia	67	63	66	64	80	77	83	82	89	77	77	78	84	85	83	92	98	106	136	150	405
West																					
Alaska	92	99	101	105	119	139	152	166	176	197	214	234	256	277	287	299	319	334	358	386	420
Arizona	75	127	133	143	170	194	219	252	288	306	339	355	361	348	345	327	446	317	473	451	484
California	129	146	147	151	170	209	223	247	256	212	257	328	350	375	396	409	430	384	416	322	475
Colorado	80	88	93	98	114	135	150	162	181	212	231	257	311	311	318	256	262	289	292	249	342
Hawaii	89	93	90	95	92	77	109	104	134	115	145	174	207	209	205	164	198	202	217	319	288
Idaho	44	57	58	65	77	88	103	124	133	144	141	136	142	150	153	209	234	245	283	235	323
Montana	87	91	92	87	99	107	121	127	136	135	147	157	165	176	183	180	182	204	228	502	255
Nevada	187	204	224	230	245	301	354	380	397	447	432	452	438	444	439	448	434	468	493	261	518
New Mexico	126	123	112	106	100	126	142	133	144	176	200	180	235	196	191	197	206	211	231	226	256
Oregon	122	117	122	120	124	146	157	170	165	108	110	215	223	142	228	174	166	157	174	194	232
Utah	64	69	68	64	73	77	77	84	98	108	110	115	137	142	149	146	152	157	174	224	205
Washington	118	122	113	106	125	148	155	156	156	147	134	124	142	162	182	192	196	201	212	307	233
Wyoming	98	102	95	113	117	135	138	143	148	168	190	199	216	237	237	226	238	254	289	307	326

Source: Kathleen Maguire and Ann K, Pastore, eds., *Sourcebook of Criminal Justice Statistics, 1997.* U. S. Department of Justice Bureau of Justice Statistics, Washington, DC: USPGO, 1998

Table 2.8
Crime Rate by Incarceration Rate by State

State	Crime Rate					Incarceration Rate				
	1973	1980	1988	1994	1997	1973	1980	1988	1994	1997
AL	2,512	4,933	4,561	4,903.0	4,889.7	104.5	149	300	450	500
AK	4,943	6,210	4,921	5,708.1	5,272.6	56.3	143	355	317	420
AZ	6,703	8,170	7,471	7,924.6	7,195.0	81.0	160	328	459	482
AR	2,538	3,811	4,219	4,798.7	4,718.7	82.2	128	230	353	392
CA	6,304	7,833	6,635	6,173.8	4.865.3	96.7	98	257	384	475
CO	5,495	7,333	6,178	5,318.4	4,650.4	77.5	96	174	289	342
CT	3,664	5,881	5,097	4,548.0	3,984.3	54.2	68	146	285	397
DE	4,582	6,776	4,799	4,147.6	5,782.9	57.1	183	331	393	443
DC	N/A	10,236	9,914	11,085	9,839.1	324.2	426	1078	1,583	1,682
FL	5,960	8,402	8,937	8,250,0	7,271.8	32.5	208	278	406	437
GA	3,430	5,603	6,326	6,010.3	5,791.7	173.3	219	281	456	472
HI	4,958	7,482	5,989	6,680.5	6,022.9	37.3	65	136	202	288
ID	3,457	4,782	3,973	4,077.0	3,925.2	54.6	87	157	258	323
IL	4,324	5,275	5,620	5,625.9	5,141.1	50.3	94	181	310	342
IN	3,533	4,930	4,150	4,592.8	4,466.3	63.4	114	202	258	301
IA	2,831	4,746	4,076	3,654.6	3,815.8	49.0	86	107	192	243
KS	3,513	5,378	4,879	4,893.8	5,152.4	60.6	106	232	249	304
KY	2,265	3,433	3,134	3,498.6	3,127.0	89.4	99	191	288	372
LS	3,402	3,811	5,760	6,671.1	6,449.2	108.3	211	370	530	672
ME	2,544	4,367	3,577	3,523	3,131.7	43.8	61	100	118	124
MY	4,791	6,630	5,704	6,122.6	5,653.1	144.0	183	291	395	413
MA	4,521	6,079	4,990	4,441.0	3,675.2	34.3	56	109	171	278
MI	5,489	6,675	6,084	5,445.2	4,916.9	86.8	163	298	428	457
MN	3,535	4,799	4,314	4,341.0	4,413.8	36.0	49	64	100	113
MS	1,926	3,417	3,592	4,837.1	4,630.2	75.5	132	277	408	531
MO	4,141	5,433	4,844	5,307.7	4,814.5	79.4	112	236	338	442
MT	3,395	5,024	4,267	5,018.8	4,408.8	43.5	94	158	194	255
NE	2,811	4,305	4,140	4,440.4	4,283.8	66.0	89	129	159	200
NV	6,632	8,854	6,453	6,677.4	6,064.5	134.9	230	452	460	518
NH	2,329	4,679	3,333	2,741.0	2,639.6	34.8	35	93	177	184
NJ	4,082	6,401	5,295	4,660.9	4,057.0	73.5	76	219	310	351
NM	4,707	5,979	6,606	6,187.8	6,906.5	66.4	106	180	220	256
NY	4,306	6,911	6,309	5,070.6	3,910.9	71.4	123	248	367	386
NC	2,811	4,640	4,862	5,625.2	5,491.5	183.9	244	249	322	370
ND	2,078	2,963	2,728	2,735.9	2,711.4	24.9	28	62	78	112
OH	3,495	5,431	4,645	4,461.4	4,510.1	71.9	125	243	377	429
OK	3,366	5,052	5,589	5,570.1	5,494.7	120.4	151	323	508	617
OR	5,297	6,686	7,058	6,296.4	6,269.8	74.7	120	215	176	232
PA	2,458	3,736	3,176	3,271.9	3,431.5	55.0	68	149	235	291
RI	4,678	5,932	5,204	4,119.1	3,654.4	43.2	65	118	186	213
SC	3,327	5,439	5,412	6,000.8	6,134.0	130.1	238	369	494	536
SD	2,175	3,243	2,581	3,102.2	3,245.0	34.9	88	143	240	303
TN	3,060	4,497	4,469	5,119.8	5,511.8	84.2	153	157	277	309
TX	4,046	6,143	8,017	5,872.4	5,480.5	146.6	210	240	636	717
UT	4,247	5,880	5,578	5,300.9	5,995.5	44.7	64	115	155	205
VT	2,498	4,988	4,240	3,250.3	3,139.1	40.3	67	98	168	140

Table 2.8
Crime Rate by Incarceration Rate by State (Continued)

State	Crime Rate					Incarceration Rate				
	1973	1980	1988	1994	1997	1973	1980	1988	1994	1997
VA	3,238	4,620	4,176	4,047.6	3,876.2	107.9	161	230	395	407
WA	5,089	6,915	7,113	6,027.5	5,926.3	77.1	106	124	201	233
WV	1,471	2,551	2,238	2,528.4	2,469.1	60.8	64	78	106	174
WI	3,176	4,798	3,972	3,944.4	3,677.6	47.2	85	130	187	283
WY	3,413	4,986	3,967	4,289.7	4,180.8	76.6	113	199	254	326

Source: Federal Bureau of Investigation. *Crime in the United States*, 1973, 1980, 1988, 1994 and 1998. Uniform Crime Reports for the United States. (Washington, D.C.: U.S. Department of Justice, 1994).
Source: Kathleen Maguire and Ann K. Pastore, eds., *Sourcebook of Criminal Justice Statistics 1993 and 1997*. U.S. Department of Justice, Bureau of Justice Statistics (Washington, D.C.: USGPO, 1994 and 1998).

minor amount of drugs) be placed in a treatment program. Table 2.8 provides the crime rate and incarceration rate for all states.

Irwin and Austin (1994) point out that criminal justice system employment has increased from 1,146,350 in 1979 to 1,721,622 in 1990. In 1998 state and local criminal justice system employees totaled nearly 1.7 million employees. This is good news in a sense. It means that we have the same number of police officers, corrections and court workers responsible for policing our neighborhoods, handling trials, and working with offenders in spite of an increase in total U.S. population, an increase in court dockets, and prison populations. We are indeed getting a good deal for our tax dollar.

In 1998 nearly $5 billion was spent on payroll. Anyone who has worked in a prison or as a police officer will attest to the fact that they are underpaid. In fact, we demand more form criminal justice system employees than perhaps any other endeavor in the world of work. We also continue to subsidize the well-to-do by paying those in the most dangerous occupations a salary that is at times pitiful. Nevertheless, there is more to employing someone than simply a salary. Benefits of some sort are necessary such as medical/dental care, social security, and retirement. As a consequence, when we hire 100 new police officers or corrections workers we will continue to pay far into the future in the form of retirement. As a consequence, any public figure who says he or she knows how much money police, corrections, or the courts consume each year is lying.

Take the case of corrections. In a previous book (Houston, 1995) the author cites McDonalds (1989) excellent discussion of corrections budgets and points out that there are direct and indirect costs. Direct costs include: food for inmates, salaries, and utilities for example. Indirect costs are often overlooked and include:

> *Amortizing capital expenditures.* Most analysis of correctional costs do not amortize capital spending over time. As a consequence, capital spending is often understated.

> *Financing.* If financed by borrowing, the costs of acquiring assets should be considered current operating costs. In public accounts this is rarely done.

> *Expenditures of other agencies.* Direct costs incurred by other agencies that help the corrections agency accomplish its mission should be counted. Teachers salaries, utility bills, and transportation are examples of costs often paid by other branches of government.

> *Disentangling costs within an agency.* Agencies often perform a variety of functions, and it is often difficult to disentangle the costs. For example, a probation agency may conduct pre-sentencing reports for the court and supervise parolees once the inmate has been paroled from prison.

> *Expenditures from other accounts.* Some costs are paid out of general government accounts. Examples include pension and fringe benefits which are handled for all state employees by one branch of government.

The above examples are illustrative of all criminal justice agencies. It is also an example of what is wrong with contemporary thinking on how to approach the issue of crime. It appears that we are spending money on solutions that will require our children and grandchildren to pay the bill.

Proposition #3: We cannot sustain the present policy of
imprisoning the non-violent offender.

Alternatives to Prison

In an effort to fight crime we aimlessly set goals of putting more people into jails and prisons, regardless of consequential costs or the complete denigration of dignity and resulting human sacrifice.... The knee-jerk reactions by angry executives, politically conscious legislatures and vindictive judicial officers is taking us down a primrose path with little success in combating crime. The resulting approach is accomplishing nothing more than exorbitantly wasting tax dollars, creating a warehouse of human degradation and in the long run breeding societal resentment that causes more crime (Lay, 1990 in Durham, 1994).

Judge Lay clearly recognizes the folly of placing everyone in prison. However, many citizens are unaware of viable alternatives. We seem to feed on the perceived notion that everyone else wants a stricter use of prisons and that anything less than prison is being soft on crime. That is not true. Most Americans support punishments other than prison for non-dangerous law-breakers. While the American public is uncertain about what prisons and corrections in general should do, 60% of the public would favor restitution over imprisonment for some criminals, 67% of the public favors diversion programs, and of lawyers and judges polled 87% of the judges and 92% of lawyers favor restitution over prison. Seventy-five percent of the public also sees overcrowding in prisons as a contributor to the crime rate and 62% of respondents stated that they would favor higher taxes in order to build new prisons (Gilbert, 1988).

In another study by the Public Agenda Foundation for the highly respected Edna McConnell Clark Foundation, (1987), the authors learned that instead of a fierce desire for retribution on the part of the American public, they instead wanted an assurance of public safety and for prisons to promote rehabilitation. The study was conducted through the use of focus groups that represented all segments of the American public. Among the "discoveries" were:

* Americans feel that criminals are products of their environment and totally reject the idea that they are born.

* Americans have a low regard for the nation's prison system.

* Americans feel that a primary goal of the prison system should be to rehabilitate prisoners, especially young or first offenders. But, they feel that the prison system is falling far short of that goal.

*   Americans believe that prison overcrowding is caused by an increase in crime. They simply do not believe that the crime rate has leveled off or that mandatory and stiffer sentencing are a cause of the problem.

*   Americans strongly support the use of alternatives to incarceration in particular cases.

*   While favoring greater use of alternatives, Americans would restrict their use to certain types of offenders, excluding violent or repeat offenders and drug dealers.

A national poll conducted by the Wirthlin Group in 1991 found that 75% of Americans favor non-prison punishment for criminals who are not dangerous (in Irwin and Austin, 1994). More recently, one poll found that nearly 50% of those queried state that rehabilitation should be the main goal of the prison. In the same poll, respondents seem to believe that such alternative as probation, electronic monitoring of offenders, boot camps, and so on are either "very effective" or "somewhat effective" at protecting citizens against crime (Maguire and Pastore, 1998). Apparently the American public has a good deal more common sense than those we elect to represent us in Congress and the state legislatures.

Americans are not a mean spirited people. We have a reputation for generosity and allowing the individual spirit to soar. However, with the crisis mentality that has been created among the public, we have failed to question the claims of many people running for political office who are loose with the facts. Polls seem to verify that most Americans support alternatives to prison for nonviolent offenders. Therefore it is time we begin to seriously consider alternatives to prison for non-dangerous criminals.

As illustrated in Table 2.5, some states have funded and continue to fund alternatives to imprisonment. Presumably if they were not considered successful, those programs would not be included in the budget. The following alternatives are ones that have been tried and are accepted by experts in the field of criminal justice. Nearly every community has an example of each of the programs, we simply do not use them enough for nonviolent offenders. We must remember that punishments in the field of corrections lie on a continuum--from fines and probation to execution. There is a lot of room between the two extremes and it is often not necessary for the majority of sentenced felons to be sent to prison as the first reaction if other alternatives have not been tried.

Diversion Programs. Diversion programs are those attempts to keep the individual out of the criminal justice system rather than bring them into the system. The philosophy is one of attempting to deal with social, economic, and mental health (including substance abuse) problems if the court believes that the condition played a major role in causing the individual to violate the law. An individual may be referred to such a program by the police, the prosecutor, or by the probation department prior to sentencing.

Home Confinement Home confinement is usually used in conjunction with electronic monitoring. It allows the individual to remain at home except for designated times when the person is allowed to be out of the home for work or other appointments as agreed upon by the Probation Officer. It allows for regular intensive contacts by the probation officer, the offender is allowed to maintain employment and relationships and it saves the taxpayer a good deal of money. Usually, the offender is required to pay a daily fee to cover costs of maintaining the electronic equipment and to defray the costs of hiring a probation officer to supervise the probationers.

Electronic Monitoring. Technology is now available for the authorities to monitor the location of probationers and parolees. There are two systems: active and passive. The active system is one where the probation officer and the probationer agree to a schedule and the probationer must be in his home at certain times. To check up on the probationer, the probation officer programs a computer to call the offenders home at random hours. The probationer must answer the phone and after identifying himself, has a few seconds to match his wrist bracelet with a corresponding place on the terminal box in his home. If he or she is unable to manipulate the box and bracelet, perhaps because they are too drunk or high on drugs to do so, a print out makes a note for the probation officer to review. In addition, the conversation between the computer and the subject is recorded on tape for the probation officer to listen to and determine if there is cause to believe individual is high on drugs or alcohol. The probation officer can then require a urine sample the next day and, if positive, the results will be considered as cause for remand to custody.

The passive system is somewhat more simple. The probationer must wear an ankle bracelet that emits a signal to the terminal box connected to the telephone in the residence. If the probationer leaves a certain radius, usually 150 feet, the terminal signals the computer in a central location and it makes a note for the probation officer to see on a print-out. Thus if the probationer leaves the residence at a time not agreed upon by the probation officer, he or she has committed a violation of the terms of supervision.

The bracelets worn by the subjects are tamper proof and, if cut or tampered with, a signal is sent to the computer and is noted on a print-out. Further, neither system prevents the probationer from engaging in some form of skullduggery while at home. Therefore it is necessary for the sentencing court to assure adequate supervision by a community programs officer to assure the integrity of the system.

Fines and Community Service. Two distinguished experts (Morris and Tonry, 1990) point out that the fine is a vastly underutilized sanction in the United States. In their view, we should "let the fine serve as a powerful penal disincentive rather than a mere adjunct to other punishments." They have a point, in a nation were the spirit of capitalism has achieved a purity of form unknown in most other nations of the world, we do not think of financial sanctions in any way other than as an adjunct to prison or probation. We have the technology to now deduct a portion of one's paycheck for payment on an automobile or to make a mortgage payment, so why not payment to the Court?

Community service is also underutilized. Some of the opposition has come from public employee unions and they are wrong to oppose such a program. Temporary employment will not substitute for experience and commitment, but community service offenders can augment the efforts of regular employees. In addition, if adequate supervision is obtained by the sponsoring agency, community service offenders can put valued skills to work in hospitals, schools, parks and recreation programs to maintain the infra-structure of the county or state. There has been a move to revive the chain gang in some southern states. This is a viable alternative to idleness and boredom in a prison or jail. In addition, valuable work can be accomplished by the inmates on behalf of the state.

Probation. Probation is an often misunderstood alternative to prison. For adults, the individual is never sentenced to probation, rather he or she is sentenced to a term in prison. After reviewing a Pre-sentence Report to determine if the offender is eligible, the Judge can sentence the individual to a term in prison and then set aside the sentence and allow the individual to remain free in the community under the supervision of the court and subject to certain conditions. If, while on probation the probationer commits a new crime he or she is liable to be sentenced to a prison term (assuming it is a felony offense) and his or her probation will be revoked and the sentence imposed. Thus, if the probationer was sentenced to prison for 5 years which was set aside and he was placed on probation for five years, then if found guilty for the new offense, he will serve the five years and any new sentence often consecutive to each other. As a result the subject, who could have lived at home and held a job ends up spending as long as 10 years in prison.

The reason that probation does not work many times is that the term of probation ends up being a term of unsupervised release into the community. This is not the fault of the judge or the probation department. It is the result of penny wise and pound foolish policies and a short sighted public. It is approximately 14 times cheaper to supervise an adult on probation than send him or her to prison. It is approximately 10 times cheaper to supervise a juvenile on probation than send him or her to the state training school. According to experts, it costs about $2.00 per day for someone to serve his or her time on probation, compared to $35.00 -$50.00 per day if he or she was sent to prison (Durham, 1994). It may well be that if we had invested money in probation officers in the past, we would not have had to invest in new prisons and corrections workers today.

One answer to critics of probation has been to institute what are called Intensive Probation Programs. This is an approach that allows a probation officer to supervise no more than perhaps 15-20 probationers at a time. The Probation Officer is able to continually check up on his or her caseload and take a proactive approach to supervision. That is he or she can take urine samples from suspected drug users, check up on employment, counsel, and in general be available for supervision and social work activities. In regard to cost, Georgia's Intensive Probation Program is $4.36 per day (Durham, 1994).

Work Release and Restitution Centers. Many offenders are eligible for placement in a semi-secure setting and allowed to hold a full time job. Most states have legislation that allows the sponsoring agency to collect a portion of the prisoners salary for reimbursement for room and board and also require the prisoner to make payments for restitution and any other court ordered payments such as child support. In addition, the prisoner can be required to work at least part-time on public projects such as cleaning up parks and so on until he or she finds employment. Once full time employment has been found, the prisoner can be required to continue to put in several hours per week on public service.

The benefits to the taxpayer and the prisoner are many fold, including the building of a work ethic in the prisoner and saving money for the taxpayer. Obviously violent offenders are not eligible for such a program and policies and procedures must be thoroughly thought out to maximize accountability of prisoners. However, some states have cut back on such programs because of a misguided idea of accountability. In Michigan, all work release centers have been closed, or are slated to close, and prisoners will be released from prison with little or no supervision during their critical first few months of freedom. Thus it is important that adequate staff be allocated to community residential programs to ensure accountability and public safety. Since in the long run nearly all prison inmates will be released to the community it makes good sense to implement such programs.

Summary

There is no doubt that the economic and social cost of crime is more than we want to bear. More than 105 million households were victimized in 1998 costing far more than $17 billion in direct costs. Stolen property was recovered in 35% of the crimes: 64% of all stolen automobiles were recovered, 20% of stolen clothing and furs, 10% of stolen firearms, and 13% of all stolen household goods were recovered. Clearly, victims suffer financial hardships and when one considers that the bulk of victims are lower or working class individuals, the losses are even more substantial.

While these amounts are substantial and the social costs cannot to calculated, reports from the Bureau of Justice Statistics and the FBI **Uniform Crime Report** do not substantiate a crime wave. Nor do they verify claims of those running for political office that the last 25 years have wwitnessed a steady decline into barbarism. For example, from 1988 to 1993 there was a relatively insignificant rise in dollar amounts lost to burglary and from 1994 to the present there has been a significant decline. Violent crime rose significantly for young males, but they seem to only attack each other. Since 1973, the crime rate in many states has gone up only a fraction and again violent crime has declined significantly since 1994, but the incarceration rate has doubled, quadrupled and even gone up five times the rate of 1973. We have embarked upon a prison building spree that threatens to bankrupt us and we simply cannot continue to ignore alternatives to imprisonment for nonviolent offenders.

There are a number of alternatives to prison including: diversion programs, work-release and Restitution Centers, increased use of fines, community service, and Intensive Probation. All of these programs have proven themselves to be effective in dealing with the nonviolent offender. The advantage of alternative programs is that they allow the offender to maintain employment or serve the community in some capacity. If the offender is allowed to work, he or she can contribute to their family income and alleviate further drain on welfare, food stamps and other relief measures that are commonly sought when the head of the household is sent to prison. In addition, in many instances such as electronic monitoring and work release centers, at least part of the cost is defrayed by charging the offender a fee for the privilege of being a part of the program. However, such programs do not work based solely upon good intentions. They must be funded and staffed properly. Clearly, they are much cheaper than prison.

Bibliography

The Corrections Compendium. CEGA Publishing, 3900 Industrial Avenue North, Lincoln, Nebraska.

Frank T. Cullen, Gregory A. Clark, and John F. Wozniak. "Explaining the Get Tough Movement: Can the Public be Blamed?" **Federal Probation,** 49 pp. 16-24.

John Doble. **Crime and Punishment: The Publics View.** A report prepared by The Public Agenda Foundation. New York: The Edna McConnell Clark Foundation, 1987.

Alexis M. Durham, III. **Crisis and Reform: Current Issues in American Punishment.** (Boston: Little, Brown and Company, 1994).

Federal Bureau of Investigation. **Crime in the United States,** 1988 and 1993. Uniform Crime Reports for the United States. (Washington, D.C.: U.S. Department of Justice, 1994).

Dennis A. Gilbert. **Compendium of American Public Opinion.** (New York: Facts on File Publications, 1988).

James Houston. **Correctional Management: Functions, Skills, and Systems,** 2nd ed. (Chicago: Nelson-Hall, Inc. 1995).

John Irwin and James Austin. **It's About Time: America's Imprisonment Binge.** (Belmont, CA: Wadsworth Publishing Company, 1994).

Patsy Klaus. "The Costs of Crime to Victims," **Crime Data Brief.** Washington, D.C.: Bureau of Justice Statistics, February, 1994.

Kathleen Maguire and Ann K. Pastore, eds., **Sourcebook of Criminal Justice Statistics 1993 and 1998.** U.S. Department of Justice, Bureau of Justice Statistics. Washington, D.C.: USGPO, 1994.

Hans W. Mattick, "The Contemporary Jails of the United States: An Unknown and Neglected Area of Justice," in Daniel Glaser, ed. **Handbook of Criminology** (Chicago: Rand McNally Publishing Company, 1974)

Douglas C. McDonald. "The Cost of Corrections: In Search of the Bottom Line," National Institute of Corrections, **Research in Corrections,** 2:1 (February, 1989).

Norval Morris and Michael Tonrey. **Between Prison and Probation: Intermediate Punishments in a Rational Sentencing System**. (New York: Oxford University Press, 1990)

National Insurance Crime Bureau. "Insurance Fraud: The $20 Billion Disaster," **FACTPAGE**. (Palos Hills, IL.: NICB News Bureau, 1994).

Chapter 3

The Courts and the Legal Process

Introduction

We are often confused and even angered by court decisions that seem to fly in the face of justice. Many politicians and columnists have made political gain by reviling the courts and sentences meted out to convicted criminals. However, with a few exceptions, the sentences handed down at the time of sentencing are sound and thoughtful and the sentencing judge makes every effort to take into consideration the needs of the community and the offender.

However, with the advent of sentencing grids, much of the discretion of judges at the time of sentencing has been taken away. During the 1980s many elected officials determined that the courts were too lenient and that many criminals were getting off with light sentences. A related problem was that two offenders with the same offense, and of similar backgrounds could, and sometimes did, receive very different sentences, one harsh and the other not so harsh. In reaction, the US Congress and most state legislatures devised grids that allowed very little discretion to sentencing judges and made many offenses punishable by time in prison. Once grids were implemented, prison populations began to swell.

Courts and their operation are something of a mystery to most Americans and the media and various BAR associations do very little to dispel the mystery surrounding courts and court decisions. The nature of American criminal law is rooted in English common law and adopted common law continues to guide state legislatures (Eldefonso and Coffey,1981).

There are a number of sanctions available to the courts in the event a defendant is found guilty of a crime. At present, prison is a much overused sanction and this is the result of the pressure of overly zealous legislators. However, in our rush to be "tough" on crime we often forget that prisons are simply, in many instances, graduate schools of crime. As a consequence, sending a first time offender to prison is accelerating a social process in which the individual may have matured out of further criminal behavior.

The Process

Judges, prosecutors, and defense attorneys play the leading roles in formal court proceedings. The degree of "justice" that the defendant gets is often proportional to the amount of money the local jurisdiction has for such things as public defense and competent prosecutors. Most Americans are probably unaware that over 90 percent of criminal court decisions are the result of plea bargaining.

There are several stages that the defendant must go through during the course of legal proceedings: Grand Jury or prosecutorial information, arraignment, the assignment of counsel, arraignment, pre-trial motions, trial, and sentencing. Each has several separate steps that must or can be taken as the defendant works his or her way through the process. Fortunately, this process ensures that the system of American criminal justice is one of the fairest in world. We may rant and rave about criminals getting off, but we must always keep in mind that those rules protect the freedom of us all.

Grand Jury. The grand jury is an investigative body whose function is to hear the facts as presented by the prosecuting Attorney and determine if there is probable cause to believe that a crime has been committed and that the individual in question should stand trial. The grand jury does not determine the guilt or innocence of the individual, it must only answer if the person should come to trial. However, about half of the states substitute a preliminary hearing for a Grand Jury indictment. The United States Constitution requires a Grand Jury only in Federal criminal proceedings.

The Grand Jury returns an indictment, that is an accusation in writing charging a person with an offense. If the person is not in custody, the state may decide to issue a bench warrant for the arrest the individual. Once arrested he or she must be allowed the opportunity to post bail. However, the grand jury must make a recommendation as to the amount of bail for that particular offense. The court then has the discretion to set bail at an amount it deems appropriate.

Witnesses appearing before a grand jury are not allowed the right to counsel as the grand jury is only an investigative body, not an adjucative body. Still, witnesses have the right to plead the fifth amendment against self incrimination. The grand jury decides whether to return an indictment. The indictment issues from the grand jury and under the signature of the foreman. By contrast, an information issues from the prosecutors office, is signed by the prosecuting attorney and endorsed by the court.

The First Appearance. Among other actions, the subject appears before the magistrate in order for him or her to determine whether or not there is probable cause to detain the individual if he or she has been arrested. Most states require that when defendants are held in the jail, that they be brought before them with out unnecessary delay, often within hours, but for defendants not in custody there may be a lapse of several days or weeks between being charged and the first appearance.

The first appearance only takes a few minutes and the magistrate performs several functions: they determine probable cause to detain arrested suspects, they make certain that the individual before them is indeed the proper person and the one named in the complaint, they read the charges against the defendant and advise them of their rights, and they assign counsel if the subject is too poor to afford one (Samaha, 1990).

Preliminary Hearing. A preliminary hearing is often called a judiciary inquiry into the existence, validity, and sufficiency of probable cause (Eldefonso and Coffey, 1981). While a grand jury or preliminary hearing can precede a trial, there is a difference. The purpose of the preliminary hearing is to advise the individual of his or her rights. It also serves other purposes as well: to determine the existence of probable cause for which a warrant was issued for arrest, to inquire into the reasonability of the arrest and search, determine whether or not the executing officer complied with the demands of the warrant, afford the magistrate who issued the warrant the opportunity to hear the case of the accused, and to determine bail (Eldefonso and Coffey, 1981)..

The preliminary hearing follows the first appearance, usually by a few weeks. During this time plea bargaining may change the nature of the proceedings. The preliminary hearing permits the magistrate to "screen the prosecutor's decisions to charge, in order to avoid when possible, or justify if necessary, further intrusion against defendants and expenditures of government resources" (Samaha, 1990). For the first time the adversarial process comes into play and the defendant is allowed to address the probable cause. Charges can be dismissed for lack of evidence or faulty investigation. If the magistrate finds probable cause, they "bind over" the defendant, that is they send the case forward for trial.

Several things come to mind at this point. Bail is an important issue and the history of bail is rooted in medieval England. At that time the Sheriff had the authority to release someone instead of keeping them in jail in exchange for money or barter. The early colonists brought the practice to North America and it has remained a cornerstone of American criminal law.

Release on Recognizance, often called ROR or OR (shorthand for **own recognizance**), is a form of bail. During the 1960's reformers called attention to the disproportionate number of poor people in jail awaiting trial. As a result, several projects were started around the country releasing defendants if they met certain criteria such as having a job, owning property, from an intact family, and so on. The projects met with great success in that most defendants returned for trial. Other jurisdictions adopted the practice, thereby decreasing the numbers of people in jail and saving money for the taxpayers.

Grand Jury Review. About half of the states require that grand juries indict, or make a formal charge against defendants before the courts tries them (Samaha, 1990). The grand jury requires only a majority vote to indict. Their task, in secret session, is to determine whether or not there is probable cause to require the suspect to answer the charges against him or her.

Arraignment. Once the government has proven that enough evidence exists to require the defendant to answer the charges against him or her, the court arraigns the defendant. Arraignment means to bring the defendant to court, inform them of the specific charges and ask them to plead guilty or not guilty. There are three choices: Guilty, not guilty, or nolo contendere. Nolo contendere means that the defendant does not admit guilt, but will not fight the case. Those who refuse to plead, will have a not guilty pleas entered for them.

Pretrial Motions. If the defendant has objections of one sort or another, they enter a pretrial motion. The most common motions are ones that challenge the court's jurisdiction or authority to hear the case, or request discovery. Discovery is the requirement that the government and defendant must reveal to the other side information in their possession. In addition, motions claiming double jeopardy and speedy trial violations are also entered at this time. Contrary to conventional wisdom, "getting off on technicalities" occur in less than 10 percent of cases (Samaha, 1990).

Trial. The 6th Amendment of the United States Constitution ensures a trial by an impartial jury. The defendant must waive that right in order to receive a bench trial, that is a trial without a jury and with the judge making all determinations. A trial is the hearing of the facts before a judge or jury by duly constituted actors in a court of established jurisdiction. That is, the matter must come to trial in the county or district in which the offense occurred and the judge must be duly appointed or elected as provided for in the state constitution. In federal court, the offense must be tried in the state in which the offense occurred. In state court a change in venue can be obtained in a pretrial motion if the defense believes, and can prove to the judge, that the defendant will not receive a fair and impartial trial.

If a change in venue is granted, it will only be within the state in which the offense occurred, usually to a neighboring county. There are a number of people surrounding the defendant as he or she goes through a trial. This is commonly known as the courtroom work group. The work group consists of: judge, prosecutor, defense attorney, clerk, court reporter, bailiff, police officers, and various representatives of groups that support one public or another.

I have included the First Ten Amendments to the Constitution (Bill of Rights), as well as the 14th Amendment, below in order for the reader to begin gain a real grasp of the uniqueness of our rights as American citizens (as if we all are not aware). This document assures us that we are indeed free from the oppression of government and that includes those charged with crimes as well as those of us not charged with crimes. After all, in a repressive society, the tables can change very quickly and with no warning.

Bill of Rights

I. Congress shall make no law respecting an establishment of religion, or prohibiting the free exercise thereof; or abridging the freedom of speech or of the press; or the right of the people peaceably to assemble, and to petition the government for redress of grievances.

II. A well regulated militia being necessary to the security of a free state, the right of the people to keep and bear arms shall not be infringed.

III. No soldier shall, in time of peace, be quartered in any house without the consent of the owner, nor in time of war, but in a manner to be prescribed by law.

IV. The right of the people to be secure in their persons, houses, papers, and effects, against unreasonable searches and seizures, shall not be violated, and no warrants shall issue but upon probable cause, supported by oath or affirmation, and particularly describing the place to be searched and the persons or things to be seized.

V.   No person shall be held to answer for a capital or otherwise infamous crime, unless on a presentment or indictment of a grand jury, except in cases arising in the land or naval forces or in the militia when in actual service in time of war or public danger; nor shall any person be subject for the same offense to be twice put in jeopardy of life or limb; nor shall be compelled in any criminal case to be a witness against himself, nor be deprived of life, liberty, or property, without due process of law; nor shall private property be taken for public use without just compensation.

VI.   In all criminal prosecutions the accused shall enjoy the right to a speedy and public trial, by an impartial jury of the state and district wherein the crime shall have been committed, which district shall have been previously ascertained by law, and to be informed of the nature and cause of the accusation; to be confronted with the witnesses against him; to have compulsory process for obtaining witnesses in his favor, and to have the assistance of counsel for his defense.

VII.   In suits at common law, where the value in controversy shall exceed twenty dollars, the right of trial by jury shall be preserved, and no fact tried by a jury shall be otherwise re-examined in any court of the United States, than according to the rules of the common law.

VIII.   Excessive bail shall not be required, nor excessive fines imposed, nor cruel and unusual punishments inflicted.

IX.   The enumeration in the Constitution of certain rights, shall not be construed to deny or disparage others retained by the people.

X.   The powers not delegated to the United States by the Constitution, nor prohibited by it to the States, are reserved to the States respectively, or to the people.

XIV.   All persons born or naturalized in the United States, and subject to the jurisdiction thereof, are citizens of the United States and of the State wherein they reside. No State shall make or enforce any law which shall abridge the privileges or immunities of citizens of the United States; nor shall any State deprive any person of life, liberty, or property, without due process of law; nor deny to any person within its jurisdiction the equal protection of the laws

Constitutional Rights When
Charged With a Crime

Eldefonso and Coffey (1981) offer an excellent summary of everyone's constitutional rights if they are charged with a crime.

> The person charged with a crime has certain protections set up by the Constitution and by code provisions. The United States Constitution protects the people from the federal government, and generally the first 10 Amendments (known as the Bill of Rights) do not protect from the actions of a state. The "due process" clause of the United States Constitution has by inclusion and exclusion covered some of these rights of the people against the state (Eldefonso and Coffey, 1981).

As a result, it is necessary to look to the various state constitutions which outline the protections of the citizens against the state. It is important that police officers and others who deal with the public and with law breakers know these protections in order to avoid misunderstandings, avoid law suits, and not jeopardize the prosecution of a case.

Right to Jury Trial

Every person brought to trial has the right to a jury to decide the facts of a case. This right may be waived by the defendant and the number of persons on a jury may vary according to the state. Some states require only six persons on a felony jury and others require twelve. The number of twelve persons on a jury is a historical accident and has little relevance to the twentieth century. The Supreme Court has ruled that numbers sufficient to protect the innocent from unfounded prosecution, provide checks and balances, arrive at the truth, and enable community representation in law enforcement satisfied the right to a jury trial requirement (Samaha, 1990). In most states, a finding of guilt must be unanimous, but some states allow a non-unanimous decision. The defendant may also agree to a trial where the judge, and not a jury, hears the case.

Double Jeopardy

Double jeopardy means no one can be tried for the same crime more than once, that is the government is allowed one "fair shot." A "hung jury" is not included as it is not an acquittal and as a consequence a retrial is not double jeopardy, but usually state procedural rules set a time limit on the prosecutors ability to retry a case. Two jurisdictions may try someone for what appears to be one crime. However, the trials are actually for different offenses. For example, someone may steal a car in North Carolina and drive it to Tennessee. North Carolina may try the individual for car theft and the federal government may try the person for violation of the Dyer Act (Interstate Transportation of a Stolen Motor Vehicle). Another example is one of murder where the state may try the defendant for the crime of murder and the federal government may try the defendant for violation of the victim's civil rights.

Right to Bail

The defendant always has the right to bail unless the offense is punishable by death or bail is prohibited by statute. The right to bail also extends to conviction after trial, but in that instance as well, bail is discretionary with the judge. The 8th Amendment of the Constitution prohibits excessive bail. However, state rules will usually weigh the safety of the community against the likelihood of the person appearing in court as required. If bail is not granted the Sheriff will attempt to hold the defendant in a cell with other legally innocent defendants.

Right to a Speedy Trial

Everyone accused of a crime has a right to a speedy trial. After arrest the accused has a right to demand arraignment within a reasonable time--usually 48 hours, sometimes 24 hours. Under Supreme Court decisions, there is no particular time limits. The accused has a right to a trial in a reasonably short time and unless he or she waives this right, the matter must be brought to trial within a certain number of days after the indictment or filing of information by the prosecuting attorney.

Right to Counsel

The defendant has the right to an attorney of his or her choice. However, in the case of felonies, if the defendant is indigent and cannot afford an attorney, one will be appointed at the expense of the court. Further, the defendant does not have freedom to choose who will represent him or her. The defendant must also be advised of this point because he or she has the right to waive counsel and act as his or her own attorney. The waiver, however, must be rational and the judge must also agree. The right to a court appointed counsel does not extend to misdemeanors.

Right not to Testify Against Oneself

The Fifth Amendment allows the defendant to refrain from providing testimony that would be incriminating. This privilege has two purposes: (a) the defendant can refuse to take the stand and the prosecution cannot make comment on the refusal (some states do allow comment), and (b) to protect the individual from making incriminating statements at the time of arrest. This privilege can be waived by the defendant.

Right to Confrontation of One's Accuser

The framers of the Constitution sought to avoid secret inquisitions, they determined that the defendant always has the right to have a witness testify against him in his presence. The one exception is in the case of child molestation where the court believes that such confrontation would harm the child in some way. However, in the case of children the defendant has the right to confrontation through video. The defendant also has the right to cross examine the witness and to "impeach the witness to show he or she may be lying, mistaken, hostile, prejudiced, or whatever" (Eldefonso and Coffey, 1981). The Supreme Court has held that informers who testify against a criminal defendant must reveal their name and address. However, if the testimony is not directly related to the guilt or innocence of the defendant he or she does not have to reveal his name or address. Also it is not necessary for police to reveal the name and address of an informer in order to establish probable cause for a search warrant.

Statute of Limitations

Statute of limitations means that an indictment, complaint, or information must be filed within a specific period of time. Generally speaking, felonies have a statute of limitations of three years, misdemeanors have a statute of limitations of one year, and there are no time limits for murder, embezzlement of public money, or falsification of public records. There have been instances where criminals have used the statute of limitations to their advantage. However, the benefit to the average person is that it motivates government to act promptly.

The Structure of the Courts

It is the responsibility of the courts to arraign defendants, assign a lawyer to indigent defendants, and to dispose of cases in adversarial proceedings. The courts exist in a tier system ranging from the lower courts to the U.S. Supreme Court.

Lower criminal courts are of limited jurisdiction. The most common names are: municipal courts, county courts, justice of the peace courts, and magistrates courts. Lower criminal courts are limited to trying misdemeanants and other minor offenses, conducting preliminary hearings, and issuing warrants. Generally speaking, defendants in the lower courts have fewer procedural protections than those appearing in courts of general jurisdiction. The truth is that most cases appearing in lower criminal courts are tried without a jury and trials in lower courts can be retried in the trial courts without regard to the lower court's decision, although the appeals process on simple misdemeanants vary from state to state.

Nearly all felony proceedings begin in the lower courts with a presentment or initial appearance. This is the time where the magistrate reads the charges, establishes bail, and assigns a defense attorney to indigent defendants. There is some diversity in lower courts due to differences in community standards. For example, many states do not require judges to have legal training and one court may have a heavy emphasis on keeping misdemeanants out of jail and another may have a heavily punitive approach. Whatever the general philosophy of the lower court, its activities are defined by the state constitution.

Trial courts are more formal. They receive the greatest public attention such as the O.J. Simpson trial and the Susan Smith trial (a young woman who was accused and found guilty of murdering her two children in South Carolina). It was pointed out in chapter 1 that these trials are celebrity trials and receive the entire range of court services, but they also proceed more formally than cases in a lower court.

Trial courts possess general jurisdiction, that is, the authority to hear and determine all criminal cases occurring in their jurisdiction. Original and exclusive jurisdiction means that felony adjudication belongs in trial courts and that trial courts alone can adjudicate felony cases. Adjudicate means the settlement of a case.

Appellate courts are the most formal of courts and they exist to hear and decide appeals of trial court decisions. The federal system and thirty-nine states have a two-tiered appellate system. The intermediate appellate courts will hear the case at first and then it can be appealed up to the Supreme Court, or the court of last resort. It is the responsibility of the Supreme Court to hear decisions of the appellate court. In all jurisdictions in the United States defendants have the right to appeal lower court and trial court decisions based upon allegations of errors in the original proceedings.

Society expects a lot from the courts and they perform several functions: they work for justice, they must reflect the values of the community, they interpret the U.S. and State Constitutions, they insure the protection of the innocent, and they must determine the truth from two conflicting stories. It is not an easy task and it is up to a select group of people to shepherd cases through the system. The issue is not that they do a poor job at times, but rather how they manage to do such a remarkable job nearly all the time.

The Work Group in the Courtroom

Every work place and every job is characterized by a group of people who work together, depend upon each other to get the job done, and even depend upon each other for promotions and pay raises. The courtroom is no exception and it should not be a surprise that the people who work together day after day in an overheated environment such as a prosecutors office make decisions in a certain way and that there is an agreed upon way to approach cases brought to them for prosecution. We must remember that the courtroom work group is comprised not only of judges, prosecutors, and defense attorneys, but also the clerk, bailiff, court reporter, police officers, probation officers, family court liaison official, matron and all others who work together day in and day out in the court room.

Walker (1994) summarizes what we know about the courtroom work group and he points out that "people administer justice and what we call the administration of justice is actually the sum total of a series of decisions made by individual criminal justice officials working with other officials." The common understandings that are developed in the courtroom help get the job done with as little conflict as possible. In one study cited by Walker, Frederic Suffett (1966) found conflict in only three percent of bail decisions and some disagreement in only nine percent of the others.

Walker's point is that there is a specific way of going about the courts business and the pace is maintained by the courtroom work group. It is exceedingly difficult to change that way of doing business because change is often nullified or moderated by the work group. When the work load changes beyond the capacity of the group to handle it, adaptation is made, often in ways that are not intended or anticipated.

Sentencing

Once the defendant pleads guilty or is found guilty, he or she will receive the sentence prescribed by law. This may not satisfy the victim or an outraged public, but the court often has no discretion because of a sentencing grid. Adults can receive a prison sentence, probation or a combination of the two usually called a split sentence and usually for no more than six months in jail or prison followed by probation. The split sentence is often used for it's supposed shock effect, but there is no evidence that there is any "shock;" but it is an effective tool for judges to prove to a public that they are tough on crime.

Often along with probation the defendant will be offered the opportunity to pay a fine or restitution. This is an often overlooked sanction and according to Morris and Tonry (1990), "It is paradoxical that a society that relies so heavily on the financial incentive in its social philosophy and economic practice should be so reluctant to use the financial disincentive as a punishment of crime." They go on to relate how the fine is used much less frequently in the United States than in Europe. In West Germany in 1979, 82.4 percent of all sentenced offenders were ordered to pay a fine. Sweden and England also rely heavily on the fine. In the United States, fines have been largely relegated to a regulatory sanction and where they are imposed in criminal cases, the fine is usually so low as to be ineffective.

Prisons were an American innovation by the Pennsylvania Quakers at the beginning of the nineteenth century as a reaction to the harshness of punishments and against the use of corporal punishment. It was believed that a period of time in the penitentiary would give the offender time to contemplate his transgressions and sins and become penitent, hence the term penitentiary.

Prior to the Civil War prison sentences were determinate, that is, they had a specific beginning and end. If someone was sentenced to five years, they would serve five years. With increasing urbanization, the asylum was discovered and the penitentiary was a major part of that "discovery." There was a conviction that the only way to save the errant individual was to separate the criminal from temptation and place him in a penitentiary.

> Since the convict was not inherently depraved but the victim of an
> Upbringing that had failed to provide protection against the vices
> at loose in society, a well-ordered institution could successfully
> reeducate and rehabilitate him. The penitentiary, free of corruptions
> and dedicated to the proper training of the inmate, would
> inculcate the discipline of negligent parents, evil companions, taverns,
> houses of prostitution, theaters, and gambling halls had destroyed.
> Just as the criminal's environment had led him into crime, the
> institutional environment would lead him out of it (Rothman, 1971).

At the first American Prison Congress meeting in Cincinnati in 1870, the indeterminate sentence was proposed and the Prison Congress concluded "Sentences limited only by satisfactory proof of reformation should be substituted for those measured by mere lapse of time" (Tappan, 1960). The indeterminate sentence gradually gained favor and by 1922 thirty-seven states had adopted some form of the indeterminate sentence. The indeterminate sentence is a sentence with a spread of time that can be served between a minimum time for parole eligibility to a maximum time at which the person must be released. However, today the indeterminate sentence is equated with leniency and lack of accountability.

In the last twenty years many states have abolished the indeterminate sentence in favor of the determinate sentence in addition to establishing many more mandatory sentences. Critics have stated that, on the one hand, the indeterminate sentence is unfair in that the inmate does not know how long he or she will serve in prison. Other critics meanwhile, state that inmates are released prematurely via the indeterminate sentence. Advocates of change point out that the determinate sentence will not allow criminals to be released prematurely to take advantage of an unsuspecting public.

Proposition #4: Attempts to get "tough on crime" by changing the Constitution will do nothing to change the way in which the courts go about their business or improve the efficiency of the system. We should leave the Constitution alone.

Presentence Investigation Report (PSI)

Before proceeding, a look at how sentences were determined prior to the implementation of sentencing grids. Many states have abandoned the Presentence Investigation (PSI) in favor of a shorter version that is short on usable information. Most courts have forgotten that the PSI plays a major role in decision making in the institution if the offender is sentenced to a period of time. Whether or not a PSI will be ordered depends upon the state. Some states require PSI's in all felony cases and in others the judge has the discretion to order one. However, many states have adopted a sentencing grid and the decision is not in the hands of the judge. He or she need only find the point of two intersecting lines on a chart and establish a sentence within a few months of a minimum and maximum.

The presentence investigation report is based upon the philosophy of looking at the whole person and attempting to determine his or her needs and the judge must figure out how those needs contributed to the crime. If those needs can be met, the thinking goes, then the individual will have no future need to commit crimes. Perhaps the idea is somewhat simplistic, but it does look to the long term and recognizes that deterrence is not a factor in much criminal behavior.

The PSI is ordered by the judge at the time of a finding or plea of guilty. The probation department is ordered to complete the report within a certain time and the initial interview with the defendant is usually in jail or in the office of the probation officer. The basics of a PSI are:

* The official version of the offense including co-defendants and much demographic information at a glance.

* The defendants version of the offense.

* A statement by the complainant and or a victim impact statement.

* The prior criminal record of the defendant, including his or her juvenile record.

* Family and marital history.

* Employment and military history.

* Education and related history such as behavior problems in the case of juveniles.

* Mental and physical health including substance abuse history and referrals for counseling.

* A summary, including a recommendation by the probation officer and a treatment or program plan.

There has been a good deal of research on how much the PSI influences the decision of the judge. Usually the recommendation of the probation officer carries some weight. However, some judges do not require a PSI for some crimes, and in other instances, the judge simply does not feel a need to have a PSI. But, their importance to criminal justice system employees after sentencing cannot be over stated in terms of public safety and decision making.

Loopholes, Deterrence, and Guns

There are a number of variables that affect the operation of the court and the impression the public has of the court. The issues of loopholes, deterrence and guns are of great interest to many Americans and in many ways affect public perceptions. Loopholes, conventional wisdom states, are responsible for many criminals being able to prey upon citizens after they have beaten the system and are out on the street again. Guns and deterrence are often spoken of in the same breath. Not only do we have a constitutional right to own and carry guns, many opponents of gun control state, but ownership of guns is a right that deters many criminals from committing crimes against individuals.

Contentiousness and legal debate are the hallmarks of these issues, but what are the facts? How do we separate myth and opinion from research and fact? The remainder of this chapter explores these issues in an effort to shed light on the facts and aid the taxpayer in making sound decisions at home and at the ballot box. We again turn to Samuel Walker (1994) to summarize what we know about loopholes and public attitudes.

Loopholes

There are three main loopholes that many people feel should be closed: the inability of the courts to prosecute career criminals, the insanity defense, and plea bargaining. If we can close these loopholes, the argument goes, we can then begin to get the career criminals off the street and the crime rate will decrease. There is a general attitude that dangerous criminals do not receive sufficient punishment because prosecutors simply do not spend enough time on getting them behind bars. The truth is that the American criminal justice system is very efficient.

One study highlighted by Walker is the San Diego Major Violator Unit "which targets robbery and robbery-related homicide cases in which the defendant is charged with three or more separate robbery-related offenses or has been convicted of one or more serious offenses in the preceding ten years" (1994). This project focused on the continuity of prosecution, that is instead of a case being handled by several prosecutors over the course of the prosecution, it is followed through by one prosecutor. The job of the prosecutor in the unit is to work closely with detectives, develop relationships with witnesses, and to assure limits on plea bargaining in that the defendant may only plead to the most serious charge.

Walker also reports on other projects in Kalamazoo, Michigan, Columbus, Ohio, and Phoenix, Arizona. He concludes that "career-criminal prosecution programs do not produce higher rates of prosecution or punishment." He points out that these type of programs fail for a simple reason: we are already tough on career criminals and contrary to conventional wisdom, criminals do not get off easy.

The San Diego prosecution rate prior to the implementation of the Major Violator Unit was 89.5% and after implementation of the program the prosecution rate took a jump to 91.5 percent. In Kalamazoo the prosecution rate took a slightly larger jump from 66.6% to 73.4% and in another project in Columbus, Ohio the rate went from 73.9% to 76.4 percent. A program in Phoenix, Arizona was even tougher than Kalamazoo and Columbus. Prosecutors and detectives worked together as a team with the detectives walking warrants through the system to ensure that the bond would be sufficiently high and that additional charges were filed, thus assuring that the criminal would be kept in jail within the parameters of the law. Detectives also contacted probation officers and provided information for the presentence report. The prosecution rate went from 98% prosecuted to 98.9% with the conviction rate going from 86.4% to 89.9 percent. The above studies point out that the American criminal justice system is already very efficient and somewhat unforgiving.

Another alleged loophole is the insanity defense. John Hinkley is probably responsible for the recent changes in the insanity defense. The public outrage over his attempted assassination of President Reagan caused thirty-nine states and Congress to make changes in their insanity defense laws. These changes fell into five categories: abolition of the insanity defense, changing the test of insanity, shift burden of proof to the defendant, create a new "guilty, but mentally ill" verdict, change the procedures for commitment of a person found not guilty by reason of insanity.

These changes abolished the "loophole," if it ever existed, and Walker concludes that "abolishing or limiting the insanity defense will have no impact on serious crime" 1994). The insanity defense is a defense that has been abused by the media and politicians and is overrated as a loophole (Moran, 1991 in Walker, 1994). As a consequence the general public has a distorted view of how often the insanity defense is used. Actually, according to Walker, it is seldom used. One estimate by a respected legal scholar is that the insanity plea is used in only two percent of cases that go to trial, which means that since many cases never reach trial, only in one-tenth of one percent of all felony trials is the insanity defense used. In summary, the insanity defense is rarely used and almost never used in robbery and burglary cases. The publicity of the insanity defense is a clear example of how the media and politicians are able to distort the facts to their own ends.

Plea bargaining is an issue of which everyone seems to have a dim view. According to Walker plea bargaining is the mode of settlement of up to 90% of all prosecuted cases. It appears that abolishing plea bargaining will not reduce serious crime.

A number of experiments have been attempted that evaluates plea bargaining and the conclusion is that even without the use of plea bargaining, the disposition of cases would not be affected. One such research project was in Alaska where on July 3, 1975 plea bargaining was abolished for the entire state. The good news is that the criminal courts did not collapse under the burden of increased caseloads and they continued to function about the same as before. In fact, defendants plead guilty at about the same rate and the percentage of cases going to trail increased from 6.7% to 9.6 percent.

One effect is highlighted by the abolition or reduction in use of plea bargaining. That is, since we are already tough on crime, the "get tough on crime" attitude trickles down to less serious crimes. As a result, those charged with less serious offenses, or first time offenders who would have normally received probation or a short jail term, are given more severe punishment. The result has been an expanding prison population.

In the eyes of the prosecutor, plea bargaining ensures a conviction. The accused is made to look worse than he or she really is in that the defendant is "over charged" in order to force a plea bargain. Plea bargaining according to Walker is a phantom loophole. There are no overwhelming numbers of criminals beating the system. The media and politicians have contributed to the misunderstanding of the public. It fits with the American desire to find a panacea for problems and our inability to tackle long term solutions to complicated problems.

A final loophole for discussion is the exclusionary rule. In 1961 the **Mapp v. Ohio** decision held that "all evidence obtained by searches and seizures in violation of the Constitution is, by that same authority, inadmissible in a state court" (Mapp v. Ohio), otherwise known as the "exclusionary rule." In other words, prosecutors cannot use evidence obtained in violation of the Fourth Amendment. Police work is a curious business. Many times officers will know that someone is guilty, but cannot prove it to be the case. Critics of the "exclusionary rule" point out that too many criminals get off because they are not allowed to be prosecuted by use of evidence tainted by skullduggery. In this instance, critics are also guilty of over-reacting to a few celebrity cases.

The exclusionary rule has three purposes: (1) protect the rights of all Americans against police misconduct, (2) to maintain the integrity of the judiciary, and (3) to deter the police from misconduct. It is important that these basics be protected. Walker points out that "the exclusionary rule has virtually no impact on the crime-fighting capacity of the police" (Walker). He goes on to cite a number of studies that support his assertion and he claims that the only area where the rule has any affect is in drug related cases, and here he states it is a small impact. The end result is that the exclusionary rule forces the police and prosecutor to carefully build a case relying on professionalism and hard work resulting in the prosecution rate only going up. Recent exclusionary rule changes allows "good faith exceptions" which have further closed any perceived loophole. Before discussing guns, it is appropriate to discuss the concept of deterrence because it is assumed that gun ownership is a deterrent to crime.

Deterring Criminals

Sentencing criminals to a period of time in prison is assumed by many to be a deterrent to others contemplating criminal acts. In addition, there is an assumption that a harsh sentence will deter the individual from committing further criminal acts. There are two types of deterrence: general and specific. In our desire to stop crime by sending convicted criminals to prison we are aiming for both general and specific deterrence. In regard to general deterrence, we assume that the knowledge of possible incarceration for breaking the law will cause would-be criminals to refrain from criminal activity. Specific deterrence refers to the belief that if one spends time in jail or prison he or she will be reluctant to commit further criminal acts because of the previous time spent in jail or prison.

Deterrence is highly important to the conservative notion of crime control. However, anyone who has been a cigarette smoker is aware of the ineffectiveness of deterrence. People continue to smoke in spite of the knowledge that smoking will shorten his or her life, add to medical costs in later years, and in general bring about a poorer quality of life after a period of time. In short, we are totally unable to envision ourselves dead or debilitated.

So too deterrence is ineffective as a means of preventing crime. One may argue that we ourselves have been deterred from committing one crime or another. Not likely! People who are largely law abiding are not deterred from criminal behavior, we refrain from criminal behavior because we believe that we have a moral obligation not to do harm. In a later chapter we discuss the fact that some people do not have the opportunity to learn law abiding behavior; or they attempt to obtain the material possessions that everyone else has by a process of innovation. As a consequence, deterrence is not likely to be effective.

The issue of deterrence is most complex and until recently was left largely to philosophers. Professor Don C. Gibbons (1992) summarizes what is known about deterrence. Research by William Chambliss (1966) and Jack Gibbs (1968) offer some hope for the possibilities of deterrence. On the other hand, Charles Tittle (1969) completed a study similar to that of Gibbs and Tittle and concluded that states with the lowest crime rates also had proportionately higher imprisonment rates. In his view, severity did not appear to affect the crime rate.

Based upon his review of the literature, Gibbons concludes that: (a) nothing is known about the certainty or swiftness of punishment on offenders, (b) most research suggests that certainty is more important than severity, (c) most people are relatively uninformed about the nature and severity of criminal punishments, and (d) nearly nothing is known about the effects of economic hardship, feelings of deprivation, or other attitudes on the perceived risk of punishment. In short, politicians and others may make grand pronouncements about the deterrent effect of harsh prison sentences, but they are ignorant of the true facts.

Any discussion of sentencing would be incomplete without a discussion of the death penalty. Execution is often discussed as a deterrent to such heinous crimes a murder, but nothing could be further from the truth. No research to date indicates that the existence of the death penalty is a deterrent to murder. The proper role that the death penalty plays in our society is that it is a means for the collective order to exact retribution for the commission of crimes so heinous and repulsive that a diseased cancer is excised from the body of society.

The inconclusive nature of research on the deterrent effect of the death penalty can be illustrated by the research of Brian Forst. He examined the years 1960 -1970 and found no evidence that actual executions prevented crime and he found some evidence that the executions actually encouraged homicides. In addition, because of the high cost of appeals, it is more expensive to execute someone than it is to keep that individual in prison for natural life. We now turn to guns and we can conclude that as a deterrent to crime, gun ownership is as likely as threats of the death penalty to deter crime.

Guns

The issue of guns and their control never fails to stir deeply held convictions on both sides of the political spectrum. Conservatives state that if we eliminate guns we will be over run by criminals and violence. Conservatives point out that we have a "right to bear arms" and that they are the primary means for the average citizen to defend himself against crime and a repressive government; guns do not kill people, people kill people. Liberals on the other hand state that the presence of guns act as a stimulant to crime and that it is unnecessary to have as many gun related deaths each year as we do in the United States. Surely the rancher in Wyoming and the fifteen year old alienated youth in the inner city do not have equal rights to own a gun. The task for public policy makers is to sort out the legal and social points and arrive at a solution that serves us all.

Perhaps the most quoted statement on guns is by Gary Kleck (1991). He points out that the debate over gun control is "abysmal" and that both sides argue past one another leaving everyone's biases intact.

Much of social order in America may depend on the fact that millions of people are armed and dangerous to each other. The availability of deadly weapons to the violence-prone may well contribute to violence by increasing the probability of a fatal outcome of combat. However, it may also be that this very fact raises the stakes in disputes to the point where only the most incensed or intoxicated disputants resort to physical conflict, with the risks of armed retaliation deterring attack and coercing minimal courtesy among other-wise hostile parties (Kleck, 1991).

Kleck concludes that "routine gun ownership and defensive use by civilians may have a pervasive, ongoing impact on crime," however, that impact is difficult to measure. The point, according to Kleck, is that gun ownership by private citizens may be a deterrent to criminals. Wayne LaPierre of the National Rifle Association (NRA), states, "when the public loses faith in the ability or the willingness of the government to protect it, people rely more heavily on self-protection" (1994). Mr. LaPierre points out that the criminal justice system is broken and cites a number of heinous, celebrity cases that are used to justify the purchase of weaponry to deter criminals. As we discussed in earlier chapters, there is no crime wave and the criminal justice system is not broken. The problem has more to do with the shear numbers of people being sent to the system and a lack of adequate funding to properly conduct programs and ensure accountability of inmates/probationers/ parolees.

Today there are more than 200 million guns in circulation in the United States including 66 million handguns, 72 million rifles, and 62 million shotguns. The Bureau of Alcohol, Tobacco and Firearms estimate that approximately 2 million new handguns enter the market each year along with 1.5 million rifles and 1 million shotguns. Many, if not most, of these weapons are for sport, nevertheless many end up in the hands of people who commit crimes. It remains that the United States is the only industrialized nation in the world with such laxity in gun ownership.

Attempting to deal with such a complex issue is not easy. While shotguns and assault rifles may be troublesome to a few people, they are not the weapon of choice among criminals. One research project revealed that among jail inmates, most had never owned an assault rifle and only a very few had even fired one. In addition, the gun of choice is a hand gun (Knox, Houston, Laskey, McCurrie, Tromanhauser, and Laske, 1994; see also Wright and Rossi, 1986).

Remembering that the greatest fear of the average citizen is that of random violence we need to separate, in our minds at least, those crimes that put us at peril from those that would happen anyway, regardless of the weapon at hand. Thus, if we eliminate murders and attempted murders between gang members, violence between lovers and spouses, and violence between acquaintances we are left with much fewer incidents to cause us to be fearful.

James Q. Wilson (1985) concludes that there are three views on gun ownership and any attempt to deal with the issue of guns must recognize those views: first, do nothing to disturb the present approach to gun ownership. Second, a handgun exists only to kill and its production and distribution should be tightly controlled and regulated. Third, certain kinds of behavior results when there is an available handgun and as a consequence, we ought to devise ways of reducing that availability among people likely to be involved in such behavior.

By and large the present attitude of the U.S. Congress is to do very little, owing primarily to the powerful National Rifle Association (NRA) lobby. More is being done at the local level where there is more concern about guns and where the NRA is less effective. The second view has been recognized through various attempts at legislation. Currently we have over 20,000 gun laws on the books and according to Samuel Walker (1994), what we lack are **effective** gun laws. We can safely conclude that banning ownership of guns is, or will be, ineffective. James D. Wright (1988), another respected criminologist, agrees. He states that while gun control is a laudable idea, we will never be able to marshal an effective, scientifically based argument to support more gun control. We need only look to the experiment with Prohibition to gain an idea of the business that would arise if guns were outlawed entirely. Unless we are willing to entirely trash the Constitution and the Bill of Rights, the prohibition of guns will not work. The same can be said of bullets. Even if ammunition were outlawed, Walker points out that a cottage industry would soon arise for the manufacture and sale of ammunition.

Both Walker and Wilson agree that there may be a way to deal with guns as found in the Bartley-Fox law passed in Massachusetts in 1975. This law ordered that anyone caught carrying a hand gun outside of their home without a permit would receive an automatic one year sentence. Obviously it does not challenge anyone's right to own a gun, it only attempts to cut down on crime by keeping guns at home.

Walker (1994) summarizes the research on Bartley-Fox and points out that in Boston, assaults with a gun declined by 13.5 percent between 1974 and 1975 and by 11.7 percent between 1974 and 1976. However, assaults with other weapons went up 40.4 percent, indicating a "substitution" effect. We can compare these figures with cities that did not have a similar law but. also experienced declines in gun related offenses in that period: Philadelphia experienced a 21.3 percent decline in assaults and 36.7 percent in armed robberies. Chicago experienced a 26 percent decline in assaults and a 43.5 percent decline in armed robberies.

Another approach to deterring criminals is to allow private citizens to carry concealed weapons. More than forty states have approved such legislation and only sixteen require some form of demonstrated need for a concealed gun while others require some form of demonstrated proficiency in their use. Allowing citizens carry concealed weapons may be letting the genie out of the bottle. Those states that approve carrying of concealed weapons may learn that crime does not go down and perhaps casualties will go up. The casualties will not be criminals, but perhaps by-standers and other innocents. The press will sense a good story however, and pick up the "celebrity" case in which a criminal was killed or apprehended by an outraged citizen. Ignored in the mayhem will be the numbers of casualties by inept and frightened citizens.

The 1995 bombing of the Oklahoma City Federal building focused attention on gun ownership advocates and the National Rifle Association (NRA). However, that tragic incident has not forced a serious re-examination of present policies toward guns and gun ownership. There are many issues to be resolved and in the short-term the Bartly-Fox approach to gun control may be our best hope if adopted as a federal law. In addition, the problem of "leakage" might be solved. That is many jurisdictions pass legislation or ordinances controlling guns, but one can simply travel to a neighboring state or city, make a purchase and then bring the weapon back home.

Proposition #5: Loopholes are not a factor in the increase in crime. The increased propensity of private citizens to arm themselves may ultimately result in an increase in vigilantism and disregard of the sanctity of law.

Summary

The American criminal justice system is based upon the supremacy of the individual. The framers of the Constitution had a fear that government could become so intrusive, powerful, and corrupt that they devised a series of checks and balances to offset the power of government. The Bill of Rights articulates the rights of the individual and it is important to preserve them. They serve us all.

The criminal law process is driven by common law, state codes, and by the United States and State Constitutions. There are several steps the individual must go through as he or she goes to trial, they are: arrest, preliminary hearing, grand jury or prosecutorial information, arraignment, pretrial motions and trail. The process is not perfect, but it continues to evolve and it does protect the individual from arbitrary and capricious action on the part of government.

There are several tiers of courts at the federal, state, and local levels. While lower criminal courts are courts of limited jurisdiction, all felony cases begin in the lower courts. Courts of general jurisdiction process felony cases and appellate courts review decisions made by courts of general jurisdiction. In courts of general jurisdiction, the court room work group is a complex mix of individuals who must depend upon each other in order to get the job done. They will determine who is brought to trail. Sentencing is dependent upon statute, and often on information contained in the Presentence Investigation (PSI).

In spite of myth and conventional wisdom, there are very few loopholes which criminals use to avoid prosecution. The American criminal justice system is most efficient and in some jurisdictions a conviction rate of 90% or better is obtained. Deterrence is an issue today in that many persons running for elective office wrongly state that longer prison terms or the death penalty will deter would-be offenders from committing further criminal acts. Research does not support such a contention and the most we can say about deterrence is that if the punishment is certain, it may pay some sort of dividend. Guns are also an open sore in public debate. Liberals state that we should strictly control guns and if we do so, the crime rate will decrease. Cnservatives state that guns in the hands of responsible citizens is the main deterrent to an ever rising crime rate. Whatever the answer, most people agree that we do not want to live in a society in which one must carry a gun.

Bibliography

William J. Chambliss. "The Deterrent Influence of Punishment." **Crime and Delinquency**, 12 (January 1966). pp. 70-75.

Edward Eldefonso and Alan R. Coffey. **Criminal Law: History, Philosophy, Enforcement.** (New York: Harper and Row, 1981).

Don C. Gibbons. **Society, Crime, and Criminal Behavior**, 6th ed. (Englewood Cliffs: Prentice Hall, 1992).

Jack P. Gibbs. "Crime, Punishment, and Deterrence." **Southwestern Social Science Quarterly**, 28 (March 1968). pp. 515-530.

Gary Kleck. **Point Blank: Guns and Violence in America.** (New York: Aldine De Gruyter, 1991).

George W. Knox, James G. Houston, John A. Laskey, Thomas F. McCurrie, Edward D. Tromanhauser, and David L. Laske. **Gangs and Guns.** (Chicago: National Gang Crime Research Center, 1994).

Wayne LaPierre. **Guns, Crime, and Freedom.** (Washington, D.C.: Regnery Publishing, Inc. 1994(.

Mapp v. Ohio, 367 U.S. 643 (1961)

Norval Morris and Michael Tonry. **Between Prison and Probation: Intermediate Punishments in a Rational Sentencing System.** (New York: Oxford University Press, 1990).

David J. Rothman. **Discovery of the Asylum.** (Boston: Little, Brown, 1971).

Joel Samaha. **Criminal Procedure.** (St. Paul, MN: West Publishing Company, 1990).

Paul Tappan. **Crime, Justice, and Correction.** (New York: McGraw-Hill Book Company, 1960).

Charles L. Tittle. "Crime Rates and Legal Sanctions." **Social Problems**, 16 (Spring 1969). pp. 409-423.

Samuel Walker. **Sense and Nonsense About Crime and Drugs: A Policy Guide**, 3rd ed. (Belmont, CA: Wadsworth Publishing Company, 1994)

James D. Wright. "Second Thoughts about Gun Control." **The Public Interest.** 91 (Spring 1988). pp. 23-39.

Chapter 4

Law Enforcement and the Police

Introduction

The police play a significant role in the criminal justice system. They also are the most visible component of the system and the one agency available twenty-four hours a day to respond to calls for help. To say that the job of the police officer is a difficult one is to understate the obvious. One major facet of police work is to prevent crime. That is, by their presence and related contacts with the public, they serve to prevent crime from occurring. Beyond that, a fact little noted by the public, is that an important job of the police officer is that of *peacekeeping*. That is, maintaining order and controlling the activities of persons engaged in obnoxious and frightening behavior that is not necessarily illegal. This includes panhandlers, street walkers, rowdy youths, and drunks.

The police are also responsible for the investigation of crimes against persons and property and doing so in a constitutionally correct manner. If they do not follow legal procedures, the case is likely to be lost to prosecution. Much of what the general public knows about law enforcement is gained from television and the movies. Such stories make good drama, but are far from accurate. For example, the average police patrol officer spends much of his or her shift going from call to call rather than spending time solving a murder, robbery, or burglary. The average detective spends his or her shift sifting through a mountain of information, making telephone calls, and interviewing people on a number of cases; not spending his or her time on one case until it is solved. Community policing is changing the face of policing and is responsible for allowing the police to be pro-active in the fight against crime. More on this subject later in the chapter.

The police see themselves as being alone in the fight against crime and the public as wanting to remain disengaged. On the whole, the average citizen does not fully understand the role of police. Perhaps if they did understand, they could become more fully involved. This chapter explores how the police evolved, what the job entails, what their role in society is, and how we as citizens can help improve law enforcement in general.

Crime, Law, and Building a Nation

In 1790 there were 3.9 million people huddled along the eastern seaboard. By 1921 the population of the United States had reached 105.7 million with 51 percent of the population living in urban areas. The 1990 census revealed that we have over 250 million people with 75 percent living in an urban area. From 1790 to 1920 the immigration of people from eastern and western Europe as well as the migration of people from the east to the frontier of the west changed not only the landscape, but also the manner in which we enforced the law.

The early colonists brought those institutions with which they were most familiar to the new world and that included the concept of sheriff and the watch system. The sheriff was responsible for the jail and law enforcement outside of the cities. However, the position was not as prominent in the east as it was to be in the west as the frontier was pushed westward. Under the supervision of a town Marshall, The Watch was a group of men who would patrol the cities at night and look-out for criminal activity. However, they were primarily a fire patrol as they were often intimidated or paid-off by gangs of thugs and thieves. In the day time order was maintained by constables, often against nearly overwhelming odds.

As the major cities such as New York, Boston, Philadelphia, and Charleston grew, they also became increasingly rowdy and violent. The problems of crime and riots were not however, limited to those cities. Lest anyone think of early America as we see it in the movies, Inciardi (1993) quotes the **Bristol Journal** (Massachusetts) of March 16, 1760:

> The watch burn tobacco while houses are burning, and the glass, not the watch, goes its rounds, a burning shame this and sad subject of mourning, that our Guard's such a mute pack of hounds.

The sheriff was not responsible for seeking out crime, but he was charged with investigating crime in the counties. In addition he was responsible for collecting taxes, supervising elections, and for maintaining the jail. The sheriff did not receive a salary, but did collect fees for arrests and from prisoners in the jail. Needless to say the opportunity for corruption was present.

The modern police department is rooted in the urban violence and unrest that typified American cities in the nineteenth century. Prior to the earliest police departments, the members of the city council were usually responsible for assisting the constable, but in 1838 Boston, Massachusetts created the first police department. New York followed in 1844 and Philadelphia in 1854.

It isn't a surprise to learn that the early police departments were somewhat primitive and responsible for other tasks. For example, Boston police were responsible for maintaining public health until 1853 and in New York they were responsible for sweeping the streets until 1881; no small task in days of horse drawn transportation. Police work was also unsophisticated in that given the crowds and gangs of toughs they had to deal with, it was important that officers be tough, and the bigger the better. Because they were often roughed up and hoodlums were prone to use intimidation, the police often answered in kind.

Conditions and pay improved for the policeman throughout the 1800's and by 1880 the average pay for a factory worker was about $450 per year. On the other hand, the average pay for a policeman was about $900 per year. Because of the pay, appointment to the police department represented an important step up the social ladder for various immigrant groups.

During the middle 1800's police departments began to take on the look that they have today. Police departments began to departmentalize and in Boston, at mid-century, the first detective bureau was established. Elsewhere uniforms were introduced, call-boxes appeared, and a more corporate approach to management was introduced. Non-police functions were soon eliminated, and towards the end of the century, Theodore Roosevelt introduced the first merit system to the New York City Police Department when he was Police Commissioner.

However, as police moved into the 20th century they were largely incompetent, corrupt, and disliked by the people they were supposed to serve. Their activities were only minimally aimed at law enforcement and they served primarily as an arm for the reigning political party and protected the property of the wealthy and controlled immigrant groups.

Politics and the spoils system took their toll on many departments as the police were often the tools of politicians and wealthy capitalists who were interested in stopping a growing labor movement seeking to improve the pay and working conditions in the factories. Police were also directly involved in criminal activities (Lincoln Steffens 1904, McClure, Phillips & Co, 1957). Steffans wrote of the notorious "Doc" Ames and the Minneapolis police department.

> Immediately upon his election, before he took office (on January 7, 1901), he organized a cabinet and laid plans to turn the city over to outlaws who were to work under police direction for the profit of his administration...Norman W. King,[Chief of Detectives] a former gambler, who knew the criminals needed in the business ahead. King was to invite to Minneapolis thieves, confidence men, pick pockets and gamblers, and release some that were in the local jail. They were to be organized into groups, according to their profession, and detectives were assigned to assist and direct them (Steffans, 1904, 1957).

Steffans documented many other abuses of civic trust and responsibility and all were related to the spoils system prevalent in politics from the time of Andrew Jackson. Clearly, the police had degenerated into a gang of thugs and thieves that served only other thieves. It was time for reform.

Reform of the Police

In an effort to control corruption, many cities appointed police administrative boards and filled the positions with civic leaders. In some states, the legislatures took over some big city police departments and it was decades before control was wrested from rural legislators and control was once again in the hands of the cities. While these efforts were well intentioned, they failed to accomplish what they were supposed to do: create a police department that served all the people.

The real impetus to police reform came in 1919 when the Boston Police Department went on strike. By 1919 the income of factory workers and police officers had reversed. The factory worker, because of advances pushed by unionization, had improved their income to twice that of the average police officer. The dissatisfaction felt by police in Boston was also aggravated by the low esteem in which the police were now held due to the rampant corruption.

In early September, 1919 the Boston Police Officers Association voted to go on strike and become affiliated with the AFL. The officers went on strike on September 9, 1919 and almost immediately rioting and looting broke out. The

Governor called in the State militia to take over the city and public opinion, which had favored pay increases for police, turned against the police and the strike was broken. Eventually all strikers were fired and replaced with new officers and the efforts to unionize police was halted for decades.

There was some good that came out of the Boston Police Strike in that the public became aware of police conditions and pay and in the wake of the strike, a Commission was appointed to study crime in Boston and improvements were made. However, it was another decade before a serious look at crime and related issues were made.

In 1930 President Herbert Hoover appointed the Wickersham Commission to study crime issues nationally. This was the first attempt to understand the dynamics of police work and seek ways to improve efforts to fight crime. The Commission report, issued in 1931, made a number of observations and suggestions, among them:

* Police supervisors were too closely allied to political officials and their term of tenure too short to really accomplish anything.

* They found a lack of effective, efficient, and honest patrolmen.

* No intensive effort was being made to educate and train officers, there was no effective discipline of wayward officers or those who were incompetent.

* There was poor interorganizational communication, poor or non-existent communication equipment thereby inhibiting pursuit of task completion.

* The cities were growing so rapidly with the various nationalities the police could not keep up with the change.

* There were too many duties thrust upon the individual police officer.

There were a number of improvements to police operations that grew out of the Wickersham Commission, but police operation continued to lag behind comparable organizations in the private sector in terms of technology and management. It took another three decades for elected officials to get serious about true improvements in the police. Local communities had abdicated their responsibilities and the lead came from the federal level.

During the 1960's the public and the elected officials again became concerned about crime and violence and in 1965 President Johnson appointed The President's Commission on Law Enforcement and the Administration of Justice. He instructed the Commission "to inquire into the causes of crime and delinquency" (Commission, 1967). The Commission released its report in 1967 and made a number of recommendations that substantially changed American criminal justice for the better, such as improving communications within and between police agencies as well as the increased use of alternatives to prison.

Congress was also concerned with crime and passed into law the **Omnibus Crime Bill and Safe Streets Act of 1968**. This legislation was responsible for creating the Law Enforcement Assistance Administration (LEAA) that enabled local communities to improve services in law enforcement, courts, and corrections. There were legitimate complaints about the management of the LEAA in that it was too heavily weighted towards law enforcement, but it is undeniable that communications, training, technology, and programs were initiated that substantially improved criminal justice. The LEAA was abolished by the Reagan administration with the reasoning that crime is a local issue and that resources to fight crime should be shouldered by local citizens.

The Organization of the Police

There are over 40,000 different police departments and state and federal law enforcement agencies in the United States. Depending on whether or not it is rural, urban, or suburban, its organizational structure will differ. Most are organized along departmental lines, that is like functions are grouped together. Another popular variation on this theme is when a department is spread out over a very large area such as a large county, for example, it may be organized along geographic lines. Regardless of the distribution of manpower and lines of authority, the job of the police department is to protect the public.

Most departments are hierarchically arranged and Figure 4.1 simplistically illustrates the pyramidal organization of a typical police department. However, the implementation of community policing in many communities has altered the organizational structure of the police department. The decentralization that occurs via community policing changes the lines of communication, alters the distribution of power, and pushes decision-making down to the lowest possible level. This is a frightening thing to many of those who have succeeded in the old structure and they often will do all they can to prevent its implementation, at least in its most efficient form. More on this later in the chapter.

Figure 4.1 illustrates the typical pyramidal organizational structure. Note that the department in this illustration is organized along departmental lines. In addition, the Administrative Services Division uses non-sworn staff in many positions in order to get the sworn officers on the street where their powers of arrest can be used.

There is a good deal of variation in how police departments go about their task, but most departments allocate the bulk of officers to patrol activities. According to the International Association of Chiefs of Police, the staffing of

---

Figure 4.1

Police Organization Chart

Mayor or
City Manager

Chief of Police

Deputy Chief Administration	Deputy Chief Operations	Deputy Chief Research and Personnel	Deputy Chief Investigations

Captain		Captain		Captain		Captain	
Supv	Lt	Lt	Lt	Lt	Lt	Lt	Lt

SGT	SGT	SGT	SGT	SGT	SGT	SGT	SGT

Officer	Officer	Officer	Officer	Officer	Officer	Officer	Officer
Staff	Staff	Officer	Officer	Officer	Officer	Officer	Officer
Officer	Officer	Officer	Officer	Officer	Officer	Officer	Officer
Staff	Staff	Officer	Officer	Officer	Officer	Officer	Officer
Officer	Officer	Officer	Officer	Officer	Officer	Officer	Officer
Staff	Staff	Officer	Officer	Officer	Officer	Officer	Officer
Officer	Officer	Officer	Officer	Officer	Officer	Officer	Officer
Staff	Staff	Officer	Officer	Officer	Officer	Officer	Officer

---

patrol is a complicated task dependent on such things as philosophy, priorities, number of calls for service and population density, among other variables. However, when considering patrol needs, the following must be allowed for: responding to the needs of citizens, engage in preventive patrol, community-policing activities, to meet administrative requirements properly, to deploy officers to meet the special needs for policing according to time and neighborhood, and to provide for an adequate number of supervisors.

Some departments have three shifts responsible for patrol, in addition, others use an overlap shift, that is a patrol shift that begins at 6:00PM and ends at 2:00AM when there are more calls for service. Since crime is also not evenly distributed across a city, some areas of a city will have a higher density of police on patrol than in other areas. In this day and age of computers, specialists have devised rather sophisticated ways of determining where and when particular areas should have increased patrols.

Not all of the positions illustrated in Figure 4.1 are officers on patrol. In addition to patrol, there will be departments or divisions devoted to: administration, traffic, Investigations, juvenile, vice and narcotics, records, communications, training, personnel, intelligence, gangs, research and planning, and community relations. There are variations on each of these divisions, for example, some police departments combine street crime (vice and narcotics) with gangs.

Costs of Policing

According to Crime in the United States (UCR) 1998, more than $97.5 billion was spent on all criminal justice activities. Of that amount, 44 percent was spent by all governments on law enforcement. Since 1988, full-time, sworn law enforcement officers have increased from 485,566 officers to 641,208 officers, a net increase of 155,642 officers. During that time the U.S. population increased 24.4 million people. In other words the number of sworn officers has dropped from .5 per 1,000 population in 1988 to .4 officers per 1,000 population in 1998.

In the same time period civilian employment by police departments increased from 166,877 employees to 253,327 employees. This represents an increase of 86,450 employees or a 65.8% increase. The civilian employees do clerical and other support activities that allow sworn officers to work in positions necessary for the public good and where their powers of arrest can be used.

Tables 4.1 and 4.2 compare the growth of police departments between 1988 and 1998. They illustrate that some areas of the country have kept pace with the rate of population growth and, in some instances, have gone ahead of the population growth. Perhaps the only conclusion one can reach about the numbers of law enforcement officers is that as the citizens of a particular jurisdiction have felt a need to increase the numbers of law enforcement officers, they have done so. Other areas have not felt the need and as a consequence, have not funded the positions. Of course, since 1988, the economy has experienced its ups and downs and that dynamism has affected the numbers of police officers. The provision to put 100,000 new officers on the street as part of the 1994 Crime Bill has had a negligible effect as many jurisdictions have not been able, or willing, to provide matching funds or obligate themselves to fund the position after the grant.

Table 4.1

Full Time Law Enforcement
by Geographic Region
1988

Region	Total	Small Towns			Large Cities		
		Group I	Group II	Group III	Group IV	Group V	Group VI
New Eng	26,816	2,618	3,344	5,906	5,203	6.002	3,743
# emp per 1,000 pop	2.5	4.5	3.2	2.4	2.2	2.2	2.3
Mid Atlantic	88,290	46,532	3,699	7,105	9,163	11,298	10,493
# emp per 1,000 pop	3.0	4.6	3.1	2.3	2.4	2.0	2.0
E. No. Cent	73,014	27,485	5,484	8,165	9,152	11,362	11,366
# emp per 1,000 pop	2.5	3.9	2.2	2.0	1.9	2.0	2.6
W. No. Cent	22,023	6,592	1,375	1,899	3,014	4,085	5,058
# emp per 1,000 pop	2.2	3.0	1.8	1.6	1.7	2.0	2.4
So. Atlantic	60,287	16,329	9,193	6,541	7,187	7,685	13,352
# emp per 1,000 pop	3.3	3.9	2.8	3.2	2.8	2.9	4.0
E. So. Cent	20,822	4,782	3,300	755	2,752	3,414	5,819
# emp per 1,000 pop	2.7	2.7	2.5	2.5	2.4	2.3	3.2
W. So Cent	43,460	17,800	4,228	4,952	3,196	5,299	7,985
# emp per 1,000 pop	2.4	2.6	2.1	2.2	1.9	2.1	3.2
Mountain	22,099	8,876	2,857	2,220	1,940	2,138	4,068
# emp per 1,000 pop	2.5	2.7	2.3	1.8	2.1	2.2	3.4
Pacific	56,587	24,588	8, 335	8,108	6,648	3,534	5,374
# emp per 1,000 pop	2.3	2.6	1.9	1.9	2.0	2.1	4.0

Source: U.S. Department of Justice. **Crime in the United States, 1988.** Washington, D.C.: Federal Bureau of Investigation, 1989.

Table 4.2

Full Time Law Enforcement
by Geographic Region
1996

Region	Total	Small Towns			Large Cities		
		Group I	Group II	Group III	Group IV	Group V	Group VI
New Eng	25,862	2,218	3,574	5,326	5,268	5,632	3,844
# emp per 1,000 pop	2.2	4.0	3.1	2.1	1.9	1.8	2.1
Mid Atlantic	81,548	46,845	2,637	6,319	7,850	9,507	8,390
# emp per 1,000 pop	3.0	4.8	2.7	2.1	2.0	1.8	2.0
E. No. Cent	68,564	25,216	5,445	7,716	8,168	10,757	11,264
# emp per 1,000 pop	2.3	3.8	2.0	1.7	1.6	1.7	2.4
W. No. Cent	21,659	5,569	2,162	2,348	2,691	3,667	5,222
# emp per 1,000 pop	1.9	2.6	2.7	1.4	1.4	1.7	2.3
So. Atlantic	58,218	13,463	8,803	7,622	5,394	7,548	15,388
# emp per 1,000 pop	3.0	3.3	2.4	2.4	2.3	2.6	4.8
E. So. Cent	20,889	4,188	2,877	1,254	2,442	3,970	6,158
# emp per 1,000 pop	2.5	2.5	2.2	2.2	2.3	2.3	3.2
W. So Cent	43,357	16,960	5,324	4,098	3,496	5,027	8,452
# emp per 1,000 pop	2.2	2.3	1.9	1.8	1.7	1.9	3.2
Mountain	21,200	8,636	2,562	2,576	1,828	1,685	3,913
# emp per 1,000 pop	1.9	2.0	1.6	1.4	1.6	1.8	3.1
Pacific	49,293	22,217	7,408	6,485	5,141	2,823	5,219
# emp per 1,000 pop	1.8	2.1	1.3	1.3	1.4	1.6	3.5

Source: U.S. Department of Justice. **Crime in the United States -
1996.**Washington, D.C.: Federal Bureau of Investigation, 1997.

Salaries

Adequate salaries are important if we are to attract intelligent, competent men and women into the field of law enforcement. No other occupational group experiences death as a consequence of employment, except perhaps for the military, as do the police. Every shift has the potential for violence and occasionally the violence results in death to the officer or suspect. In that light, it is odd that we continue to subsidize the wealthy by pushing for lower taxes and insisting on low salaries for those who put their lives on the line every shift. It is amazing that we attract the quality of men and women to police work when we factor in the variables of danger, lack of esteem for the position, and low salaries. For the officer working his or her shift, a wealthy businessman complaining about his taxes is a difficult pill to swallow when he or she remembers a comrade slain in the line of duty protecting a businessman's property.

In all fairness, since 1978 average salaries have improved somewhat, from an average of $11,472 in 1978 to an average of $28,238 in 1997. However, the bottom quartile averaged only $23,588 in 1997. When one considers that the figures are an average, that is some are higher and others are lower, then the cheapness of some salaries are quite evident. In fact in some jurisdictions the pay is so low that police officers are expected to supplement their meager salaries by moonlighting as security officers at supermarkets and football games just to adequately provide for their families. It appears that the best pay for starting officers are found in cities with populations between 50,000 and 99,999. In addition, best starting salaries are found on the pacific coast. The Pacific Coast also takes the prize for best average maximum salary with the Mid-Atlantic a close second. Worst starting pay is found in cities with a population between 250,000 and 499,999 as well as in the East South Central. Shame on the Old South who insist on paying poor salaries and continue to push the idea that is it cheaper to live in the South than in other areas of the country. The standard of living is not that different between rural Alabama and rural Oregon. Table 4.3 illustrates the average annual salaries of police officers in 1997.

Just like most other workers in the American economy, police officers and corrections workers, as we will discuss in a later chapter, realized a real loss in the purchasing power of their paychecks. In 1980, for example, the average government worker earned $14,686. In 1993 the average government worker

Table 4.3

Entrance and Maximum Salaries
for Police Officers in Cities
of 10,000 Persons and Over, 1997

Size of City	Number of cities Reporting	Average Entrance Salary	Maximum Salary
Over 100,000,000	3	30,770	46,632
500,000 to 1 mil	6	31,176	44,417
250,000 to 499,999	24	30,474	41,486
100,000 to 249,000	61	30,929	42,084
50,000 to 99,999	163	31,058	41,530
25,000 to 49,999	313	29,357	39,969
10,000 to 24,999	686	26,689	36,551
Geographic Region			
New England	99	28,859	36,256
Mid-Atlantic	158	30,006	46,848
East North Central	252	29,350	39,134
West North Central	118	26,469	35,614
South Atlantic	172	23,845	35,214
East South Central	57	20,639	28,058
West South Central	152	23,680	30,907
Mountain	68	26,841	36,932
Pacific Coast	180	36,926	46,472
Metropolitan Status			
Central City	263	28,195	38,118
Suburban	707	29,933	41,523.
Independent	286	24,085	31,275

Source: Kathleen Maguire and Ann K. Pastore, eds., **Sourcebook of Criminal
Justice Statistics 1997.** U.S. Department of Justice, Bureau of Justice Statistics.
Washington, D.C.: USGPO, 1998.

earned $18,842, a 22.1% increase. On the other hand, inflation increased approximately 107% during the same period.

On the other hand, some top executives in industry and commerce who depend on the police for their safety are more generous to themselves and peers. According to **The State of Working America** (1991), "in inflation adjusted terms, average hourly wages fell more than 9% between 1980 and 1989." During the past decade the **State Of Working America** (1999. P.5) points out that "after adjusting for inflation, hourly wages stagnated or fell between 1989 and 1997 for the bottom 60% of all workers..." In real terms, earnings of the median worker in 1997 were about 3.1% lower than they were in 1989. At the other end of the workforce, between 1989 and 1997 the pay of chief executive officers of major corporations grew 44.6 percent (Mishel and Frankel, 1997).

So, in the decade of the 1990s while the rich got richer, and working men and women lost ground, police officers were being asked to do more, in an increasingly difficult and chaotic environment, at a salary that continues to lag behind inflation and to spiral downward in purchasing power. Clearly, the American citizen is getting a good deal for their dollar.

Proposition #6: Police officers are not evenly distributed across the nation according to need. In addition, the pay of police officers, in general, is not in accordance with the level of performance and danger present on the job. Adequate pay and benefits will recruit better Officers.

The Police Officer and the Job

Everyone understands that our job influences the way in which we view the world. Teachers may view the world through the classroom, a factory laborer sees things in terms of overtime and boring repetitive work and the police officer is suspicious. The above examples may be stereotypical and simplistic, but they illustrate the idea that we often cannot help taking on certain characteristics that reflect the work we do.

Jerome Skolnick (1994) provides us with a working sketch of the police officers "working personality." According to Skolnick, the police officers working personality is forged through an apprenticeship and is the result of two principle variables: danger and authority. Those variables must be interpreted in light of a "constant pressure to appear efficient." Skolnick points out:

> The element of danger seems to make the police officer especially attentive to signs indicating a potential for violence and law breaking. As a result, the officer is generally a 'suspicious' person. Furthermore, the character of police work makes an officer less desirable than others as a friend, because norms of friendship implicate others in the officer's work. Accordingly, the element of danger isolates the police socially from that segment of the citizenry that they regard as symbolically dangerous and also from the conventional citizenry with whom they identify (Skolnick, 1994).

The element of authority reinforces the variable of danger, according to Skolnick, and serves to further isolate the policeman from the public. The police are called upon to enforce puritanical laws prohibiting drunkenness as well as law that regulate the flow of public activity.

> In these situations, the police direct the citizenry, whose typical response denies recognition of the officer's authority and stresses their obligation to respond to danger. The kinds of people who respond well to danger, however, do not normally subscribe to codes of puritanical morality. As a result, the police are unusually liable to the charge of hypocrisy. That the whole world is an audience for the police further promotes police isolation and in consequence, solidarity. (Skolnick, 1994)

The symbolic assailant, according to Skolnick, is central to the development of the policeman's working personality. The policeman develops a sort of perceptual shorthand to recognize situations that are pregnant with danger. Sometimes he or she is wrong, but there is no penalty for being mistaken, but the penalty for being wrong is often physical harm or death.

A symbolic assailant is defined as "persons who use gesture, language, and attire that the police have come to recognize as a prelude to violence" (Skolnick, 1994). Violence is not necessarily predictable, rather the police officer responds to the vague indication that violence is possible due to the appearance of the individual. To qualify as a symbolic assailant, one does not need to have ever used violence.

For example, in the late 1970's there was a motorcycle gang in southern California that would ride the freeways assisting motorists in trouble. They affected the typical biker costume and rode a "hog" and by all outward appearances were the typical biker that had earned a bad reputation. The difference was that members of this group were Christians and had no intention of harm to anyone. But, it was probably very hard for one of the Samaritans to convince an elderly lady with a flat tire that he would change her tire for the sake of Christian charity. The elderly lady associated the biker with stories she had heard, and perhaps even identified with victims of reported assaults of outlaw bikers even though, in this case, the biker may never have used violence and had no intention of using violence.

With the police, the same dynamics are at work. The police officer responds to potential violence based upon dress, gestures, costume, and demeanor. Gang members affect certain jackets and colors, use signs, sometimes behave in a threatening way that the police officer has come to signify danger and the officer responds accordingly.

Proposition #7: Police officers are subject to a unique set of variables that cause them to react as they do towards people in their environment.

Community Participation

The police welcome the participation of the public in the war on crime. However, they do not want armed vigilante groups patrolling the neighborhoods because they see that aspect of public safety as their job and do not want to see others endangered by the good intentions of citizens. What police do want is cooperation, extra eyes and ears, and prompt reporting of crime. Standing on that foundation, police and citizens can forge a partnership that preserves neighborhoods and provides the police with the support that is necessary for safe cities. Following are four programs that are of interest to citizens and are worth exploring in order to improve the quality of life in one's neighborhood or city.

Community Policing

Community policing is an approach to policing that has gained a great deal of attention in recent years. It is more of a philosophy than approach that states that the police and members of the community can effectively maintain safety and security together. This *synergy*, as Miller and Hess (1994) call it, can be powerful, drawing upon the team efforts of all members of the community.

Community policing can be defined as police and citizens working proactively to solve crime-related problems and prevent crime. A secondary value of community policing is that it allows the flexibility to give officers in the neighborhoods secondary responsibilities such as working with the elderly and youth, as crime prevention officers, and on domestic disputes

There are many contributors to the concept of community policing, but the concept grew out of what is called the Kansas City Preventive Patrol Project. This classic study set out to determine the best way to patrol a neighborhood. Certain areas of the city were cited for the experiment and patrol beats were matched as closely as possible. Within each patrol area certain districts were patrolled either by automobile, on foot, or not at all with police only responding to calls for service. Before and after the experiment citizens and businessmen were interviewed to determine if they had been the victim of a crime, what they thought of police service, and how fearful they were of crime (Wilson, 1983).

The results were analyzed and surprised a great many people, including the experts. After one year, "no substantial differences among the three areas were observed in criminal activity, amount of reported crime, rate of victimization as revealed in the follow-up survey, level of citizen fear or degree of citizen satisfaction with the police" (Wilson, 1983). Thus, if there is no difference in crime or citizen satisfaction, then it does not make much sense to tie up police officers in the relatively unproductive task of simply patrolling the streets.

The conclusion is that we can use police officers more productively. One such approach is the community service approach. This is based on the assumption that if officers are more familiar with the neighborhood in which they work, individual citizens will take more responsibility for what is going on in the neighborhood. The other payoff is that intelligence gathering will improve and the citizenry will be more confident of the police.

Miller and Hess (1994) reviewed Greene and Taylor's (1991) description of several studies on the effectiveness of community policing. One study in Flint, Michigan was conducted from January, 1979 to January 1982. The officers involved in the study were given great discretion, but contact with citizens was a primary objective. "The Flint Neighborhood Foot Patrol Program" appeared to decrease crime, increase general citizen satisfaction with the foot patrol program, reduce citizens' fear of crime, and create a positive perception of the foot patrol officers" (Miller and Hess, 1994).

Two experiments were conducted in Newark, New Jersey; one between 1978 and 1979 and the other in 1983 and 1984. In the first experiment, where foot patrols were added, citizens reported a decrease in the severity of crime, but business owners believed that public disorder had increased and the neighborhood had become worse. In the second experiment, the coordinated foot patrol was thought to reduce the perception of property crime and improve assessments of the police. The police Foundation concluded that" if vulnerable and weak people feel safe as a result of specific police activity and if that feeling improves the quality of their life, that is terribly important" (Miller and Hess, 1994).

Further studies in Oakland, San Diego, Houston, Boston, and Baltimore County all demonstrated that at worst, routine patrol of officers in cars is relatively unproductive. At best, crime either decreased and/or citizens felt safer even though crime did not decrease in the area studied. Overall, community policing appears to decrease crime and increase citizen satisfaction with police services.

Not all cities are likely candidates for community policing with a heavy reliance on intensive use of foot patrol. However, there is room for the philosophy to take hold and for the police to engage the public in its fight against crime. Police can get out of their cars and get to know the people in the neighborhood in which they are working and spend time listening to the citizens. What this entails is a change in the thinking of police management and a reorganization the department. That is, the organization chart is flattened out, decision-making is pushed down to the lowest possible level, power is redistributed and the lines of communication are rearranged so that decisions affecting the day to day operation of the department are made by the personnel responsible for results.

Perhaps the most important part of community policing is contact with the public. Once regular home visits are a part of every shift for every officer involved, things will begin to improve. Many jurisdictions involved ask the officer to visit each home in his or her beat and speak to the occupants and leave a card with the request that they contact him or her if they have a concern other than an immediate need for assistance. This aspect can be completed whether or not the department implements foot patrol.

In areas of high density or in a particularly troublesome area of a city, one answer may be to open storefront precinct offices and ask welfare, probation, and other community service agencies to join in and base workers in the office. Abandoned fire stations are excellent sites for such an endeavor. In a large facility, part of the building can be used as a teen drop in center and community organizations can offer after school classes, such as cooking for latch key children, parent effectiveness training in the evening, pre-natal classes and medical checks for unwed mothers. The possibilities are numerous and limited only by the imagination and desire to work with the members of the community. In the meantime, officers can patrol the neighborhood on foot, bicycle, or moped.

Domestic Abuse and the Minneapolis Domestic Violence Experiment

Perhaps no call for service is more dreaded by individual officers than calls regarding family violence. Our attitudes about family violence have changed dramatically over the past decade, but the problems for officers have changed very little. Research indicates that between 21% and 56% of all marriages experience some form of violence (Frieze and Brown, 1989). Conventional wisdom among police officers is that combatants are just as likely to join together and turn on the responding officers as they are likely to continue fighting with each other.

One research effort is worth mentioning. In an effort to stem the recidivism of those involved in domestic abuse, the Minneapolis Police Department conducted an experiment during 1981-1982 (Elliott, 1989). This study called for two of four precincts in Minneapolis to assign suspects in violent family disputes to one of three police actions: arrest, separation of the parties, and advise or mediate. The results are interesting and have been influential throughout the field of police work.

There were two measures of recidivism: (1) a subsequent police report for domestic violence during the six month follow-up period and (2) the occurrence of a repeated violent incident as reported in victim interviews. The analysis of police records over a six month period showed that those automatically arrested had the lowest recidivism rate (10%), while the advise disposition had a 19% recidivism rate and those who received the separate disposition had the highest recidivism rate (24%). While there are questions about the results, such as did the lower recidivism rate for the arrestees reflect a wait and see attitude while court action was pending? Over all, however, the "accumulating evidence from all available studies, experimental and quasi experimental, supports the claim that arrest is more effective than advisement, separation, or no action in reducing subsequent violence in misdemeanor family violence" (Elliott, 1989).

The Minneapolis Domestic Violence Experiment appears to offer some hope for decreasing domestic violence. However, the study has some internal research design problems. Dunford, Huizinga, and Elliott (1990) were not able to duplicate the Minneapolis success in an experiment in Omaha, Nebraska. Further, Hirschell, Hutchison, and Dean were not able to duplicate the Minneapolis success in an experiment in Charlotte, North Carolina. Their conclusion is that "based on prevalence, arrest was no more effective at preventing subsequent abuse than the other two responses" [mediation/separation and cite and release] (Hirshel, et. al., 1991). What may be important here is that arrest can open the door for intervention in the form of counseling and may offer hope for the future.

Neighborhood Watch

The Neighborhood Watch Program can be an important adjunct to police patrol. It's purpose is to act as additional eyes and ears for the police, not act as police officers. Neighborhood Watch (NW) represents a "willingness of people to enforce standards of behavior in their own neighborhoods [and is seen as a] key element in the prevention of crime and disorder" (Garafalo and McLeod, 1989).

. A NW program is generally established at the request of residents of a neighborhood. A representative of the police department meets with concerned citizens and he or she explains why citizen involvement is important, how NW works, and what the residents of a neighborhood must do in order to get police department approval. The meeting may conclude with the formation of a NW group and the election of a leader of the group.

Generally the group must meet with some frequency, usually two or three times per year is needed for certification. Meetings are not the purpose of the groups, however, it is to observe and to report. The police department will provide instructions about how to identify suspicious persons, to note important details such as descriptions if individuals and license plate numbers, and to notify police immediately of such occurrences. In addition, the presence of such a group is announced by the presence of signs stating that a NW group is active in the area. Very few groups do anything other than function as part of their daily activities, some however, do institute routine patrols.

Very few groups receive funding for start up purposes or receive money for operations. Often they function as part of a neighborhood association. In the survey completed by Garafalo and McLeod (1989), most groups are characterized by white, middle income home owners who have lived in the neighborhoods for five or more years. The groups are also responsible in some areas for instituting crime tip hot lines, improving street lighting, and block parents.

The success of a program depends upon the level of activity. Usually, there is a spurt of activity just after the formation of a group and then activity declines and the presence of signs are the primary reminder that a NW group exists. Garafalo and McLeod (1994) found that NW groups do not usually get a foothold in disorganized or depressed areas because there is not a very high level of trust and the program demands a high level of trust. The areas they found to be "fertile areas" are those "threatened" neighborhoods commonly found in middle and working class areas of large cities that are bordered by high crime areas. They found that groups in these areas are the most active and most successful. Other groups further out on the fringe soon fall into passivity due to a lack of crime.

Generally speaking, Neighborhood Watch programs are useful in promoting a crime free environment if the residents work with each other and with the police. However, a successful group requires a time commitment from residents and they can be used as vehicles to generally improve the neighborhood.

Guardian Angels

Curtis Sliwa and the Guardian Angels are a well known group who seek to re-awaken traditional community values by involving people in reaching out to others in an effort to take the streets back from the "crudballs and slimebuckets." Since 1977 their red-bereted patrols have been visible in the parks, subways, and public areas of many large cities. They are unarmed and always travel in pairs, often with radios to call for help. They seek only to prevent crime by their presence and to offer assistance when needed.

As of October 1983 Curtis Sliwa reported 48 chapters of the Guardian Angels in the United States. Attempts to speak to someone to find out how many chapters now exist were unsuccessful. However, given the success of the program, there may be more than 48 chapters in 2000. Recruits must complete a three month training program in order to earn the red Beret and a T-shirt. Originally, all members of the Guardian Angels received training in the martial arts, physical and mental conditioning, citizen arrest procedures, cardio-pulmonary resuscitation, and first-aid (Pennell, Curtis, Henderson, and Tayman, 1989).

Pennell, et al. (1989) found that in the experimental area of San Diego, the area where the Angels patrolled experienced a 22% drop in major violent offenses. However, a drop of 42% was noted in the control area. That is, there was more of a drop in areas not patrolled by Guardian Angels suggesting that there is more to be reckoned with than just the presence of Guardian Angels. The Angels may have had an impact on property offenses, but the researchers point out that figure is inconclusive due to the San Diego Police initiating a foot patrol in the experimental area.

One important aspect of Guardian Angel patrols is to increase citizen feelings of safety. When citizens were asked to rate the effectiveness of Angels in increasing feelings of safety, over half of the respondents stated that they felt more safe as a result of Angels patrolling in their neighborhood.

Curtis Sliwa's comments about Angel autonomy has not endeared him to law enforcement. But, Pennell, et al. (1989) found that of officers surveyed who were knowledgeable of Angel activities agreed that Angels had helped citizens in one way or another (66%), made citizens arrests (66%), detained a suspect (61%), identified a suspect (51%), and, on a negative note, acted inappropriately on occasion (70%).

Certainly the presence of Guardian Angels may impact the occurrence of crime in certain neighborhoods. To what extent, we do not know. However, the Angels do give an opportunity for youth, particularly minority youth, to serve their community in a way that has meaning for them. It is exciting, demanding, and perhaps for the first time they must meet high expectations to serve a cause that is beyond personal gain.

Jails

I have decided to include the topic of jails in the chapter on police rather than corrections because they are the responsibility of the County Sheriff and are a part of the local law enforcement apparatus. Whether jails serve a law enforcement function or a corrections function is debatable. Still, they are managed by the Sheriff who has a law enforcement orientation and they are a part of the governmental structure of every county in the United States.

Today there are 3,016 jails in the United States employing more than 130,000 people and with more than 557,974 inmates (NIJ, 1997). Most of us never give much thought to the jail until a scandal occurs and then there is much hand wringing and many recriminations. We send fellow citizens to work every day without thought for their health or safety. Our wives, husbands, children, and neighbors often work in wretched, unsafe, and unsanitary conditions that would frighten the average citizen. Needless to say the inmates of such places often suffer much more and this is unfortunate because, under our system of government, everyone is presumed innocent until proven guilty and the vast majority of prisoners in the local jail have not been proven guilty.

The county jail is an institution brought to North America by early settlers. By 1166 in England, jails as we know them today had made their appearance. The primary purpose of those jails was not only to hold political enemies, but also to confine persons accused of crimes until their guilt or innocence could be determined. The Sheriff, as the official representative of the King, was responsible for maintaining the gaol (as it was known at that time).

Early jails in England and in the North American Colonies were a fee for service type of institution, that is prisoners paid for such things as food, blankets, fresh straw to sleep upon and even gin and sex. Nearly half of the jails in England in the early 1700's were privately owned. For example, the Duke of Leeds owned Halifax Prison, Lord Derby owned Macclesfield Prison and the Duke of Portland owned Chesterfield Gaol, which he rented out for eighteen guineas a year. In a private prison at Exeter, there was no chimney, sewer, or water, and the men were chained to the floor on their backs with spiked collars around their necks and heavy iron bars over their legs, unless they were able to pay for removal of the bars (Hibbert, 1963).

What we now of the present state of jails today is limited because unfortunately the last national survey of jails in the United States was completed in 1982. The National Sheriff's Association (1982) pointed out that jails of that period were plagued by extensive problems of inadequate personnel, lack of modernization, overcrowding, and underfunding. Anecdotal evidence tells us that very little has changed in the past eighteen years.

Jails are the most neglected area of corrections, but perhaps the most important. One scholar points out that the jail is the major intake center for the entire criminal justice system and as a consequence plays host to a variety of disguised health, welfare, and social problem cases (Mattick, 1974). It is unfortunate that twenty-six years after Mattick described jails in the United States, we still have not addressed many of the problems he called to our attention. Such an attitude towards safety, training of personnel, and programs are shortsighted and often expensive in light of the willingness of courts to hold Sheriffs accountable for conditions in their jails.

The truth is that most old jails (constructed prior to 1960) are unsafe and out of date. Even more shocking is the fact that most jails constructed today are obsolete and unsafe by the time they are opened. Many communities will build a jail only when they are forced to do so by a court or when they simply have too many inmates for the space. Once the bond measure is approved, an architect is hired and the jail is designed and constructed without much thought given to the users.

An important innovation in the evolution of jails is the New Generation Jail, that is a direct supervision jail. There are three types of jails: linear intermittent surveillance jails, podular remote supervision jails, and podular direct supervision jails. Old jails are usually of the linear intermittent surveillance jail and are the most dangerous for both inmates and staff. In this type of jail construction supervision is intermittent at best, if a less sophisticated person is placed in a cell with a predator the worst things imaginable are apt to happen to the victim. New innovations are the podular remote supervision and the podular direct supervision jails which provide a great deal more safety for both staff and inmates.

The remote surveillance jail represents an attempt to save money by not placing the officer in the pod with the prisoners and is more popular with rural counties of limited funds. In this type of design the housing for the prisoners is secure and an officer in a control room is able to observe all activities in the pod. He or she communicates with the prisoners via intercom and if help is needed, it can be summoned from another part of the jail. The direct supervision jail is called the new generation jail and calls for the officer to work in the pod with the prisoner. In this situation the officer can be proactive and recognize and deal with problems as they occur rather than waiting for a problem to arise.

It is important to remember that once the decision is made to build a new jail, an important source of information is the National Institute of Correction's (NIC) Jail Center located in Longmont, Colorado. The Jail Center that has been a leader in the construction of New Generation Jails and the NIC offers eight principles that are applicable to the New Generation Jail (Nelson, O'Tool, Krauth, and Whitmer, 1983):

1. They offer effective control for inmates
2. Supervision of inmates is improved.
3. They allow staff to be proactive rather than sit back and wait for something to happen.
4. They require competent staff who are leaders.

116

5. Safety of staff and inmates is increased.
6. It offers manageable and cost effective operations.
7. Communication between staff, between staff and inmates, and between administration, staff, and inmates is improved.
8. Classification of inmates is improved.

In her text on new generation jails, Linda Zupan (1991) concludes,

> The direct supervision facility deals with the interrelationship between fear, disorder and predation by imposing an architectural design that functions to reduce environmental sources of stress that stimulate inmate violence and allows corrections officers to control a specifically-defined territory in order to prevent opportunities for violence.

The jail plays an important part of community institutional life. It serves to hold unsentenced prisoners until they are released on bail or personal recognizance or go to trial. The jail serves as a clearing house for the mentally-ill, as a place to hold sentenced misdemeanants, and as the central intake center for the entire criminal justice system. As a consequence, it is important that resources be devoted to the upkeep of the jail and that it be used cautiously and prudently. We cannot afford to keep individuals indiscriminately in the jail. It costs between $35-$80 per day to maintain a prisoner in jail and we have reached the point where alternatives must be used.

Proposition #10: Local citizens must be willing to work with the police in order to have an impact on the amount of crime.

Summary

The police are the most visible component of the criminal justice system. They are called upon at all hours of the day for assistance simply because they are available 24 hours a day. Most calls for service are not calls relating to the law enforcement aspect of police work, rather they are calls for help.

We have progressed from a nation of nearly 4 million in 1790 huddled along the eastern seaboard to a nation of 250 million stretching from the Atlantic to pacific coasts. In the intervening 200 years police practices have changed for the better. No longer are officers hired based upon size and ability to fight. While salaries have increased, since 1974 the policeman has witnessed an erosion of the purchasing power of his or her paycheck.

Today we need intelligent, capable leaders who can handle the demands of a diverse and sophisticated society. The working personality of the policeman is developed by the interaction of danger and authority as they combine to form a personality geared to identify potential danger. The concept of symbolic assailant arises from the potential danger an officer senses when individuals by gesture, dress, and mannerisms are perceived as a prelude to danger. The symbolic assailant need never have used violence, but he is associated with danger because the officer identifies with fellow officers who have been injured in the past by similarly dressed or acting individuals.

Community policing has developed as one answer to increase services and to involve the community. Research has found that programs such as Neighborhood Watch and Guardian Angels have some value in deterring crime. Clearly, what is needed is increased citizen involvement under the guidance of police professionals.

Jails are an important part of the community. It is expensive to maintain a jail and as a consequence we must use the jail only for those persons who need the strict confinement. Alternatives such as Restitution Centers, community service, and electronic surveillance be used in conjunction with home confinement.

118

Bibliography

Federal Bureau of Investigation. **Crime in the United States**, 1974, 1988, and 1993.

Franklin W. Dunford, David Huizinga, and Delbert Elliott. "Omaha Police Experiment," **Criminology**. 28:2(May, 1990). pp. 183-206.

Delbert S. Elliott. "Criminal Justice Procedures in Family Violence Crimes," in Lloyd Ohlin and Michael Tonry. **Family Violence**. (Chicago: University of Chicago Press, 1989).

Timothy J. Flanagan, Michael J. Hindelang, and Michael R. Gottfredson, eds,. **Sourcebook of Criminal Justice Statistics** - 1979. U.S. Law Enforcement Assistance Administration, National Criminal Justice Information and Statistics Service. (Washington, D.C.: U.S Government Printing Officer, 1980).

Irene Hanson Frieze and Angela Browne. "Violence in Marriage," in Lloyd Ohlin and Michael Tonry. **Family Violence**. (Chicago: University of Chicago Press, 1989).

James Garafalo and Maureen McLeod. 1989. "The Structure and Operations of Neighborhood Watch Programs in the United States." **Crime and Delinquency**. 35:3 (July). pp. 326-344.

Jack R. Greene and Ralph B. Taylor. "Community-Based Policing and Foot Patrol: Issues of Theory and Evaluation." in Community Policing **Rhetoric or Reality**, Jack R. Greene and Stephen D. Mastrofski, eds. (New York, Praeger Publishers, 1991). pp. 195-223.

Christopher Hibbert. **The Roots of Evil**. (Boston: Little, Brown and Co., 1963).

J. David Hirschel, Ira W. Hutchison III, and Charles W. Dean. "The Charlotte Spouse Abuse Study," **Popular Government**. 57:1(1991). pp. 11-16.

James A. Inciardi. **Criminal Justice**, 4th ed. (Fort Worth: Harcourt Brace College Publishers, 1993).

International Association of Chiefs of Police. **Patrol Allocation, Deployment, and Scheduling Studies**. (Arlington, VA: IACP).

Hans W. Mattick. "The Contemporary Jails of the United States: An Unknown and Neglected area of Justice," in Daniel Glaser, ed. **Handbook of Criminology**. (Chicago: Rand McNally Publishing Company, 1974).

Kathleen Maguire and Ann K. Pastore, eds., **Sourcebook of Criminal Justice Statistics 1998.** U.S. Department of Justice, Bureau of Justice Statistics. Washington, D.C.: USGPO, 1999.

Linda S. Miller and Karen M Hess. **Community Policing: Theory and Practice.** (Minneapolis: West Publishing Company, 1994).

Lawrence Mishel and David M. Frankel. **The State of Working America.** (Armonk, N.Y.: M.E. Sharp, Inc., 1991).

W. Ray Nelson, Michael O'Tool, Barbara Krauth, and Coralie Whitmer. **New Generation Jails: Corrections Information Series.** (Boulder: National Institute of Corrections, 1983).

Susan Pennell, Christine Curtis, Joel Henderson, and Jeff Tayman. 1989. **Guardian Angels: "A Unique Approach to Crime Prevention."** **Crime and Delinquency.** 35:3 (July). pp. 378-400.

The Presidents Commission on Law Enforcement and Administration of Justice. **The Challenge of Crime in a Free Society.** (Washington, D.C.: U.S Government Printing Office, 1967).

Jerome H. Skolnick. **Justice Without Trial: Law Enforcement in Democratic Society,** 3rd ed. (New York: Macmillan College Publishing Company, 1994).

Lincoln Steffans. **The Shame of the Cities.** (McClure Phillips and Co, 1904. New York: Sagamore Press, Inc., 1957).

U.S. Bureau of the Census. **Statistical Abstract of the United States, 1994** (114th edition.) Washington, D.C. 1994.

James Q. Wilson. **Thinking About Crime,** (Revised Edition). (New York: Vintage Books, 1983).

Linda Zupan. **Jails: Reform and the New Generation Philosophy.** (Cincinnati: Anderson Publishing Co., 1991)

Chapter 5

The Corrections System

Introduction

The American corrections system is a varied and complex enterprise designed to handle the many responses to crime available to the courts. The corrections system is responsible for investigations (such as presentence investigations and investigation of crimes committed in institutions), community programs, institutions, and post institutional programs. The corrections system cost the American taxpayer nearly $32 billion in 1993 and there were 585,685 full-time employees in corrections, the last year for which complete figures are available, (Maguire and Pastore, 1998).

The corrections system can be viewed as the programs, facilities, and organizations responsible for the supervision, care, custody, and control of people who have been accused or convicted of a criminal offense. As a consequence, this includes jails, probation, prisons, camps, boot camps, half way houses and restitution centers, and parole agencies.

Throughout the 1950s, 60s and early 1970s, corrections workers subscribed to a philosophy of rehabilitation. In spite of the fact that few resources were devoted to rehabilitation, vis-à-vis custody, it provided a secure rudder for corrections. Since the mid 1970s, rehabilitation has fallen by the wayside in favor of *just deserts* and warehousing of prisoners. Generally speaking, among many corrections officials and policy makers today there is uncertainty as to whether the philosophy should be humane confinement or rehabilitation. Don C. Gibbons (1992) pointed out nearly ten years ago, "rehabilitation has been grafted onto the punitive aims of the correctional machinery" and humanitarianism and treatment did not replace punishment.

Rehabilitation

Before proceeding, it may be wise to review the concept of rehabilitation. We have heard a great deal about rehabilitation and it has been given a bad name by some members of the criminal justice community and by conservative legislators. During the debate on the 1994 Omnibus Crime Bill much was made of "pork" and prevention programs were equated with being soft on crime when most legislators did not have the foggiest notion of what works and does not work.

The truth is that much of what was passed off as rehabilitation in the 1950's through the 1960's did not work. But we did not have to throw the baby out with the bath water. Many programs may have been well meaning, but they were programs put together by inept or poorly prepared corrections workers who equated compassion with permissiveness and touchy-feelly therapy with responsible counseling. The result was the loss of confidence by taxpayers who had been given unrealistic expectations of outcome.

Another problem has been noted by Ted Palmer (1994). Scholars have attempted to measure the effectiveness of rehabilitation programs by looking at specific, isolated entities. That is, isolating the effectiveness of counseling, for example, from the impact of vocational training as part of the individuals program. It doesn't take too much intelligence to know that receiving counseling by itself will do little good, if the individual involved does not have much hope for a positive future. Put another way, if an inmate in a prison meets once a week for a counseling session with the prison psychologist, positive gains or illuminating insight are likely to be undone within fifteen minutes of returning to the cell house. Therefore, according to Palmer, any attempt to measure the effectiveness of rehabilitation programs must take into account all inputs as well as the competence of staff.

The obligation of the community to offer a measure of support and stability is illustrated by Elliott Currie (1985) in his description of New York's Wiltwyck School for delinquents. The value of reviewing this piece of research "offers a compelling look at both the genuine potential of serious efforts at rehabilitation and the roots of their frequent failure" (Currie, 1985).

William McCord and Jose Sanchez compared two groups of men who had been institutionalized at the Massachusetts Lyman School and at Wiltwyck. The Lyman School was a conventional, punitive, regimented youth prison with few programs and the population was predominately white. Wiltwyck School was a residential youth facility, with a predominantly Black and Hispanic population, for boys who were emotionally disturbed and which offered an intense therapeutic environment with an abundance of programs.

The researchers traced the histories of all 175 boys who were at Wiltwyck between 1952 and 1955. They also traced the history of a random sample of 165 boys who had graduated from Lyman in the same years. At the beginning of the 1980's the boys had reached their late thirties or early forties. McCord and Sanchez wanted to know how they had done in the intervening years. The results were somewhat confusing to the researchers.

In the first five years after release, the Wiltwyck boys did much better than the Lyman graduates. The Wiltwyck graduates were re-arrested for felonies at an 11% per cent rate and the Lyman graduates at 79%. It appears that the Wiltwyck School was able to significantly prevent the graduates from re-involvement in crime, while the Lyman boys were involved in crime almost from the time of release.

However, after about five years in the community, the Wiltwyck boys began to commit crimes that resulted in their reincarceration. The Lyman boys, who after release had picked up their life of skullduggery almost immediately, began to become more involved in legitimate activities and their involvement with the criminal justice system began to decline. The flip-flop in status also followed racial lines. That is, the recidivism of boys from the Wiltwyck school and Lyman School were entirely of black and Hispanic boys. As a consequence, the Wiltwyck School, predominately black, on paper appeared as if it was not successful at preventing recidivism. On the other hand, the Lyman school, predominately white, appeared to be doing a good job at preventing recidivism.

What was the difference? After follow-up interviews, they concluded that the fault lie in the minority student's lack of connection to a societal support structure that allowed them to successfully cope with the demands of society and "'in contrast to the Wiltwyck group, many of the men from Lyman found it relatively easy to deal with life on the outside'" (McCord and Sanchez, 1983 in Currie, 1985). Thus, it may be that the failure of rehabilitation is not only due to the failure of implementation, but is also found in the failure of the community to nurture pro-social behaviors in those who do not have the opportunity to learn such behaviors at home or who have connections to jobs, unions, and so forth.

Prior to 1974, there were a few critics of rehabilitation, but they were largely ignored. However, in 1974 the so-called "Martinson Report" was published and created a great deal of controversy that began the rush to do away with programs that attempted to "rehabilitate" offenders.

Briefly, Robert Martinson's (1974) article described a research effort he had been involved in with Douglas Lipton and Judith Wilks (Lipton, Martinson, and Wilks 1975) in which they surveyed 231 research studies that had been published purporting to assess the effectiveness of programs aimed at reducing recidivism. They began by looking at several hundred studies and refused to consider many of them due to methodological problems. All kinds of studies were looked at: those providing counseling, vocational training, work release, probation, parole, and even cosmetic surgery. The Lipton, Martinson, and Wilks study concluded was that "with few and isolated experiences, the rehabilitative efforts that have been reported so far have had no appreciable effect on recidivism" (Martinson, 1974).

The die was cast. Many correctional agencies used the "nothing works" attitude as an excuse to pare the budget, but Van Voorhis (1987) points out that "assessments of program effectiveness should not have been reduced simplistically to the matter of 'working' vs. 'not working.'" Since the mid-70's most agencies have cut back, or done away with entirely, programs that may have been effective to some degree as an intervention. This is in spite of the fact that in budgetary terms, very little was given over to rehabilitation programs. Anyone who worked in prisons during this period, knows that very few resources in terms of staff positions, time of staff involved, and physical space were devoted to such programs. Still, the attitude has prevailed with many corrections staff that there are offenders who have some potential to reform and rejoin the community as contributing citizens.

Martinson later retracted his statements and conceded that there are programs that work. Palmer reviewed a number of studies and concluded that there are programs that work, specifically: family therapy, behavioral approaches outside of the residential setting, and combined therapeutic approaches all showed results in reducing recidivating. Other specific programs show promise, such as selected counseling programs by knowledgeable volunteers and in at least one instance a program utilizing restitution and "combined therapeutic approaches" (Palmer, 1994).

In short, we cannot deny that some programs do work. The point, when it comes to rehabilitation vs. warehousing, is that warehousing of prisoners is here and now oriented. Rehabilitation is oriented to the future. Any businessman knows that one must plan for the future and that failure to invest in a plan for the future spells bankruptcy. So it is with our investment in human capital and in the corrections enterprise. Failure to plan for the future return of inmates to the community ultimately spells doom.

Forty-eight percent of people surveyed believe that rehabilitation should be the primary goal of prison (Maguire and Pastore, 1997). In addition, 52% of those queried in an earlier survey (Maguire and Pastore, 1994) believe that we should spend money on social and economic problems up front rather than wait to put the criminal in prison. Thus we see that elected representatives sometimes act in opposition to what their constituency think ought to be done when it comes to crime. Perhaps this is a further example of the fashionability of being tough on crime.

Since parole has been either abolished or severely cut back, one final point about the attitude of offenders in regard to playing the "parole game" is necessary. Much has been made about inmates becoming involved in counseling programs and other such endeavors in their efforts to gain a parole. There has been a good deal of derision thrown at the notion of a tough looking con admitting to a problem begun in childhood because he lost his teddy bear, which in turn caused him to rob a bank. Corrections workers do not buy into such nonsense, and while there may be occasional instances of repressed trauma resulting in crime, corrections workers do not subscribe to pseudo-Freudian explanations of criminal conduct. Such insults are tossed about by conservatives who wish to do away with programs altogether and who believe that punishment will deter future criminal behavior. More on this subject later, but suffice it to say that idleness in prison makes for some very long days for both inmates and employees. Programs at least occupy the time of inmates and at best offer hope and the possibility of a future. Further discussion of rehabilitation aside, we now turn to a discussion of the various components of the corrections system and the tasks they are supposed to accomplish.

Proposition #8: Rehabilitation is not dead. Adequate resources Must be devoted to the development and implementation of programs that meet the needs of the offender and the community.

Probation

As of the end of 1997 there were in excess of 3.2 million persons on probation in the United States. The use of probation for first time offenders and those who are relatively unsophisticated represents the best hope in corrections for diverting offenders away from further involvement in criminal behavior. However, it is important that we do not have unrealistic expectations of probation, on the other hand, probation is only as effective as the desire to succeed by the probationer. It is also only as effective as the devotion of the probation officer and the resources devoted to it by the community. Table 5.1 illustrates the numbers of people on probation by state.

Probation is generally claimed to be an American innovation even though a man named Matthew Davenport Hill was working with offenders in England at about the same time and using the same approaches. The beginnings of probation can be found in such concepts as: benefit of clergy, recognizance, judicial reprieve, and bail. All of these alternatives to incarceration were used in England as early as the 1300's when any person who could read and write was automatically assumed to be a member of the clergy and was tried for criminal offenses by an ecclesiastical court rather than the King's court. As time went on other alternatives were conceived to circumvent the harshness of prisons.

The credit for being the "father" of probation is given to John Augustus, a Boston bootmaker. One day in 1841 he was in the Court of Common Pleas when a man was brought before the judge for public drunkenness. Augustus was so impressed with the man's sorrow that he pleaded with the judge to allow him to take him home and counsel him. He was allowed to do so with the admonition to return in three weeks. Upon his return the judge was so impressed with the man's progress that he fined him one penny and sent him on his way. John Augustus continued to work with offenders to the extent that his business suffered.

In Augustus' account of his experience with the drunk, we find the elements of modern probation: (1) a suspended sentence, (2) counseling, (3) freedom, and (4) conditions placed upon that freedom. The main difference is that Augustus was not an officer of the court. That was to come later. Massachusetts was the first state to have a paid probation officer beginning in 1869. It was many years before all the states followed suit, but finally in 1956 Mississippi was the last state to approve probation as an alternative to imprisonment.

Many people have a mistaken idea of probation. Probation is not leniency, the individual must be sentenced to a term in prison. The sentencing judge then has the prerogative, for certain offenders, to set aside the sentence and place the individual on probation subject to rules imposed by the court. Therefore, if the probationer abides by the rules, he or she will remain in the community and be discharged at the appropriate time. If he or she violates the rules of probation, or commits a new sentence, then they will have the probation revoked and be sent to prison to serve the original sentence.

The rationale of probation is based upon the idea that certain offenders can be reasonable risks while in the community and that it would not be helpful if they were sent to prison. Being placed on probation is predicated upon the offender providing evidence of qualities that leads the sentencing judge to believe that he or she will benefit substantially and that they intend to take up a law abiding life. The rationale makes sense if we as a people have not entirely given up on the human race and still hold to that fundamental American characteristic that men and women can change and sometimes need a break. If, however, that characteristic has been abandoned, then the rationale makes no sense at all.

Given the rationale, the aims of probation are to help offenders through services designed to solve those difficulties that brought the individual into contact with the court in the first place. It is the aim of probation to make the individual more comfortable with the demands of a civilized society and impart to them a sense of future and the confidence to succeed.

The decision to grant probation is rather complex. There are two factors that need to be emphasized in regard to the granting of probation. First, it is the responsibility of the sentencing court to grant probation. Second, even though it is the responsibility of the court to grant probation, that decision must be made within the limits and restrictions imposed by state or federal law. In other words, some offenses are not eligible for probation, such as murder, sexual offenses, and those who fall under the habitual offender statutes.

One of the traditional tools available to the court in determining whether or not to grant probation is the Present-

Table 5.1

Adults on Probation Under State and Federal Jurisdiction – 1997

Region and jurisdiction	Probation population Jan 1, 1997	1997 Entries	1997 Exits	Probation Population Dec. 31, 1997
United States, total	3,161,030	1,725,834	1,628,403	3,261,888
Federal	34,202	14,756	16,331	32,627
State	3,126,828	1,711,078	1,612,072	3,229,261
Northeast	551,727	249,991	229,955	572,594
Connecticut	55,978	38,275	38,264	55,989
Maine	7,753	NA	NA	8,584
Massachusetts	44,858	39,021	37,449	46,430
New Hampshire	4,414	3,585	3,123	4,876
New Jersey	125,881	59,641	54,967	130,565
New York	174,406	47,634	36,159	185,881
Pennsylvania	110,532	47,366	45,405	112,493
Rhode Island	20,446	8,473	9,271	19,648
Vermont	7,459	5,986	5,317	8,128
Midwest	704,965	491,274	465,678	730,005
Illinois	115,503	63,296	59,318	119,481
Indiana	93,509	81,799	78,263	97,045
Iowa	15,386	15,428	13,980	16,834
Kansas	15,732	19,502	19,029	16,205
Michigan	147,598	124,731	117,525	154,236
Minnesota	90,202	55,258	55,509	90,707
Missouri	42,368	20,718	16,785	46,301
Nebraska	14,363	14,696	14,534	14,525
North Dakota	2,599	1,498	1,440	2,657
Ohio	116,865	64,512	61,957	118,761
South Dakota	3,548	4,768	4,764	3,467
Wisconsin	47,292	25,068	22,574	49,786

Table 5.1 – Adults on Probation Under State and Federal Jurisdiction – 1997 (Continued)

Region and jurisdiction	Probation population Jan 1, 1997	1997 Entries	1997 Exits	Probation Population Dec. 31, 1997
South	1,272,488	667,472	651,235	1,292,339
Alabama	37,865	2,153	1,669	35,723
Arkansas	25,178	8,829	7,315	26,392
Delaware	16,628	NA	NA	17,872
District of Columbia	9,740	9,875	8,818	10,797
Florida	237,117	196,263	196,902	239,932
Georgia	143,457	65,452	60,489	148,420
Kentucky	11,689	6,087	5,683	12,093
Louisiana	35,375	11,815	11,737	35,453
Maryland	70,553	39,163	35,104	74,612
Mississippi	10,376	3,547	3,926	10,997
North Carolina	102,483	59,327	56,394	105,416
Oklahoma	28,090	13,812	13,131	28,733
South Carolina	42,417	15,046	15,059	42,404
Tennessee	37,002	20,305	19,056	38,251
Texas	429,329	193,128	193,364	429,093
Virginia	29,620	22,970	22,588	30,002
West Virginia	5,669	NA	NA	6,149
West	597,648	302,341	265,204	634,323
Alaska	3,999	2,038	1,659	4,378
Arizona	40,607	29,604	25,398	44,813
California	286,526	164,882	146,877	304,531
Colorado	42,688	20,153	16,051	45,447
Hawaii	14,027	7,521	6,147	15,401
Idaho	5,855	2,308	1,796	6,367
Montana	4,473	1,257	1,052	4,678
Nevada	9,760	NA	NA	10,902
New Mexico	8,903	7,470	7,478	8,895
Oregon	42,292	16,210	14,522	43,980
Utah	9,306	4,107	3,952	9,461
Washington	125,780	44,511	38,016	1322,014
Wyoming	3,432	2,280	2,256	3,456

Source: Kathleen Maguire and Ann K. Pastore, eds., *Sourcebook of Criminal Justice Statistics, 1997*. U. S. Department of Justice Bureau of Justice Statistcs, Washington, DC: USPGO, 1998

ence Investigation which is discussed in chapter 3. There are other tools available to the court such as sentencing guidelines and these guidelines have been developed to take as much risk as possible out of the decision-making process, but the sentencing judge may elect to disregard their use.

Offenders are placed on probation subject to certain rules as specified by the court. There are two kinds of conditions that the probationer must abide by. General conditions and specific conditions. General conditions are those that every probationer must abide by, such as:

* Obey all federal and state laws and local ordinances.
* Refrain from the use of all drugs unless prescribed by a physician and the abuse of alcohol.
* Maintain steady employment.
* Must not leave the district without permission.
* Will not enter into any legal contract without permission.
* Will report at the times and places as ordered by the probation officer.

Specific conditions are those conditions that apply only to the individual offender and usually are related to programmatic aspects of the probationers offense. These can be such orders as:

* Providing urine samples upon demand by the probation officer for drug testing.

* Participate in family counseling, substance abuse counseling, or educational programs such as GED classes, and so on.

* Attend AA or NA meetings.

* Refrain from contact with a former spouse.

The use of conditions are an important tool in maintaining control of probationers. Obviously, the probation officer cannot be with the individual twenty-four hours per day, but the limits on the probationers activities lets the probationer know that any attempt to circumvent the orders of the court, will bring a measure of grief. Any violation of the conditions of probation is referred to as a technical violation.

According to U.S. Department of Justice Statistics (Maguire and Pastore, 1998), 14.1% of federal probationers had their probation revoked for technical violations in 1995. Only 3.8% of federal probationers violated their probation by committing a new offense. State prisoners who had their probation revoked amounts to a considerably larger number. Still, the number of technical violations are considerable and we are short sighted in that we rely on punitive sanctions for those who use drugs or are guilty of violating a rule of probation or parole. This creates a problem of nearly monumental proportions.

According to the Bureau of Justice Statistics (August, 1995), in 1991 45% of all state prison admissions were for probation and parole violation. An estimated 41% of the violators were using illegal drugs daily. On the other hand, only 2% of the violators were violated for failing to pass a drug test. Thus, nearly 39% were violated for failure to report. We can assume many knew they would fail a drug test and were hoping to catch a break that never came.

A forty-five percent violation of probation and parole is much too high. Many critics will point to that figure as proof that the criminal justice system is not working. Quite the contrary, it is proof that the system works very well. Not very well at assisting the offender, but very well at suppression and law enforcement. What we need to ask is, "Do we really **want** 45% of all probationers and parolees to be sent back to prison where they will consume valuable resources and make no contribution to the national welfare and hone their rationalizations for deviant conduct and criminal skills?" The rational law-abiding citizen will respond with an emphatic **No!** Therefore, we need to look at the reasons for the recidivism and most experts will point out that we devote too few resources to effective community supervision and programs. We should not have unrealistic expectations of success, but we can cut the recidivism rate considerably.

Pre-trial release of defendants is a valuable tool in keeping the population of jails down. In 1994 the Bureau of Justice Statistics reports that in the 75 largest counties of the United States, only 32% of felony defendants were charged with misconduct while on some form of community supervision. Of those arrested for violent offenses, 77% were not charged. This is an important point. For selected individuals awaiting trial, there is a greater probability that they will behave themselves while on pre-trial release. In addition, research reveals that those not in jail at the time of trial and sentencing receive lighter sentences. Pretrial release is a good idea that is sometimes managed poorly and is always at the bottom of the allocations budgetary ladder. Pre-trial release makes good sense and is a valued part of the criminal justice process. It simply needs more attention and perhaps if the court released the offenders under some form of supervision, there would be even fewer failures. It is a matter of allocation of resources.

In regard to revocation of probation, it can only be done by the sentencing court and only after certain due process requirements have been met. As stated above, there are generally two ways in which probation can be revoked: a technical violation and by committing a new crime. In the past revocations were relatively easy, but due to abuses, the courts have determined that probationers are entitled to certain procedural safeguards. Probation revocation requires a two step process including determining that a violation did occur and secondly to notify the defendant of the specific charges against him or her. In all instances the probationer must have adequate twenty-four hour notice of the hearing, and he or she has a right to counsel at the time of a revocation hearing where the imposition of the sentence has been suspended.

Intensive probation has become one of the most widely accepted variations of probation (Polk and del Carmen, 1992). Intensive probation varies widely, but is generally defined as "a form of probation distinguished by the degree of increased contact between the probationer and the supervising officer" (Polk and del Carmen, 1992). In 1995 10.1% of all probationers were on Intensive Supervision (Maguire and Pastore, 1998). The caseload of an intensive probation officer is around 25 probationers, however the range varies from a high of 61 (South Carolina) to a low of 10 in Illinois and Montana (Maguire and Pastore, 1993).

The program will vary from jurisdiction to jurisdiction, but generally the offender is required to meet with the probation officer 2-3 times per week. In addition, the probation officer will work several evenings per week in order to get out into the community and surprise probationers at home or even on the job. The probationer is required to provide a urine sample upon request, which is three or more times per week if the individual has a history of drug use.

The job of the intensive supervision officer is made even more effective if there is wide use of electronic surveillance. The concept requires the probationer to wear a bracelet on the wrist or ankle and allows the probation officer to develop a program that allows the officer to track the travels of the individual offender. In addition, the technology has developed to the point where bracelets are available that emit a signal allowing the officer to drive by the home or work place of the probationer and aim a devise, much like a radar gun, at the home and determine whether or not the offender is at home or work.

The savings of probation are significant when compared to the cost of maintaining an offender in prison. The costs of imprisonment conservatively range from $10,000 to $15,000 per year with construction costs per bed at around $50,000. Even with greater costs associated with intensive probation due to lower caseloads we can see that probation, when adequately conducted, is still a cost effective alternative to imprisonment. The costs of placing an offender on intensive probation varies, but in Georgia the estimated cost is $1,622 per year (Erwin, 1986), in New Jersey the cost is given as $5,208 per year (Harper, 1987) and Kentucky and Lucas County Ohio reported significant savings in their programs (Latessa, 1986).

Probation is the most used form of punishment and correction in the United States. It is not always successful and many times the probationer will fail to complete his or her term of probation. What is important is that non-violent offenders be given a chance to succeed in the community before sending them to prison. It is less costly than imprisonment and serves the offender well if the sentencing judge believes that going to prison will only harden the offender. It is important that competent, dedicated, and clear-headed officers be appointed to supervise the offenders if the dual needs of the community and offender are to be met.

Institutions

Prisons have jumped to the forefront of possible answers to today's crime problem. However, most people have only a vague notion of what a prison is and how it impacts the people who are kept in them and who work in them. If we are going to make rational decisions at the voting booth, to disagree with our elected representatives, and, if necessary, agree to adequate funding for prisons once they are constructed, it is important that we understand the culture that exists inside a prison.

A prison is a unique organization and if judged by the standards of the private sector, it serves no real purpose. It doesn't manufacture things to be sold, it does not handle finance, underwrite insurance or serve any other purpose other than to keep people locked up for years at a time. In order for a prison to function it must have an administrative staff with a chief executive and a body of workers.

One authority points out that the warden and his associates in the form of guards, cooks, counselors and so on have specific duties geared to:

* Maintain order (that is to keep down internal disruption and violence and prevent escapes).

* Supply the prisoners with their life necessities (usually on a skimpy budget) and

* Manage the prison industries, which are restricted to the production of commodities consumed within state institutions--furniture, clothing, and food--and items sold by the states, such as license plates (Irwin, 1980).

Prison social organization is composed of the synchronized actions of hundreds of people, all of them hating some, loving others, and all vying for prestige, recognition, favors, power, and sex. The amazing thing is that somehow they work. Somehow, the personnel--including the prisoners--are bound together in such a way that most misunderstandings are not critical (Cressey, 1961). Prison social organization is complex with subtle nuances and invisible aspects.

The prison is a total institution, that is it is cut off from the rest of the world to a certain extent, but the barriers are not that impenetrable. The walls, barbed wire, and bars are there to keep prisoners in, but they do not keep the world out. Television, radio, visits, and the coming and going of staff influence and keep the inmates abreast of what is going on in the world. In addition, the constant influx of new inmates constantly renews and invigorates the inmate culture and brings about change within the inmate world.

There are two views of the inmate culture, that is the system of values and attitudes that give meaning to life and are used as a yardstick against which to judge everyone's behavior. One view states that the inmate culture grows out of a response to what are called the "pains of imprisonment" (Sykes). The other view is that the prison inmate culture is imported into the prison and is a reflection of street culture (Cressey and Irwin, 1962).

The "pains of imprisonment" cannot be rejected for they must influence life behind the walls to a certain extent. According to Sykes the pains are:

* The deprivation of liberty. This is obvious because the inmates life is restricted to a few small acres. This also represents a deliberate rejection by the community.

* The deprivation of goods and services. Most prisoners are kept in a rather Spartan environment. Even with TV and a radio, few would admit they had it worse on the street, even if it were true. However, the deprivation has another meaning in a world that measures ones worth by material possessions. They find themselves poor without the edifying reasons of principle, religion, or deferred gratification. They are poor by their own misdeeds, and this is perceived as a bitter attack on their personal esteem.

* The deprivation of heterosexual relationships. We are not discussing the physical aspects of male-female relationships, but rather the psychological aspects. The psychological damage done by being confined to a world with members of the same sex, creates havoc with self-concept. The absence of one half of one's audience from which one normally relates and from whom one normally draws a good portion of one's self concept causes the self-concept to become distorted and cracked from the lack of contrast.

* The deprivation of autonomy. The prisoners inability to make choices, along with the administrations unwillingness to explain decisions and commands, threatens the inmate's self-image by reducing him or her to the same status as a three year old child.

* The deprivation of security. The prisoners being locked up with others whom he views as dangerous or unstable is anxiety provoking to say the least. In recent years the introduction of gangs into the prison has resulted in a culture that demands that the gang member be willing to steal or assault others, especially independents. The waiting and stress call into question the inmates ability to cope--"Can he take it?"

The importation perspective (Cressey and Irwin, 1962) states that the culture of the prison is a reflection of the individual inmates and their orientation. Cressey and Irwin identified three distinct subcultures in a prison: a prison subculture, a criminal subculture, and a legitimate subculture. The criminal and legitimate subcultures are a reflection of the orientation of those who look to the outside. The prison subculture is a reflection of those who look to the inside. For example, the legitimate subculture is composed of those who perhaps are bank clerks convicted of embezzlement. They have no relationship to criminals or convicts and do not perceive themselves as criminals. The criminal subculture is composed of those who are, for example, professional burglars. They identify with other burglars and look to the outside and their next job. The importation perspective is given credence by the rise of gangs in prisons. We find the same gangs in prison as we do in the community. Their allegiance is to the gang both in and outside of prison and it is a matter of the gang member doing gang time, not his own time.

We have to admire those who work in prisons. Daily they enter through the gates and spend their days in prison with nothing more for protection than their wits and a two-way radio. In addition, their purpose and job is usually misunderstood by the taxpayer and even their family. They are underpaid and see only their failures and rarely meet a success case. The continual stress of working inside leads to a high incidence of stroke, heart disease, substance abuse, and family problems. The question is not why they do it, but how do they survive?

Inside the walls there is a staff culture that is a mirrored reflection of the inmate subculture. Staff have certain values such as: always go to the aid of an officer, don't lug drugs, don't rat, never make a fellow officer look bad in front of inmates, always support an officer in a dispute with an inmate, and so on (Kauffman, 1988). While the inmate subculture reflects a general value of solidarity against staff, the prison employee culture reflects a value of employee safety and solidarity against inmates.

Prisons and their Organization

The organization of a prison depends on the size and mission of the particular institution. All prisons are not alike. Some are designed as maximum security, some for medium security, and others as minimum or community security. Generally speaking, a maximum security prison will house the most vicious prisoners and those serving long term sentences. All inmates undergo a classification process upon arrival in the Department of Corrections. They are usually initially transported to a separate institution for the classification of inmates and then transported to the properly designated institution.

At the institution designated for classification, the inmate will undergo a series of educational, psychological, and medical testing. These tests are not a goody two-shoes attempt to help the inmate, but rather they are necessary to properly determine where the inmate should be placed. Mistakes at this point could result in death or injury to the inmate, danger to staff, other inmates, and even escapes. Once the inmate is properly classified, he or she is transported to the proper institution for service of sentence.

At the home institution of the inmate, he or she is free to participate in appropriate programs available to the inmate. Programs make good sense for two reasons: first, a person with a high school diploma or vocational training certificate is more likely to find employment upon release and thus may not commit further crimes; second, busy inmates are less apt to engage in forms of skullduggery that bring harm to other inmates, staff, or result in escape attempts. It is important to remember that institutional programs may, or may not, be helpful. We all know of people for whom a high school diploma or even a college degree was not a factor in keeping him or her out of trouble.

Medium custody prisons are for those prisoners who commit serious crimes, but are not deemed dangerous or as much of an escape risk as those who go to the maximum security prison. Socially, life is a little easier and one is less likely to be killed or assaulted in a medium custody prison, but still the inmates are younger, more volatile, less sophisticated, and more immature.

Minimum custody institutions are those places often referred to as "country clubs." They are available for those inmates with a minimal criminal record, offenders who did not commit a violent offense, are not associated with organized crime, and who have a relatively short time to serve on their sentence. Perhaps just as importantly, minimum custody institutions are cheaper to operate than a major prison and the inmates are less likely to be victimized by more predatory inmates. All custody level prisons can receive inmates straight from the court or they can be transferred from another institution, either as a means to begin easing an inmate back to society after serving a long sentence (a transfer to a less secure prison, assuming good behavior) or the prisoner can be transferred to a higher custody level prison because a stricter custody is required.

Table 5.2 shows the number of prisoners in custody of state and federal institutions in 1996 and 1997. Table 5.3 also illustrates prison population projections to the year 2002. Clearly, prison population projections are not good. Community-based facilities are a valuable alternative for non-violent offenders and allow the offender to take advantage of programs not available in prison. Community-based facilities also serve a valuable purpose in three additional ways: first, the soon to be released inmate has a chance to decompress, find a job, and affect a reconciliation with his or her family. Second, the state has a means to intensively supervise the releasee in the critical weeks before release and if

Table 5.2 – Prisoners in Custody in 1996 and 1997

Region and jurisdiction	Total			Total		
	1996	1997	Percent change	1996	1997	Percent change
United States, total	1,183,368	1,244,554	5.2	1,138,984	1,197,590	5.1
Federal	105,544	112,973	7.0	88,816	94,987	6.9
State	1,077,824	1,131,581	5.0	1,050,169	1,102,603	5.0
Northeast	169,261	172,244	1.8	161,324	163,836	1.6
Connecticut	17,851	18,521	3.8	12,465	13,005	4.3
Maine	1,426	1,620	13.6	1,351	1,542	14.1
Massachusetts	11,796	11,947	1.3	10,880	10,847	-0.3
New Hampshire	2,062	2,164	4.9	2,062	2,164	4.9
New Jersey	27,490	28,361	3.2	27,490	28,361	3.2
New York	69,709	70,026	0.5	69,709	70,026	0.5
Pennsylvania	34,537	34,964	1.2	34,535	34,963	1.2
Rhode Island	3,271	3,371	3.1	2,031	2,100	3.4
Vermont	1,119	1,270	13.5	801	828	3.4
Midwest	204,657	216,757	5.9	203,701	216,391	6.2
Illinois	38,852	40,788	5.0	38,852	40,788	5.0
Indiana	16,960	17,903	5.6	16,791	17,730	5.6
Iowa	6,342	6,938	9.4	6,342	6,938	9.4
Kansas	7,756	7,911	2.0	7,756	7,911	2.0
Michigan	42,349	44,771	5.7	42,349	44,771	5.7
Minnesota	5,158	5,326	3.3	5,158	5,306	2.9
Missouri	22,003	23,998	9.1	22,003	23,980	9.0
Nebraska	3,287	3,402	3.5	3,223	3,329	3.3
North Dakota	722	797	10.4	650	715	10.0
Ohio	46,174	48,002	4.0	46,174	48,002	4.0
South Dakota	2,063	2,239	8.5	2,063	2,239	8.5
Wisconsin	12,991	14,682	13.0	12,340	14,682	19.0

Source: Kathleen Maguire and Ann K, Pastore, eds., *Sourcebook of Criminal Justice Statistics, 1997.* U. S. Department of Justice Bureau of Justice Statistcs, Washington, DC: USPGO, 1998

Table 5.2 – Prisoners in Custody in 1996 and 1997 (Continued)

Region and jurisdiction	Total 1996	1997	Percent change	Total 1996	1997	Percent change
South	469,252	491,956	4.8	458,671	480,061	4.7
Alabama	21,760	22,290	2.4	21,108	21,680	2.7
Arkansas	9,407	10,021	6.5	8,992	9,936	10.5
Delaware	5,110	5,435	6.4	3,119	3,264	4.6
District of Columbia	9,376	9,353	-0.2	8,668	8,814	1.7
Florida	63,763	64,565	1.3	63,746	64,540	1.2
Georgia	35,139	36,450	3.7	34,328	35,722	4.1
Kentucky	12,910	14,600	13.1	12,910	14,600	13.1
Louisiana	26,779	29,265	9.3	26,779	29,265	9.3
Maryland	22,050	22,232	0.8	20,980	21,088	0.5
Mississippi	13,859	15,447	11.5	13,143	14,548	10.7
North Carolina	30,647	31,638	3.2	27,751	27,726	-0.1
Oklahoma	19,593	20,542	4.8	19,593	20,542	4.8
South Carolina	20,446	21,173	3.6	19,758	20,264	2.6
Tennessee	15,626	16,659	6.6	15,626	16,659	6.6
Texas	132,383	140,729	6.3	132,383	140,729	6.3
Virginia	27,655	28,385	2.6	27,062	27,524	1.7
West Virginia	2,749	3,172	15.4	2,725	3,160	16.0
West	234,654	250,624	6.8	226,473	242,315	7.0
Alaska	3,716	4,220	13.6	2,335	2,571	10.1
Arizona	22,493	23,484	4.4	21,523	22,353	3.9
California	146,049	157,547	7.9	142,865	154,368	8.1
Colorado	12,438	13,461	8.2	12,438	13,461	8.2
Hawaii	4,011	4,949	23.4	2,954	3,424	15.9
Idaho	3,832	3,946	3.0	3,832	3,946	3.0
Montana	2,293	2,242	-2.2	2,293	2,242	-2.2
Nevada	8,439	9,024	6.9	8,439	8,884	5.3
New Mexico	4,724	4,688	-0.8	4,506	4,450	-1.2
Oregon	8,661	7,999	-7.6	7,316	7,589	3.7
Utah	3,972	4,284	7.9	3,946	4,263	8.0
Washington	12,527	13,214	5.5	12,527	13,198	5.4
Wyoming	1,499	1,566	4.5	1,499	1,566	4.5

Table 5.3 – Number of Inmate, Design Capacity, and Prison Population Projections in State and Federal Correctional Facilities

(Population figures, 1995; projections 1998, 2000, and 2002)

Jurisdiction	1995 adult prison population	Adult prison capacity	Prison population projections								
			1998			2000			2002		
			Total	Male	Female	Total	Male	Female	Total	Male	Female
Alaska	2,789	2,603	3,354	NA	NA	3,588	NA	NA	3,823	NA	NA
Arkansas	8,430	8,060	9,930	9,405	525	10,237	9,694	543	10,335	9,787	548
California	134,718	77,884	179,737	168,279	11,458	214,963	201,522	13,441	250,115	234,756	15,359
Colorado	8,071	8,447	13,357	12,413	944	15,419	14,327	1,092	NA	NA	NA
Connecticut	14,744	NA	15,685	14,600	1,085	NA	NA	NA	NA	NA	NA
Delaware	4,258	3,745	4,748	4,444	304	4,865	4,551	314	4,890	4,576	314
District of Columbia	10,029	10,986	12,745	11,917	828	13,125	12,272	853	NA	NA	NA
Florida	64,076	67,616	84,249	78,637	5,612	106,255	100,230	6,025	116,036	109,598	6,438
Hawaii	3,171	1,750	3,435	3,172	263	3,771	3,485	286	NA	NA	NA
Idaho	2,886	2,721	4,118	3,912	206	4,838	4,597	241	5,558	5,280	278
Illinois	37,881	27,087	46,105	43,835	2,270	51,216	48,633	2,583	55,790	52,863	2,927
Indiana	14,905	12,539	15,491	14,604	887	16,086	15,147	939	NA	NA	NA
Iowa	5,905	3,603	7,091	NA	NA	7,851	NA	NA	NA	NA	NA
Kansas	7,342	7,095	7,812	7,346	466	7,985	7,509	476	NA	NA	NA
Kentucky	9,225	10,160	15,250	14,337	913	17,336	16,299	1,037	8,115	7,650	485
Louisiana	16,857	17,099	NA	NA	NA	22,000	NA	NA	19,273	18,142	1,131
Maryland	21,850	NA	22,254	21,091	1,163	23,609	22,429	1,180	25,000	NA	NA
Massachusetts	19,750	6,565	NA	NA	NA	NA	NA	NA	23,711	22,525	1,186
Michigan	38,964	39,002	44,708	NA	NA	49,339	NA	NA	NA	NA	NA
Minnesota	4,794	4,464	5,568	5,337	231	6,013	5,767	246	6,124	5,874	250
Mississippi	10,256	10,541	17,321	16,241	1,080	22,150	20,640	1,510	26,377	24,523	1,854

Source: Kathleen Maguire and Ann K. Pastore, eds., *Sourcebook of Criminal Justice Statistics, 1997*. U. S. Department of Justice Bureau of Justice Statistics, Washington, DC: USPGO, 1998

Table 5.3 – Number of Inmate, Design Capacity, and Prison Population Projections in State and Federal Correctional Facilities (Continued)

(Population figures, 1995; projections 1998, 2000, and 2002)

Jurisdiction	1995 adult prison population	Adult prison capacity	Prison population projections								
			1998			2000			2002		
			Total	Male	Female	Total	Male	Female	Total	Male	Female
Missouri	18,704	19,132	22,940	21,388	1,552	25,816	23,990	1,826	28,692	26,592	2,100
Montana	1,865	950	2,171	2,076	95	2,401	2,296	105	NA	NA	NA
Nebraska	2,934	2,103	3,663	NA	NA	4,350	NA	NA	4,803	NA	NA
Nevada	7,889	7,661	9,530	8,933	597	10,437	9,808	629	11,361	10,673	688
New Hampshire	2,033	1,786	2,796	NA	NA	3,260	NA	NA	3,801	NA	NA
New Jersey	20,326	13,869	29,850	28,475	1,375	NA	NA	NA	NA	NA	NA
New Mexico	4,200	3,647	NA	4,691	NA	NA	5,244	NA	NA	NA	NA
New York	68,889	67,701	71,500	67,679	3,821	76,927	72,946	3,981	NA	NA	NA
North Carolina	28,724	25,159	33,301	NA	NA	33,434	NA	NA	34,131	34,131	NA
North Dakota	671	600	(d)	X	X	X	X	X	X	X	X
Ohio	44,365	26,058	48,810	45,838	2,972	54,123	50,894	3,229	58,735	55,249	3,486
Oklahoma	1,433	14,153	22,354	NA	NA	23,746	NA	NA	24,901	NA	NA
Oregon	7,801	7,202	10,107	9,645	462	12,858	12,246	612	15,736	14,970	766
Pennsylvania	31,062	20,550	33,628	32,081	1,547	34,973	33,364	1,609	36,406	34,731	1,675
Rhode Island	3,048	3,471	3,257[b]	NA	NA	3,335	NA	NA	3,439	NA	NA
South Carolina	19,174	17,586	20,768	19,740	1,028	NA	NA	NA	NA	NA	NA
South Dakota	1,873	1,565	2,243	2,093	150	2,665	2,496	169	23,314	NA	NA
Tennessee	13,228	13,328	20,537	18,119	948	22,033	19,689	1,024	23,314	20,872	1,037
Texas	126,123	131,616	148,019	135,133	12,886	148,019	135,130	12,889	NA	NA	NA
Vermont	1,010	1,052	NA	NA	NA	NA	NA	NA	NA	NA	NA
Virginia	23,785	15,518	34,512	32,448	2,064	38,946	36,460	2,486	43,792	40,842	2,950
Washington	11,679	8,269	12,978	12,154	824	13,887	13,040	847	14,762	13,887	875
West Virginia	2,458	2,600	(d)	X	X	X	X	X	X	X	X
Wisconsin	11,150	7,499	13,458	12,966	492	15,846	15,309	537	NA	NA	NA
Wyoming	1,190	NA	1,326	1,236	90	1,416	1,316	100	1,483	1,373	110
Federal Bureau of Prisons	90,159	72,039	109,389	101,732	7,657	117,278	109,069	8,209	122,607	114,025	8,582

necessary return him or her to prison before a new offense is committed. Third, the court has a tool to use for confinement, supervision, and programming of non-violent, unsophisticated offenders that do not belong in prison. Cast in these terms, community facilities are vastly underutilized.

Anyone who has served in the military knows about culture shock and remembers the difficulty of transition back to civilian life upon discharge. One of the main purposes of work-release (which is a community based facility) is to allow an inmate to be transferred to a community based facility with 4-6 months left to serve before parole or mandatory release. The inmate has lived for months, if not years, in a situation where he or she was told when to get up, when to shower, when to go to recreation, when to eat, how to get to work and so on. It doesn't take much common sense to realize that any individual would be somewhat disorganized upon release into free society with only $100.00 and a suit of clothing. Research indicates that most parole violations occur in the first six months of an inmates release.

As a consequence, the inmate upon transfer, is given a very short leash, but allowed to look for work and begin to adjust to free society. At this time he or she will undergo a classification process to determine what his or her needs are relative to work, substance abuse counseling, education, family and so on. A program is devised with the inmate to begin the transition. Some do not make it. For whatever reason, it is too difficult and perhaps even frightening to the inmate and he or she will commit some violation to be returned to the institution. Experienced corrections workers will tell us that some community program participants seem to violate deliberately, even though they would not admit it. Others simply do not have the capability to successfully complete their stay at the work-release facility. They will be returned to the prison, be released on the appointed day, and most likely begin committing new crimes shortly after release. Most residents of a work-release facility, however, do make it and go on to be released to the supervision of a parole officer.

Proposition #9: Institutions are complex organizations that require capable, intelligent workers. It is important that programs be available for inmates to take advantage of in order to alleviate boredom and to acquire social and educational/vocational skills that will aid them in successfully being a contributing member of the community.

Parole

Parole is an often misunderstood concept. Parole is the conditional release of an inmate from custody subject to the same rules of conduct under which he or she lived in the institution. The parolee must report to a parole officer and abide by the rules of parole. That is, get a job, don't do drugs, avoid fraternizing with other parolees or known felons, report when told to do so, and obey all federal and state laws, and local ordinances. As of December 31, 1997 there were 685,033 people on parole in the US, up from 658,601 people on parole in the United States in 1993. Table 5.4 illustrates the numbers of people on parole by states at years end 1997.

Today many states have enacted statutes that in effect either eliminate parole or cut the time to be served on supervision. Prior to the decline in use of the indeterminate sentence, 85% of inmates released were released via parole (Clear and Cole, 1990). Traditionally the parole board determines who is eligible for release by looking at whether or not the inmate has participated in institution programs. In addition, such things as his or her institutional work history and numbers of disciplinary reports as well as his or her criminal history and how many, if any, times he or she absconded from probation or parole in the past.

There are at least three kinds of conditional release that the layman would associate as being some kind of parole and which require the releasee to report to a parole officer and be subject to supervision in the community. Depending on the state of residence they are: mandatory release, expiration of sentence, and parole. Mandatory release is the point at which the inmate cannot be held in custody any longer, usually due to the accrual of earned good time. Expiration of sentence is that point at which the inmate must be released and often refers to statutory release due to the loss of earned good time and in this instance, the inmate is released without some sort of supervision. In some instances it is possible that an inmate could be released with two or more years left on a sentence without receiving a parole due to earning good time. In most, if not all, instances the releasee must report to a parole officer and submit to the conditions of release and supervision until the end of the statutory sentence.

Parole has its origins in the nineteenth century and is principally the result of the efforts of Alexander Maconochie who was the superintendent of the prison colony in Australia. He developed a "ticket-of-leave" system based upon rewards for good conduct. By using a mark system he developed a five stage release that

Table 5.4 – Adults on Parole Under State and Federal Jurisdiction, 1997

Region and jurisdiction	Parole population Jan 1, 1997	1997 Entries	1997 Exits	Parole Population Dec. 31, 1997	% Change in Parole Population during 1997	No. on parole on 12/31/97 per 100,000 residents
United States, total	675,986	420,615	410,839	685,033	1.3	346
Federal	56,591	23,884	21,648	58,827	4.0	30
State	619,395	396,731	389,191	626,206	1.1	316
Northeast	154,959	78,667	72,493	160,37	3.7	413
Connecticut	1,083	1,058	1,145	996	-8.0	40
Maine	57	4	2	59	3.6	6
Massachusetts	4,836	3,809	3,653	4,596	-5.0	98
New Hampshire	1,066	872	855	1,083	1.6	124
New Jersey	14,545	14,608	12,250	16,903	16.2	279
New York	57,137	27,096	24,563	59,670	4.4	439
Pennsylvania	75,013	30,211	28,992	76,232	1.6	833
Rhode Island	573	587	629	531	-7.3	70
Vermont	649	422	404	667	2.8	150
Midwest	87,987	62,604	61,922	88,683	0.8	192
Illinois	30,064	23,595	23,311	30,348	0.9	348
Indiana	3,580	4,549	4,085	4,044	13.0	93
Iowa	2,200	2,343	2,506	2,051	-6.8	96
Kansas	6,004	4,650	4,504	6,150	2.4	323
Michigan	14,609	8,758	9,016	14,351	-1.8	197
Minnesota	2,377	2,632	2,563	2,446	2.9	71
Missouri	13,087	4,720	5,293	12,514	-4.4	313
Nebraska	688	770	770	688	X	57
North Dakota	100	212	193	119	19.0	25
Ohio	6,331	5,258	4,786	6,803	7.5	81
South Dakota	725	675	540	860	18.6	159
Wisconsin	8,222	4,442	4,355	8,309	1.1	217

Source: Kathleen Maguire and Ann K, Pastore, eds., *Sourcebook of Criminal Justice Statistics, 1997*. U. S. Department of Justice Bureau of Justice Statistics, Washington, DC: USPGO, 1998

Table 5.4 – Adults on Parole Under State and Federal Jurisdiction, 1997 (Continued)

Region and jurisdiction	Parole population Jan 1, 1997	1997 Entries	Exits	Parole Population Dec. 31, 1997	% Change in Parole Population during 1997	No. on parole on 12/31/97 per 100,000 residents
South	241,668	98,173	104,626	234,780	-2.9	336
Alabama	4,966	0	0	4,742	-4.5	146
Arkansas	5,459	3,225	2,817	5,867	7.5	315
Delaware	591	196	196	591	X	107
District of Columbia	7,120	2,310	2,363	7,067	-0.7	1,676
Florida	9,243	3,596	4,362	8,477	-8.3	76
Georgia	21,146	11,567	10,587	21,915	3.6	399
Kentucky	4,621	2,853	3,241	4,233	-8.4	144
Louisiana	19,082	10,819	9,974	19,927	4.4	630
Maryland	16,246	9,732	10,215	15,763	-3.0	412
Mississippi	1,326	1,233	1,181	1,378	3.9	70
North Carolina	12,358	8,774	12,984	8,148	-34.1	147
Oklahoma	2,159	442	673	1,928	-10.7	79
South Carolina	5,036	1,343	1,369	5,010	-0.5	179
Tennessee	8,934	4,294	4,535	8,693	-2.7	215
Texas	112,594	27,682	30,839	109,437	-2.8	789
Virginia	9,918	9,538	8,746	10,710	8.0	210
West Virginia	869	569	544	894	2.9	64
West	134,781	157,287	150,150	142,006	5.4	330
Alaska	642	466	356	752	17.1	179
Arizona	3,785	6,141	6,548	3,378	-10.8	103
California	99,578	134,345	129,514	104,409	4.9	448
Colorado	3,294	3,744	2,899	4,139	25.7	144
Hawaii	1,733	699	639	1,793	3.5	203
Idaho	692	600	472	820	18.5	95
Montana	771	444	409	806	4.5	124
Nevada	3,216	NA	NA	3,304	2.7	268
New Mexico	1,426	1,617	1,417	1,626	14.0	132
Oregon	15,800	6,649	5,634	16,815	6.4	691
Utah	2,920	2,329	1,930	3,319	13.7	242
Washington	560	32	112	480	-14.3	12
Wyoming	364	221	220	365	0.3	105

included, (1) strict imprisonment, (2) labor on a chain gang, (3) freedom within a specific area, (4) ticket-of-leave or parole, and (5) full liberty. From this beginning, developed what we know as parole.

In the United states the development of parole was linked to the spread of the indeterminate sentence, which was discussed in Chapter three. The U.S. Board of Parole was created in the 1930's and beginning at that time, states that did not already have parole, approved legislation that created indeterminate sentences and allowed for parole. Parole has been controversial throughout its history and whenever an inmate convicted of a particularly heinous crime is up for parole, the media often lead the reader to believe that release is imminent. However, one function of a parole board is to gauge community sentiment before making a decision. As the case of Richard Speck and Charles Manson demonstrate, the parole board is not interested in creating a public uproar.

Today, even though many states have abolished the indeterminate sentence, most still have a mechanism to release an inmate into the community under some form of supervision. As pointed out earlier it makes good sense to assign newly released inmates to supervision in order to assist them and to protect the public. This forward thinking approach has the benefit of preparing inmates for release and supervision in the community. If an individual is apt to violate, there is a better probability of catching a propensity for skullduggery than if on traditional parole.

Work Release Centers and Half-way Houses

The use of work release centers is an important part of the correctional program for any state. Not to have a program that releases inmates into the community under supervision is short sighted and most likely drives up the chance that released inmates will return to prison at a greater rate.

An example of politics playing a large role in terminating reliable programs can be found in an incident that occurred in Indiana in September, 1989. An inmate serving a sentence at the Indiana Reformatory at Pendleton was released on a day long furlough to visit with his mother. Prior to his incarceration he was estranged from his wife who lived in Mishiwaka, Indiana. On the day of the furlough, the inmate who was supposed to spend the day with his mother, persuaded her to drive him to Mishiwaka to see his estranged wife.

The incident concluded with the inmate brutally murdering his wife in full view of many witnesses and created a great public outcry. A number of citizens were rightly outraged at the offense and the Governor, in a knee-jerk response, canceled all community programs throughout the state. His response caused a degree of short-term over crowding throughout state correctional institutions and eliminated a legitimate program designed to safeguard the public.

In this case, it would have been better to review the furlough program in question, including all associated policies and procedures, and change any procedures that needed to be changed. In this particular instance, the procedures broke down due to a failure of communication in the prosecutor's office who failured to send to the Department of Corrections the woman's statement that she wanted to be notified of her husband's release into the community. Had the case manager in this instance known of the woman's desires, the inmate would not have been approved for the program and she would not have been murdered. As a consequence of that one incident, the Indiana Department of Corrections still has fewer than 300 inmates in community programs and many inmates in need are released into the community without the stringent kind of supervision needed the first few weeks of their release.

In all fairness, however, since the Mishawaka incident, Indiana has increased the numbers of participants in community programs as a diversion from prison sentences through the implementation of a Community Corrections Act. It may be that this is an example of politics in action. The public usually blames the governor or a "lenient" prison system if a resident of a community program commits a new offense. Therefore, if no inmates (or relatively few inmates) are in community programs, there is less likelihood that there will be controversial incidents, thereby allowing the Governor to maintain a "tough on crime" stance or at least to avoid a measure of public indignation. As an alternative, if an inmate or resident of a community program is involved in a criminal act, it is the "fault" of the program or Sheriff, not the Governor.

There are two stated aims of work release centers and half-way houses: (1) to aid the offender in his or her adjustment back into the community, and (2) to assure the community that the inmate will make a successful transition into the community.

Halfway houses have been on the American scene since the 1800's, but it wasn't until Congress passed the **Federal Prisoner Rehabilitation Act** in 1965 that they finally became more widespread. Today there are more than 700 halfway houses, work-release centers, and restitution centers in operation in the United States (Houston, 1998). There have been a number of research projects on half-way houses and work-release centers with mixed results. What we can say with some assurance is that they are more cost effective than prison, and that in one research population, the inmates who participated had a recidivism rate that reflected less serious crimes than those who were not released through a half-way house. The general conclusion is that release through a half-way house or work-release center may be better for some individuals than for others.

Predicting who will make a good adjustment to the environment of a work release Center or Half-way house is difficult. One thing is certain, however, and that is that institutional disciplinary reports are not a good indicator of adjustment (Houston and Koch, 1993). Before an inmate can be transferred to a half-way house or work-release center he or she must be within 6-9 months of guaranteed release. Prior to a transfer to a half-way house or work-release center is even considered, the institutional counselor or case manager will prepare a packet for review by a committee of administrators and the warden or his or her representative. A final decision will be made as to the worthiness of the individual based upon need, prior record, and present offense. Usually, sex offenders, those serving sentences reflecting involvement in organized crime and those persons with a history of escape or absconding from probation or parole will not be considered for transfer to a community residential center. If the committee approves a transfer the packet is sent to the manager of the center who then reviews the materials with staff to determine eligibility and probability of adjustment. If acceptable, notice of acceptance is sent to the institution with a transfer date.

Upon arrival at the community residential center, the inmate immediately undergoes classification and is informed of the rules and, with staff, develop a program to follow while in the Center. Usually, he or she will be required to spend 7-14 days in the center without contact with the public. This serves as a period of observation by staff and to allow the inmate to become adjusted to a less rigorous security schedule and he or she may undergo a series of appointments with mental health staff or substance abuse counselors. Some programs provide the opportunity for the inmate to meet with family, both with and without staff. The purpose of the latter is to explain schedules and expectations to the spouse and in documented instances of abuse, develop a counseling program or arrange a referral to a family counselor.

Once the staff is reasonably assured that the inmate will meet expectations, he or she is allowed to leave the center for a few hours each day for a job search. This aspect is closely monitored and, depending on the program, the inmate is escorted or at least must bring a list of contacts and a staff member will check on the contact by telephone. The inmate is also required to undergo urinalysis at least three times per week as a deterrent to drug use. If a positive report is received, the inmate is subject to a disciplinary report. Most centers have a zero tolerance and a few others are more lenient, but in no instance should the leniency be extended to more than two "dirty" samples.

Once the inmate has employment, he or she must faithfully report to work, perform duties around the center, and should (most states have legislation that requires the inmate) pay for a portion of his or her room and board. The amount varies, but is often $25.00 per week, or a percentage of gross income, whichever is greater. In addition, after a period of weeks, the inmate is allowed to spend an occasional night with family if he or she is working, is participating in agreed upon programs, and has no disciplinary reports. If all is well, the inmate is terminated from the program at the appointed time and must report to a parole officer and will continue on supervision until the end of his or her sentence.

Are Halfway houses and work-release centers effective as instruments of rehabilitation? The research is mixed; what we can say is that placing an offender in a work-release center or halfway house is cheaper than jail or prison. Waldo, Chiricos, and Dobrin (1971) investigated the type and extent of inmates' attitudinal change while in work-release programs. They conclude "that there is no discernable improvement in the levels of perceived opportunity, achievement, motivation, legal self conecpt, and self esteem expressed by work-release participants." In addition, they point out that work release appears to have a harmful effect upon self-esteem. Waldo and Chiricos (1977) also looked at recidivism of inmates released from work-release centers in Florida and determined that it does not have any real rehabilitative impact.

Latessa and Allen (1982) investigated halfway houses, their goals, and their objectives on a national level. They conclude that halfway houses may be as effective as any other parole program and stratgegy and theat they may be more cost effective. Mrad, Kabakoff, and Duckro (1983) validated Magargee's calssification system using he population of a halfway house. They suggest that such a profile would be valuable to community program managers in their efforts to manage inmate populations.

Dowell, Klein, and Krichmar (1983) reviewed a group of female residents of a halfway house and compared them with a matched group of parolees who did not receive the benefit of halfway house services. They conclude that release through a halfway house reduced both the number and severity of offenses once the women were released. Latessa and Travis (1991) looked at matched sample of probationers and halfway house residents and found no difference in post-release behavior. They conclude that halfway house placement may be better for some offenders, but that such a placement might best be based on the offenders need rather than on a desire to increase the penalty.

Halfway houses and work-release centers are a part of the corrections continuum, but are limited in what they can do to and for an inmate in regard to behavior change. Boot camps were conceived as a means to get the attention of first-time offenders and to "teach them a lesson" short of going to prison or jail. How do they operate and are they effective? We take a look at boot camps in the next section.

Boot Camps

Boot camps are one of the latest efforts to deal with first time offenders and are looked at by many members of state legislatures as a panacea to the problem of crime by youthful offenders. The approach is to provide a highly regimented program that involves strict discipline, hard physical labor, and physical training. Programs are typically of short duration, 90-180 days and offenders who complete such a program are usually placed on probation immediately after leaving the program. Failures are usually brought back to court for resentencing by the judge.

Many policy makers assume that Boot Camps are effective because "I went through boot camp when I joined the Army and it really straightened me out". Such thinking is wishful at best and makes the assumption that most offenders are similar to themselves. Perhaps military boot camp has straightened out many youth, but most likely the average military recruit is fairly well socialized and well adjusted. As we will learn in the next chapter, the causes of criminal behavior are many and varied. Most are not given to correction by doing a few push-ups every day and by enduring a harangue by a drill instructor on an hourly basis. Are Boot Camps effective? The jury is still out and preliminary data is mixed.

The costs of boot camp is no less than traditional prison, but because of short terms, there is a gain. Some programs have a high failure to compete rate which makes overall evaluation difficult as those who would fail after release may spin out of the program leaning only those who would do well any way after release. Some evaluations indicate that the recidivism rates of inmates released from boot camps are no lower than those released from prison (Sechrest, 1989). Other evaluations suggest that boot camp graduates commit fewer new crimes that parolees, but are more likely to be found guilty of technical violations while upon supervision (CJ Newsletter, 1991). There are indications however, that boot camps can provide important benefits. New York combines boot camp with intensive supervision upon release for most releasees and indications are that pparticipants and staff view boot camps as a positive experience (Burton, et al., 1993).

A more recent study by Gransky, Castellano, and Cowls (1995) looked at substance abuse programs in Boot Camps. They found that there are problems in that many programs simply copy existing programs and attempt to replicate it in their home community without regard to local custom and values. A more serious problem is that most effort is put into up-front aspects of the program. That is, money and thought are given to the actual Boot Camp, but very little thought or resources are given over to the after-care aspects of the program. The thinking is that the graduate of the Boot Camp needs to continue the efforts begun in the Boot Camp after graduating and not left to the resources of an over worked probation officer with no special training or time to devote to special needs of drug offenders.

The value of community programs such as those described above is that instead of the inmate being discharged from prison with very little money, no support structure, or job and who must rely upon his or her wits to do whatever is necessary to survive; he or she is released from custody with a job, a place to live, savings, he or she has reintegrated with family and is participating in programs that fit a need such as drug counseling and after care, AA, NA, or educational programs. Such programs are important. People are usually sent to prison because they have poorly developed decision making skills, do not know how to develop legitimate contacts in the community, and have no support structure upon which to depend. Those are the people that can be helped in a community program.

Boot Camps attempt to deal with non-violent offenders without sending them to prison and rely upon a period of probation for supervision and assistance in the community. As for the rest of the offenders, all the science and good intentions in the world cannot be of help.

Proposition #10:   Community programs are a positive adjunct to
prisons in that they enhance the supervision of the inmate as
he or she goes through the first critical weeks back in the community.

Private Corrections

The push by government to offer services without raising taxes results in some wrong-headed ideas at times and the corrections enterprise is no exception. A large problem for government is that the prison and jail population rose tremendously during the 1980s and 1990s, as we discussed in earlier portions of this book. Many jurisdictions responded to this problem by contracting with private corporations to build and/or operate facilities for unsentenced and sentenced offenders. This has raised many questions about the use of private corrections companies.

Today there are fifteen private companies offering institutional corrections services, providing more than 85,000 beds under contract to states and the federal government. In addition to residential facilities, a survey by Huskey and Lurigio (1992) reveals that there are a number of private companies that operate intermediate sanctions and services for offenders. They report that the respondent's serve those arrested for drug possession, nonviolent/property offenses, drug sales and manufacture, DUI, and personal/violent offenses. They conclude that (1) privately operated community programs serve a significant number and range of offenders; (2) the agencies appear to be responsive to correctional concerns; (3) the private agencies save the public considerable money through wages earned, restitution, and taxes paid; and (4) offenders have a low re-arrest rate, suggesting that they are a minimal threat to the public.

There are a number of issues, legal and moral, that continue to be discussed in regard to private corrections, among them are questions surrounding whether or not a private corporation has the right to forcefully hold an individual against his or her will, questions about use of deadly force, and will the corporation protect the inherent rights of the individual? There are other questions surrounding the use of inmate labor, discipline, contracting and the monitoring of contacts. There has been some research on the quality of service and the most noteworthy was completed by Archambiault and Deis (1996).

The authors studied three institutions: one operated by Wackenhut Corporation, one operated by the Corrections Corporation of America (CCA), and one operated by the Louisiana Department of Public Safety and Corrections. They concluded that the two private institutions (Allen and Winn) significantly outperformed the public state operated institution on the vast majority of variables used to compare the three prisons. An earlier study by Logan (1992) looked at a private New Mexico facility for women, the state operation of that facility one year before, and a federal prison for women. Logan found that the private prison outperformed its state and federal counterparts on all dimensions except care, where the state facility scored higher, and justice where the federal prison matched the private facility.

Thus we may conclude that the quality of care offered to prison inmates in private institutions is at least as good as that found in publicly operated institutions. However, concerns have been raised in regard to the practice of "creaming," that is the private facilities get the more cooperative and quiet inmates, while the public institution receives the more violent inmate and the individual less receptive to programs. Thus, research on inmate satisfaction will reveal inmates are more pleased with the private institution. Another issue is that the private facility pays less and as a consequence attracts less capable and committed staff with a higher turnover. However, it should be noted that most private facilities hire personnel retired from public institutions for management and executive positions at attractive salaries and as a consequence, there is not a lack of experience at the upper levels. If there is continued growth in private corrections, elected and appointed officials should consider a two-tier approach to private corrections: the privatization of community programs and retain public institutions for medium and maximum custody inmates.

Summary

The corrections system is a complex entity that is designed to carry out the orders of the courts. It ranges from institutions such as the super-maximum security institutions at Pelican Bay in California to small community corrections facilities as well as probation, parole, and various diversion programs. The system has changed greatly over the years due to a changing inmate population that reflects the changes in our society. Today prisons reflect changes in the cities brought about by the rise of gangs. Gangs have changed prisons from places where not long ago inmates were admonished to "do your own time" to places where gangs dictate the rhythm and pace of life.

We spend nearly $32 billion per year to supervise and program men and women in prison and in community programs such as probation. It may well be that in many instances, those felons sentenced to prison could do as well, or better, in alternatives to prison and thus save the taxpayer a great deal of money. It is difficult to convince men and women that they have a stake in their community when they have been taught by family and others that there is no place for them or they have the belief that there is no future for them. It is ironic that we lock up poorly socialized men and women in close proximity with others cut from the same cloth and expect them to be released as repentant, law abiding citizens.

To be sure there is a place for prisons, both public and private. There are among us evil, psychopathic individuals who have no concern for others and do not seem to learn from past experience. We must have room for these men and women for they have demonstrated that they do not deserve to live among decent citizens. As for the rest, we are obligated to take advantage of advances in technology and the social sciences to enable those convicted of crimes to advance and become contributing members of society.

Bibliography

William G. Archambeault and Donald R. Deis. "Cost Effectiveness Comparisons of Private Versus Public Prisons in Louisiana: A Comprehensive Analysis of Allen, Avoyeller, and Winn Correctional Centers," Executive Summary (Baton Rouge, LA: Louisiana State University, December 10, 1996).

Velmer Burton, James Marquart, Steven Cuvelier, Leanne Fiftal Alarid, and Robert Hunter. "A Study of of Attitudinal Change among Boot Camp Participants," **Federal Probation**. 57(1993). Pp. 46-52.

Todd R. Clear and George F. Cole. **American Corrections**, 2nd ed. (Pacific Grove, CA: Brooks/Cole Publishing Company, 1990).

Donald R. Cressey. **The Prison: Studies in Institutional Organization and Change**. (New York: Holt, Rinehart, and Winston, 1961).

Donald R. Cressey and John Irwin. "Thieves, Convicts, and the Inmate Culture." **Social Problems**. 10 (Fall, 1962). pp. 139-148.

Criminal Justice Newsletter. "New York Correctional Group Praises Boot Camp Programs." 22(1 April, 1991). Pp. 4-5.

Elliott Currie. **Confronting Crime: An American Challenge**. (New York: Pantheon Books, 1989).

David A. Dowell, Cecelia Klein, and Cheryl Krichmar, "Evaluation of a Halfway House for Women," **Journal of Criminology**. 13:3(1983). Pp. 217-26.

Billie S. Erwin. "Turning up the Heat on Probationers in Georgia." **Federal Probation**, (June, 1986). pp. 17-24, in Clayton A. Hartjen and Edward E. Rhine, eds. **Correctional Theory and Practice**. (Chicago: Nelson-Hall, Inc, 1992).

Don C. Gibbons. **Society, Crime, and Criminal Behavior**, 6th ed. (Englewood Cliffs: Prentice-Hall, Inc, 1992).

Alice Glasel Harper. "Intensive Supervision, Working for New Jersey." **Corrections Today**. (December, 1987). pp. 88-89, in Clayton A. Hartjen and Edward E. Rhine, eds. **Correctional Theory and Practice**. (Chicago: Nelson-Hall, Inc, 1992).

Laura A. Gransky, Tom Castellano, and Ernest L. Cowls. "Is there a 'second generation' of shock incarceration facilities?," in John O. Smykla and William L. Selke, eds. **Intermediate Sanctions: Sentencing in the 90s.** (Cincinnati, OH: Anderson Publishing Company, 1995).

156

James Houston. **Correctional Management: Functions, Skills, and Systems,** 2ed. (Chicago: Nelson-Hall, Inc, 1998).

James Houston and Paul Koch. **Predicting a Headache: Adjustment in Work Release Programs.** Paper presented to the Academy of Criminal Justice Sciences, Kansas City, March, 1993.

John Irwin. **Prisons in Turmoil.** (Boston: Little Brown and Co., 1980).

Bobbie Huskey and Arthur J. Lurigio. "An Examination of Privately Operated Intermediate Sanctions Within the U.S." **Corrections Compendium.** 17:12 (1992):1-8

Kelsey Kauffman. **Prison Officers and Their World.** Cambridge, MA: Harvard University Press, 1988).

Edward J. Latessa. "The Cost Effectiveness of Intensive Supervision." **Federal Probation.** (June, 1986). pp. 70-74, in Clayton A. Hartjen and Edward E. Rhine, eds. **Correctional Theory and Practice.** (Chicago: Nelson-Hall, Inc, 1992).

Edward J. Latessa and Lawrence F. Travis III. "Halfway House or Probation: A Comparison of Alternative Disposition," **Journal of Crime and Justice.** 14:1(1991). Pp. 53-75.

Edward Latessa and Harry E. Allen. "Halfway Houses and Parole: A National Assessment," **Journal of Criminal Justice.** 10:2(1982). Pp. 152-63.

Douglas Lipton, Robert Martinson, and Judith Wilks. **The Effectiveness of Correctional Treatment: A Survey of Treatment Evaluation Studies.** (Springfield, MA: Praeger, 1975).

Charles H. Logan. "Well Kept: Comparing Quality of Confinement in a publican Private Prison" in Paul Seidenstat, ed., **Privatizing Correctional Institutions.** (New Brunswick, NJ: Transaction Books, 1992)

Kathleen Maguire and Ann L. Pastore, eds. **Sourcebook of Criminal Justice Statistics 1997.** U.S. Department of Justice, Bureau of Justice Statistics. (Washington, D.C.: USGPO, 1998).

Robert Martinson. "What Works: Questions and Answers about Prison Reform." **Public Interest.** 35:(Spring, 1974). pp. 22-54.

William McCord and Jose Sanchez. 1983) "The Treatment of Delinquent Children: A Twenty-Five Year Follow-Up Study." **Crime and Delinquency.** 29:2 (March), in Elliott Currie, **Confronting Crime: An American Challenge.** (New York: Pantheon Books, 1989).

David F. Mrad, Robert Kabacoff, and Paul Duckro. "Validation of the Megargee Typology in a Halfway House Setting," **Criminal Justice and Behavior**. 10:3(September, 1983). Pp. 252-62.

Ted Palmer. **A Profile of Correctional Effectiveness and New Directions for Research**. (Albany: State University of New York Press, 1994).

O. Elmer Polk and Rolando V. del Carmen. "Intensive Probation Supervision-Fad or for Keeps," in Clayton A. Hartjen and Edward E. Rhine, eds. **Correctional Theory and Practice**. (Chicago: Nelson-Hall, Inc, 1992).

Dale Sechrest. "Prison Boot Camps do not Measure up," **Federal Probation**. 53(1989). Pp. 15-20.

Gresham Sykes. **The Society of Captives**. (Princeton: Princeton University Press, 1958).

Patricia Van Voorhis (1987). "Correctional Effectiveness: The High Cost of Ignoring Success," **Federal Probation**, (March, 1987). Washington, D.C.: Administrative Office of the U.S. Courts. pp. 56-62.

Gordon P. Waldo and Theodore G. Chiricos. "Work Release and Recidivism: An Empirical Evaluation of a Social Policy," **Evaluation Quarterly**. 1(February, 1977). Pp. 87-105.

Gordon P. Waldo, Theodore G. Chiricos, and Leonard E. Dobrin. "Community Contact and Inmate Attitudes: An Experimental Assessment of Work Release," **Criminology**. 11:3(November, 1971), pp. 345-81.

Chapter 6

Why People Commit Crimes

Introduction

No other question is as troubling to normal, law-abiding people than the question of "Why do they do it?" The answers are many and varied and this chapter simply provides an introduction to theoretical explanations to criminal behavior. Before beginning a discussion of why people commit crimes, we need to acknowledge that in America, as nearly everywhere else, a certain amount of crime, particularly violent crime will unfortunately always be with us. By that, I mean larceny, theft, fights, battering, and murders between people who are normally law abiding. We cannot logically account for a spouse who suddenly murders the lover of his or her wife or husband. We cannot logically account for the desperate attempt of a businessman to save a business on the verge of bankruptcy through cheating or larceny. Those kinds of criminal acts are a part of the human condition. Even the most reasonable of us are sometimes unable to keep a lid on our emotions or despair.

But we can explain a certain amount of crime and certain kinds of crime based upon scientific research. We intuitively know some of the answers, but usually when crime is discussed we all have an opinion, but not much real knowledge on the subject. This is illustrated by the present approach to crime control by the U.S. Congress and the various state legislatures. Most crime control efforts and legislation assumes the value of punishment and also presumes that every criminal undergoes a form of mental calculus before committing a crime. That is, he or she will weigh the benefits of the crime versus the penalty and proceed if the calculated value of the pleasure derived is greater than the pain of being caught.

Following this line of reasoning for example, if one has a fight with one's spouse and wants to kill the other, he or she will calculate the value of living without the spouse against the probability of getting caught and convicted of the crime. If the individual calculates that the probability of getting caught is too high, then we can say that he or she has been deterred from the offense and the couple will live to fight another day. Under most current legislation that attempts to deal with crime, that line of reasoning is also followed for property crimes as well as crimes of violence.

However, as we shall see, human beings are not that easy to predict. We can predict behavior somewhat based upon past behavior, but to say we can prevent or deter crime by simply making the penalties extremely severe is wishful thinking. This chapter leads the reader through some of the more recent and enduring research and thinking on why people commit crimes.

No excuses are made for criminal behavior and no one ever commits a crime because someone took away their teddy bear as a child or their toilet training was deficient in some way. What we do know however, is that a close knit family is the key to successful child rearing and that it takes more than one person to do an adequate job of rearing children. If that job is done well, there is a high probability, not a guarantee, that the child will grow up to be a responsible adult.

Crimes of passion aside, we can divide the various theories of criminal behavior into roughly three categories: biological, psychological, and sociological. These categories are presented simply as a tool for discussion. There is a good deal of overlap between the three, particularly between the psychological and sociological dimensions. Today most research by criminologists is within the sociological dimension and as a consequence most criminological theory is sociological criminology.

However, before beginning with the biological dimension, a brief discussion of the classical school of criminology is in order. The Classical School is based on the assumption that people choose how they act. Early philosophers during the period about 1500-1750 assumed that free will impelled people to undergo a form of mental calculus to determine pain or pleasure derived from a particular act. Cesare Beccaria (1738-1794) was a major proponent of classical criminology and was very critical of the judicial system of his day claiming that judges were arbitrary and capricious in administering harsh judgements. Since he believed that people were motivated by pain and pleasure, he advocated a form of punishments that were based on the harm inflicted on the victim. He felt that punishments proportional to harm should be the lot of criminals. The problem with this approach to punishment is that it eliminates judicial discretion, exactly what Beccarria had in mind. Beccarria's ideas were incorporated into the criminal code of France of 1791 and the revised code of 1819 which allowed some discretion to judges.

In spite of the arguments of critics, for example, Marxist critics point out that any punishments are defined in such a way as to protect the interests of capitalists from interference by other classes (Taylor. Walton, and Young 1973), we see many of the ideas of Classical criminology incorporated into the thinking of today's legislators who have successfully changed the criminal code of the federal government and most states. Sentencing grids eliminate judicial discretion and harsh sentences for particular crimes are assumed to be a deterrent to crime. Whatever the shortcomings of Classical criminology are, its contribution was to look at crime impartially and with some logic. We now move on to the biological explanations.

Biological Dimension

Man has searched for explanations for criminal conduct for nearly as long as civilizations have existed. Aside from supernatural explanations, one of the first attempts to explain why people commit crimes was linked to biological explanations. Form was linked to function and even today we jokingly make remarks such as "He just looks like a criminal." Shakespeare even touches on the subject in **Julius Caesar** when Cais Cassius points out that Brutus "has a lean and hungry look." As a consequence, it seemed to make sense that physical abnormalities were related to criminal conduct.

The most complete explanation, and influential for it's time, was Caesar Lombroso's book **The Criminal Man,** published for the first time in 1876. Lombroso attempted to explain criminal behavior by proposing that criminals are an evolutionary throw back to an earlier stage in human development. He identified a number of physical deformities and linked them to specific behaviors that he believed explained criminal behavior. He began his work as a physician and upon being called to perform an autopsy on a known criminal who had died in an Italian prison, he was struck by a number of physical anomalies. As a consequence, he came to believe that criminals could be identified by such things as excessive facial hair in women, a lack of facial hair in men, large ears, long arms, supernumerary nipples, webbed toes, and so on.

Lombroso divided criminals into three groups: the born criminal, insane criminals, and the criminaloid. The three categories attempted to explain criminal behavior by linking behavior to physical deformities, or by one's passions getting the upper hand. Lombroso created a third group into which all others were thrust because they did not fit into the other two groups. Over the next twenty years he gradually changed his thinking and came to rely more heavily on environmental factors (Vold and Bernard, 1986). He also admitted later in his life that the majority of criminals did not fit into the born criminal category. While Lombroso's efforts to explain criminal behavior is wrong and unscientific by today's standards, it was one of the first attempts to scientifically explain criminal behavior.

Gradually the typologies of Lombroso lost favor as an explanation of criminal behavior. However, the notion persisted that there must be a biological explanation for crime and the idea of body type continued to hold some allure as a means to explain criminal behavior. William H. Sheldon was a proponent of body type explanations in the late 1800's and he posited that as the embryo developed in the womb, it was simply a continuous digestive tube composed of three layers of tissue.

In his view, the inner layer of tissue was called the endoderm and gave rise to digestive viscera, the middle layer was called the mesoderm and gave rise to muscle, bone and tendon. The third layer was called the ectoderm and gave rise to connecting tissue, the nervous system, skin, and related appendages. The point of his writing was that an excess of tissue of a particular kind gave rise to certain behaviors that led to deviant behavior. For example, based upon his observations of prison inmates, he believed that the mesoderm gave rise to behavior of most violent criminals because of their tendency to be muscular and physically active.

The idea of body types gradually fell by the way, but the idea that there was a physical explanation for criminal conduct still persisted. As a consequence, the idea of feeblemindedness caught hold. The reasoning was, and still is to an extent, that it takes a stupid person to commit many of the known crimes. This shift in thinking was given impetus by the increasied use of I.Q. testing in the classroom. In addition, several studies were conducted that indicated that prison inmates had an average I.Q. score that was lower than the general population.

Interest in feeblemindedness theories began to decline when the results of several tests on WWI draftees and prison inmates were released. Those results indicated that the average prison inmate was smarter than the average WWI draftee. That research was flawed and psychologists and criminologists came to the conclusion that there are just as many stupid people in the draft army as there are in prison. As a result of further research, explanations of crime based upon intelligence fell by the way.

One interesting area in the study of biological influences on criminal behavior is the study of twins. Since identical twins develop from a single egg and have no hereditary differences, scientists can obtain a good idea of the influences of heredity and environment. Conklin (1992) points out that results of twin studies in Japan, Europe, and the United States between 1929 and 1962 are "consistent with the idea that inherited factors influence criminal behavior." In these studies it was found that the identical twins have a rate of between 60% and 70% for criminal behavior on the part of both. On the other hand fraternal twins have a rate of between 15% and 30% criminal behavior for both.

In probably the best twin study, Karl O. Christiansen (1974, 1977), investigated 3,586 pairs of twins born in a particular area of Denmark between 1881 and 1910. "He found that if one identical twin had a criminal conviction, the other twin also had a conviction in 35 percent of the cases. The rate of concordance was only 12 percent for fraternal twins" (Conklin, 1992). While we cannot see a consistent pattern in the influence of genetic influence on criminal behavior, clearly there is a factor, or factors, at work that precludes our dismissing the influence of genetics on criminal behavior.

Another explanation of criminal behavior is that of the XYY Chromosomal pattern. Much of the interest in XYY is drawn from Richard Speck who brutally murdered eight nursing students in Chicago in 1966. A physical examination of Speck revealed that he had the XYY Chromosome pattern. This anomaly, which occurs once in about every 400-500 live male births has been linked with antisocial behavior (Fox 1971).

The XYY Chromosomal pattern is relatively new and was only discovered in 1961. That person appeared to be perfectly normal both behaviorally and physically. Shortly afterward a number of cases turned up in Australia, France, Great Britain, and the United States. There have been some attempts to use the XYY as a defense for criminal conduct, but to date no jury has accepted it. Research on the XYY is still ongoing and it is too early to draw any conclusions.

We can, however, conclude that the XYY is responsible for some abnormalities in the male population, but the sample is much too small to be considered a major factor in explaining crime. Besides, it does not explain female crime at all (Gibbons, 1992).

There are other efforts to link biological explanations to crime, for example there are indications that delivery complications at birth are associated with violent episodes that may be linked to brain damage that reduce the inhibitory control of aggression. Research also has provided evidence that frontal lobe dysfunction has been found to be associated with adult violent behavior. Reduced spinal fluid levels have been found in people exhibiting impulsive aggression. Some antisocial individuals have been found to have reduced levels of autonomic reactiveness and poor conditioning of autonomic responses. (Brennan, Mednick, and Volavka 1995). Nutrition has also been investigated as a cause of criminal behavior with inconclusive results.

Psychological Dimension

Psychological explanations for criminal behavior are largely the product of psychiatry. Those explanations have had a lot to say about the treatment of criminals and other programs. This is called the *Medical Model*. This approach to dealing with criminals and their conduct assumes that the individual is sick and that he or she must figuratively visit a "doctor" each day and receive a "pill." This pill is in the form of group counseling, individual counseling, or some other form of therapy in which an expert assists the individual to overcome a psychological problem that is at the root of his or her deviance.

According to Freudians, the personality is made up of three distinct components: the Id, the Ego, and the Superego. The infant arrives in the world as simply a bag of protoplasm with eyes. The only instincts he or she has are sucking, blinking, sneezing, and coughing. It is dependent upon loving parents to care for it until it is able to survive by itself. This is the rub. Parents often do not do a good job and the contamination of the personality by others is what may contribute to criminal behavior.

The Id is a reservoir of instinctual energy that is basically uncontaminated and in infancy the individual is prepared to behave only at the behest of pain or pleasure. Soon after birth the Ego begins to develop and the infant begins to gain an awareness of self as distinct from its surroundings. In other words the ego gradually assumes executive control of the young persons personality. The Superego consists largely of morality or a conscience. The Superego is formed out of the Ego and is the sum total of standards and expectations of parents and significant others. In other words it serves to "police" the individual and in a way punishes us for doing "wrong."

In a well developed personality, these three components work well together, but in neurotic or otherwise disturbed individuals, problems arise. For example, the Superego may become too rigid and powerful and the person begins to have guilt feelings about repressed instinctual drives, or the Superego may be underdeveloped and anti-social behavior may develop. The psychoanalytic interpretation of criminality is summed up very nicely by George Vold:

> Criminal behavior, under this general theoretical orientation, is to be understood, simply and directly as a substitute response, some form of symbolic release of repressed complexes. The conflict in the unconscious mind gives rise to feelings of guilt and anxiety with a consequent desire for punishment to remove the guilt feelings and restore a proper balance of good against evil. The criminal then commits the criminal act in order to be caught and punished. Unconsciously motivated errors (i.e., careless, or imprudent ways of committing the crime) leave "clues" so the authorities may more readily apprehend and convict the guilty, and thus administer suitably cleansing punishment (Vold, 1958).

According to Professor Don C. Gibbons (1992) psycho-analytic theory is deficient in several ways: (a) it assumes a biological motivation, particularly instinct, (b) it stresses the impact of infancy and early childhood, (c) it minimizes the influence of social factors on human behavior, and (d) it overemphasizes sexual aspects of behavior and motivation. In spite of the deficiencies of psychoanalytic theory it gives us a clue about the importance of a strong family in raising a child.

For example, if a child is raised in a secure home where there are standards, limits on behavior, sanctions placed on negative behavior, and a consistent moral front posed to the child by all concerned, then in all probability the child will grow up to be a responsible adult. If, on the other hand, the child grows up in a home characterized by absent parent(s), discipline is non-existent or erratic, where morality is absent, and available role-models extol the virtues of deviant behavior we should not be surprised at the results.

For the sake of understanding, think of the Ego an enclosure around the Id. The Id is a bundle of instincts that seek immediate gratification and the Ego is the buffer that prevents the illegal, illogical, or self-destructive behaviors from reaching into the external environment.

Travis Hirschi (1995) asserts that the major function of the family is socialization of the young and that those youth with high levels of self-control will avoid criminal behavior. He points out that it is the family that is responsible for initial inculcation of values that will produce a law-abiding citizen. But when we consider that too many of our youth have been victimized by irresponsible parents, the media, and others to the degree that some neighborhoods are populated by an over abundance of people who are unable (or unwilling) to stop their actions before they act. Once we understand this fact we can begin to see the true dimensions of the crime problem and how a strong family is able to prevent criminal behavior.

Samuel Yochelson and Stanton Samenow provide some unique ideas on "the criminal mind." In **The Criminal Personality** (1977), they point out that traditional psychiatric methods of working with criminals are ineffective and as a consequence they began a search for effective methods to deal more effectively with criminals. Part of the problem, they state is that all criminals have certain "thought patterns," whether they are from the inner city or not, high school drop-outs or not and so on. They identify fifty-two specific errors of thinking that form the criminal personality, among them are:

chronic lying

an attitude that other people's property is theirs

supreme optimism

great energy

fear of injury or being insulted

intense anger

manipulativeness

a high self-image that cannot be bent

Don C. Gibbons (1992), states that it is hard to take Yochelson and Samenow seriously because of flaws in their methodology. The research is the result of 255 interviews that are unrepresentative of even a part of the criminal population. Many of them had been adjudged not guilty due to insanity and were sent to St. Elizabeths Hospital instead of a regular prison. Nevertheless, the fifty-two "thinking patterns" identified by Yochelson and Samenow strike a chord with those who work in prisons and are the basis for a number of treatment programs.

Sociological Dimension

As stated earlier, most criminology is sociological criminology. For the past 150 years, beginning with philosopher/reformers and then sociologists trained in scientific methods, attempts to explain crime and its causes have been an ongoing effort. We have to go back to the father of sociology to begin a sociological explanation of criminal behavior. Emile Durkheim is responsible for two main ideas about crime: the first is that crime is "normal" and the second idea is the concept of normlessness, or as he called it "anomie" (1897, 1951) (1895, 1938)

To say that crime is normal usually raises the hackles of the average person. But in Durkheim's view, behavior exists along a continuum, from angelic to satanic so to speak. He also maintained that "normal" behavior and the pathological are not different from each other, but are social distinctions that we place on certain kinds of behavior. A quick look at drinking and driving is a simplistic example of this concept. Twenty years ago, driving under the influence of alcohol and causing the death of another was viewed as reprehensible, but not criminal. Now it is viewed as both reprehensible and criminal and a social stigma has been attached to drinking and driving. As a consequence there has been a decline in the number of arrests for driving under the influence because of the re-labeling of this behavior by the general public.

Anomie, or normlessness, states that "the social needs or desires of humans are potentially insatiable, so collective order (social organization) is necessary as an external regulating force to define and control the goal-seeking of men" (Durkheim, 1897, 1951). If, as Durkheim, said, the social order is disrupted, then the aspirations of humans may increase to the point of out-distancing all possibilities of fulfillment. That is when traditional rules have lost their ability to control behavior and when the regulatory functions of the normative order have broken down, then we have a state of anomie. Anomie is brought about, according to Durkheim by sudden depression or prosperity, rapid technological change and war, just to name a few causes (1895, 1938).

This sounds depressingly like some neighborhoods we avoid when driving around town. The inhabitants have a reputation for wanting "things" like our wallets or car; these are places where the normal order has broken down in that shame, guilt, nosy neighbors and so on fail to keep behavior in check. These are places where the young people have no positive outlook for the future, where there are no decent jobs, where they have no investment in the city or neighborhood, and they simply don't care what anyone, other than peers, think.

Emile Durkheim was observing events as he saw them in the late 1800's up to WWI. However, Another sociologist by the name of Robert K. Merton (1938) kept the concept alive by publishing a paper that embellished the idea of Anomie. Mertonian anomie, as it is called, distinguishes between the **goals** that we are all told to pursue and the **means** to reach those goals. He points out that not all people have the same access to societally approved goals. This goals/means disjunction is what causes a good deal of criminal behavior.

He observed that while all citizens are told to pursue the same goals; that is an education, a good job, a house, and so on, not everyone has the same access to the means to achieve those goals as others. Consequently, humans have developed five ways of adapting to the conflict in achieving socially accepted goals. Those adaptations are: conformity, innovation, ritualism, retreatism, and rebellion. Figure 6.1 illustrates the adaptations to means.

We see in the below figure that one who conforms to the goals (+) and the means (+) are living by the rules. He or she will learn a trade or go to college, and otherwise hold down a job and work hard to achieve a piece of *the American Dream*. He or she has the support of all institutions in American life to pursue those goals: family, education, church, synagogue or mosque, and so on. He or she is able to achieve the goals that they set out to achieve.

The Innovation mode is one where the individual accepts the goals (+) that society has spelled out, but is blocked (-), or at least feels blocked, from achieving them. As a consequence, he or she is able to achieve the goals they set out to achieve.

It isn't too hard to imagine how innovation occurs. There are a number of opportunities in the illegitimate opportunity structure of society Cloward and Ohlin, 1960). According the Cloward and Ohlin, the pressure to join delinquent subcultures originate in the discrepancies between culturally induced aspirations among lower class youth and available means of achieving legitimate sociatally approved goals. Thus, Cloward and Ohlin point out, the illegitimate opportunities available to lower class youth take on a greater degree of importance, depending on the neighborhood. Sale of drugs is one example. We can take a small amount of comfort in that entreprenurialism is alive and well in the blighted areas of our cities

---

Figure 6.1

**Merton's Adaptation to
Goals/Means**

	Goals	Means
Conformity	+	+
Innovation	+	-
Ritualism	-	+
Retreatism	-	-
Rebellion	±	±

---

and depressed areas of smaller towns and cities of our nation. Innovation by selling drugs is only one small example, burglary and robbery are others.

A recent research project involving jail inmates in Iowa asked them to agree or disagree with the statement, "I believe in such things as education, having a nice home, and supporting my family." Over 93% of the respondents agreed with this statement. Respondents were also asked if they had ever felt shut out of an education or trade training. Nearly fifty percent (49.4%) said they had felt shut out of training or education. Additional surveys involving nearly 6,000 respondents agreed with the Iowa respondents (See Knox, et al. 1994 and Knox et al. 1995).

The other forms of adapting to the means/goals disjunction are of a concern, but are not as great a stimulant to criminal behavior. Ritualism refers to one who is more enamored with the means rather than the achievement. For example, a workaholic would be one who fits this mode and is rarely a concern to police and the courts. Retreatism is more of a concern in that one can retreat into drugs or alcohol and the related offenses are of a concern to police and courts. The other choice is to retreat to a mountain top and remain in seclusion. Rebellion is a concern in that those who fall into this mode reject both the means and goals of society and seek to replace them with other goals and means to achieve them. In this regard organizations on both ends of the political spectrum cause a good deal of concern. In the 1960's it was the Weather Underground on the left, today it is the Order, Posse Committatus, KKK, and other organizations on the political right that advocate the replacement of the existing order with their own view of society.

Labeling

Mother was right. How many times were we told not run around with others who they thought were trouble makers. Many times they were right and we were lucky to be at home or on our part-time job when they were arrested for one thing or another. Labeling holds that if one is part of a group that is deemed undesirable, then regardless of the honesty or "goodness" of one or several of the members, all can be labeled with the same stigmatizing tag.

There are two views of deviance, (a) those who focus on the person who commits the act and the laws he or she violates, (b) and those who emphasize the audience who observe and react to rule breaking. The second group are called the labelers and they insist that criminal conduct or deviance is the product of the social interaction between those who commit the act and those who label the behavior as deviant (Gibbons, 1992).

This is what happened to drinking and driving. The same thing happened to LSD in the 1960's when LSD was not illegal along with other substances prior to 1964. The use of LSD was not considered a problem as long as a small group of people considered to be on the social fringe used it. But, when the children of the middle class began to use LSD and became involved in bizarre behavior, even killing themselves as they tried to fly, LSD use was labeled as deviant and was declared illegal. This is an example of behavior that was tolerated for a while, but was eventually labeled deviant by a social audience.

The movie **Days of Wine and Roses** illustrates the point another way. Jack Lemmon's role was one of a drunk whose behavior was tolerated within certain limits, when his behavior exceeded those limits, he was labeled a drunk, was shunned and eventually lost his prestigious job and gradually spiraled downward to skid row. Along the way he was constantly searching for approval for his conduct. He became enmeshed in a deviant role and was excluded from resuming a normal social role.

It is labeling that often results in ex-convicts from rejoining the community. High school students experience this if they are labeled by "more popular" peers as undesirable. If youth are socially connected to a group of youth who have a reputation for deviant conduct, such as use of drugs, it is often very hard for a child to leave the group and be accepted by other, more socially acceptable, youth in the school. *He or she is excluded from resuming a normal social role.*

Social Control Theory

One of the more enduring theories of criminal behavior is one conceived by Travis Hirschi. Hirschi (1969) states that juveniles become free to commit delinquent acts when their ties to the conventional social order are severed. Obviously many delinquent acts are attractive and most youth would engage in such things as playing hooky, drinking, promiscuity, and criminal acts for financial gain. However, most are constrained from such behavior because they have strong social links to others, particularly their family.

For others, no special motivation is necessary to participate in delinquent behavior because their links to others are non-existent, or at best, weak. Hirschi (1969) identifies four dimensions along which the bond of the individual varies and the stronger the bond, the less likely the individuals involvement in delinquent behavior. Those dimensions are:

Attachment. Attachment refers to the bond between the child and parents and the child and school. According to Hirschi, children who have a significant attachment to parents will refrain from delinquency because they do not want to jeopardize that relationship. In regard to school, Hirschi states that incompetence in school leads to poor grades, which leads to a dislike of school, which leads to rejection of teachers and administrators as authorities, which leads to delinquency. Hirshi found that attachment to parents and school is more important than attachment to peers.

Commitment. This refers to the individuals investment in conventional activities. That is support of and participation in social activities that bind the individual to the morality and ethics of society.

Involvement. This is the most important dimension for us as parents. It is a dimension that stresses the importance of activities that promote the interests of society as a whole. We can foster this bond by encouraging participation in family activities, school activities such as sports, band, and/or service clubs. Hirshi points out that one who is busy with conventional things has little time for delinquent activities.

Belief. This dimension includes the belief in societies value system. This includes respect for the law, institutions, and the people who work in those institutions. Hirschi believes that if youth do not believe laws are workable or fair, their ties to society are weakened and there is a higher probability that they will become involved in delinquency.

One criticism of Hirschi's theory is that it explains delinquency and not adult crime (Adler, Mueller, and Laufer). However, it seems that if youth become involved in delinquency at an early age, then the probability of committing crimes as an adult is relatively high.

Differential Association

There is one more theory about criminal behavior that needs to be discussed in this brief review, and that regards the way people learn to commit crimes. Edwin Sutherland (1942) (see also Sutherland and Cressey, 1966) is noted for his theory of Differential Association and states that crime is learned through social interaction. Sutherland drew heavily upon the ideas of others that delinquent values are transmitted from one person to another or from one group to another and even from one generation to another.

He posited several propositions that attempt to explain criminal behavior (Sutherland and Cressey, 1966).

1. Criminal behavior is learned.
2. Criminal behavior is learned in interaction with other people in a process of communication. That is, a person does not become criminal simply by living in an environment that has a lot of criminals. Crime is learned in interaction with others.
3. The principle part of learning occurs in intimate personal groups.
4. When criminal behavior is learned, it includes how to commit the crime and how to rationalize the crime.
5. Depending on the primary reference group to which the individual belongs, he or she learns whether or not approval is forthcoming for breaking the law.

6. Becoming criminal or delinquent is dependent upon how many definitions one has that are favorable to violation of the law.

7. The differential associations may vary in frequency, duration, priority, and intensity. That is how often one associates with criminals, how intense the contact is, the meaning those associations has for the individual are important to the learning process.

8. Learning law violating behavior is the same as learning law abiding behavior. The same mechanisms are at work.

9. While criminal behavior is an expression of general needs and values, it is not explained by those general needs and values since non-criminal behavior is an expression of the same needs and values.

Thus, according to Sutherland, it appears that criminal behavior is leaned in much the same way we learn other, law-abiding, behaviors. According to Sutherland, while Differential Association explains criminal behavior of individuals, we must remember that criminal behavior is rooted in social organization and is an expression of that social organization.

Drugs and Crime

It is not the intent of this text to attempt to include a lengthy discussion on every variable related to crime, but drugs and crime are so interrelated that not to include a brief discussion on drugs would be inappropriate. So, even though it may not neatly fit into this chapter, it seems to be the least inappropriate place for such a discussion.

Elliott Currie (1993) states that we have made no headway on the drug problem and are in the midst of "the American nightmare." The news from the federal government is that we have made great headway on the drug problem, but this seems to be simply a justification for our present policies. To be sure, we have made some headway on middle-class drug use and the "crack epidemic" seems to have abated somewhat, but we are still the leading nation in the world for drug abuse. This fact has unleashed a terrible punitive streak that threatens the fabric of our society.

Because of our failure to get a grip on the introduction and use of drugs in our country:

* There are more cocaine-related arrests in our major cities than in most European nations in a single year.

* There are twice as many drug-related homicides in New York City in a single year than homicides for any reason in England.

* Nearly 25 percent of diagnosed AIDS cases are caused by intravenous drug use alone.

* Nearly 1 in 11 persons arrested are for drug abuse violations alone. this does not count those arrested for other crimes that can be attributed to drug abuse (Currie, 1993).

Drugs have permeated every level of our society and we seem helpless to do anything about it. As a consequence we can say with some certainty that drugs and crime are related. But this is like asking which came first, the chicken or the egg. Omitting casual marijuana use, it is a safe assumption that well adjusted people do not abuse drugs. However, the addictive personality will gravitate to whatever substance is available for use in order to "retreat" from the demands of family, society, and so on.

The Drug Use Forecasting Program was begun by the National Institute of Justice in 1987. It is designed to provide each of 24 cities with estimates of drug use among booked arrestees and information for detecting changes in drug use trends. In 1991 San Diego led all cities with 79 percent of arrestees showing positive for any drug with Omaha showing 42 percent positive for drug use. Clearly, drugs in these two cities were a contributing factor in one way or another to the individual being in jail during the first quarter, 1991.

More recently, in 1998 the drug testing program conducted interviews and drug tests with more than 30,000 recent arrestees in 35 metropolitan areas. A total of 20,716 adult males, 6,700 adult females, 3,134 juvenile males, and 434 juvenile females participated in the program during 1998. Twelve of the 35 sites (Albuquerque, Anchorage, Des Moines, Laredo, Las Vegas, Minneapolis, Oklahoma City, Sacramento, Salt Lake City, Seattle, Spokane, Tucson) were added during 1998. Cocaine was found to still be the most favored drug in 11 of the 35 sites. However, location was found to be a significant variable in the prevalence of use. Forty-seven percent of arrestees in Miami tested positive for cocaine while only 8% tested positive in San Jose, California. It appears the cocaine powder is increasing among young adults, especially in the Southwest and Southern United States.

In 8 of 10 sites, more than 10% of arrestees tested positive for opiates. Use of multiple drugs continues to be a serious problem among opiate users. Sixty-four percent testing positive for opiates also tested positive for cocaine, 30% tested positive for marijuana, 15% tested positive for valium or similar drugs, and 13% tested positive for methadone. In short, there was very little change between 1997 and 1998.

Data from the Bureau of Justice Statistics indicates that 82.4% of jail inmates in 1996 had ever used drugs and 60% of all jail inmates were under the influence of either drugs or alcohol at the time of their arrest. More sadly, 83 percent of all youth in long term public juvenile facilities in 1987 had used drugs at some point in their lives (BJS, 1995).

Drugs and crime are related. According to the Bureau of Justice Statistics, 10 percent of federal prison inmates, 17 percent of state prison inmates, and 13 percent of all convicted jail inmates stated they had committed their crime to get money for drugs. Further, 20 percent of Hispanic inmates, 15 percent of white inmates and 17 percent of black inmates said they committed their present offense in order to get money for drugs (BJS, 1995)

This calls our attention to the need for effective substance abuse programs in our jails and prisons. It makes no sense to keep a man or woman locked up for a period of time and then return them to the community with no preparation. Even more reprehensible, is the fact that money spent on street drugs represents a tax placed upon our society that flows into the pockets of a few corrupt, evil people who will stop at nothing to increase or preserve the flow of profits. In addition, drug money is spread around in a corrosive influence that rips away the integrity and honesty of public officials, bankers, and others who serve the needs of a few wealthy drug czars.

Drugs are directly responsible for nearly every type of crime possible from murder, bank robbery, and muggings to drug sales and public indecency. Perhaps even more insidious is the effect it has had on the moral fabric of normally "upright" citizens. Something must be done to stem the flow of drugs into the United States and perhaps the United States government should be more concerned with the plight of American citizens than diplomacy. Our future is at stake and it is time to do more than plead with the governments of Columbia,

Ecuador, and Peru. Perhaps it is time to do more than allow credits for military supplies to those governments and consider outright military intervention.

Leaping From Theory to Practice

Travis Hirschi, in an earlier discussion remarked once that if we look at all the theories of criminal behavior one at a time, they don't seem to make much sense, but if we place them end to end they make a great deal more sense. This incomplete review of some of the reasons why people commit crimes sheds some light on the subject, but we need to place them end to end in order to make some sense out of them.

Let's begin with a worst case possibility and examine a child born into a family characterized by a young unmarried mother. There are many possibilities in this example and not all of them lead to a life of deviance for the child. Nevertheless, if that child grows up neglected because the mother is out of the home for prolonged periods of time, the mother subsists on public or charitable support and if there are no responsible adults in his or her life there is little likelihood that the child will have an idea of what a "normal" family is supposed to be like. Assuming that the child lives in a neighborhood with an abundance of other similar families, where there are few external controls on the behavior of children, and the inhabitants of that neighborhood do almost as they please, we then have what we can term an anomic situation. In addition, if one, or several, of the young adults are criminal they are available to teach the child, as he grows older, how to commit certain crimes, including ways to rationalize that behavior (that it is OK to steal, rob, or sell drugs).

At the same time, the child grows up with a television in the home and it is used as a baby-sitting tool by the mother. The child learns what kind of material things are available if one has the money. Over time the child acquires a desire to have nice things, but the opportunity to achieve them legitimately are closed because of class, opportunity, and perhaps race. Therefore, using Merton's scheme, he or she innovates and decides to take advantage of one, or several, of the illegitimate opportunities available to him or her.

We see in the above example several things at work. First, the bonds that attach the youngster to society are nonexistent. There is no family, no school (or at least not an effective school), and no belief in the ethics and values of society. Secondly, a condition of anomie exists that fosters a means/goals disjunction and since the child cannot achieve societally approved goals legitimately, he innovates. Third, he or she has learned how to commit the crime or crimes through differential association. That is he or she has learned the techniques and rationalizations, and that criminal behavior is approved behavior.

This is all vastly simplified for example's sake, but we can see how some children do not have a chance from birth. The important thing to remember is that growing up in a single parent home is not a guarantee that the child will grow up delinquent and many dysfunctional homes are two-parent homes. By the same token, some homes have a child who grows up to be delinquent or criminal and there appears to be no explanation for it. These are homes in which the parents tried to do all the right things: time with children, family activities, emphasis on education, church or synagogue, and so on. Sometimes we are at a loss to explain such behavior.

If we are going to make a dent in crime at the neighborhood level, we must begin by attacking the problems that breed delinquent conduct. It is axiomatic that if we have fewer delinquents, we will have fewer adult criminals. Research indicates that children imitate parental behavior, both conforming and criminal; anti-social behavior leads to rejection by teachers and peers leading to further alienation and more criminal behavior; programs that assist single parents in supervising their children and that free them to spend more time with their children may help to prevent delinquency. The above highlights point out that there is a lot of room for program innovation to prevent delinquent and criminal behavior and which draw upon the theoretical foundations touched upon in this chapter.

Proposition #11: The search for a magical program will not bear fruit, because crime is usually learned behavior and occurs in an environment that approves of such behavior. We must deal with the conditions that cause criminal behavior.

Implications for Tax Dollars

A theoretical foundation is necessary for the development of effective programs to deal with crime. If we have some understanding of the causes of crime, we may be able to do something about it. The problem with crime theory is that we cannot seem to come to any kind of consensus. This is because there is no single reason why people commit crimes. Thus we will continue to debate causation, programs and ideology for the forseeable future. During the debate over the 1994 Omnibus Crime Bill there was a great deal of controversy over "social pork." Some members of Congress stated that programs that attempt to deal with delinquency and crime are a waste of taxpayer's money and those funds can be better spent on prisons and police. The Midnight Basketball Program was held up as an example of "pork" without a discussion of it's merits, even though President Bush had hailed the program as a "point of light." The important point in all of the rhetoric and debate is what to do with the product of dysfunctional families.

To simply send the individual off to prison after he or she has acquired an "attitude" is short sighted. Criminological research has indicated very strongly that the prison subculture is a reflection of the criminal subculture that exists on the street. It does not make sense to send a first time offender to prison where he or she will be given approval for deviant behavior by other inmates. If the individual has a bad attitude going into prison, the deprivation, boredom, monotony, and the constant assaults on his psychological and physical self may well turn a marginal character into someone beyond redemption and we have an even greater problem when that individual is eventually released.

There is a history of programs that may have been ineffective either as controlling agents or with rehabilitative value. But, that does not justify the refusal to implement programs all together. This chapter reveals that there are too many variables to simply state that prison is the only alternative to law breaking. Clearly, if we seriously attack the problem of delinquency and criminal actions head-on before it becomes habitual behavior, we will save money in the long term. One answer to the problem is found in a review of social control theory.

We learned above that people commit crimes when the social bonds that unite families and communities are severed. These attachments, involvement, and belief in community rules allow civilized behavior to flourish. Therefore, efforts to prevent crime must include the teaching of conventional values and ways must be found to strengthen individual bonds to society (Adler, Mueller, and Laufer, 1995).

Proposition #12: *It is more cost effective to work with children in the community than to send the adult to prison. It is also economically more viable to provide or develop jobs for adults than to send them to prison.*

Summary

We can view criminological theories along three dimensions: biological, psychological, and sociological. The biological theories attempt to explain behavior in terms of form explaining function. Caesar Lombroso is important in that he conceived the idea of the Criminal Man and was the first to make a scientific effort to explain criminal behavior. Included in this dimension are the body type theories, feeblemindedness, and the XYY chromosome.

The psychological explanations are largely the domain of psychiatry. Traditional Freudians hold that the personality is composed of an Id, Ego, and Superego. When these three parts are working in harmony, the person is "normal." When there is an imbalance, problems result. Whether or not there is a "criminal personality is open to debate, nevertheless, Yochelson and Samenow believe that they have identified a criminal personality and fifty-two "thinking patterns" that characterize the criminal.

The sociological dimension attempts to explain criminal behavior largely in terms of the impact of environment on the individual. Merton's Anomie is important because it points out the disjunction between the goals that society approves of and, for a segment of the American population, the means to achieve those goals are often blocked. Hirschi calls our attention to the bonds that unite the individual to society: attachment, commitment, involvement, and belief. Hirschi states that if the bonds are severed the individual is free to commit delinquent acts. Finally, Differential Association was discussed as a learning theory. That is, one learns to commit crimes through the same mechanisms that we learn law abiding behavior. Drugs play a role in crime in the United States, but to what extent drugs cause crime is difficult to determine due to the reporting practices of police agencies.

In spite of the image that the media conveys to us and the sky is falling attitude of many politicians, most non-traditional families in the United States manage to raise law abiding children. What is important to remember is that many variables enter into the life of the individual in determining whether or not he or she will enter into a life of deviance. There is hope and programs exist to teach youth and adults conventional values and that strengthen the individual's bonds to society.

Bibliography

Freda Adler, Gerhard O. W. Mueller, and William S. Laufer. **Criminology**, 2nd ed. N.Y.: McGraw-Hill, Inc., 1995.

Patricia A. Brennan, Sarnoff A. Mednick, and Jan Volavka. "Biomedical Factors in Crime," in James Q. Wilson and Joan Petersilia, eds., **Crime: Twenty Eight Leading Expert Look at the most Pressing Problem of Our Time**. San Francisco: ICS Press. 1995.

Bureau of Justice Statistics. **Drugs and Crime Facts, 1994**. Bureau of Justice Statistics: U.S. Department of Justice, 1995.

Karl O. Christiansen. "Seriousness of Criminality and Concordance among Danish Twins," in Roger Hood, ed., **Crime, Criminology, and Public Policy: Essays in Honour of Sir Leon Radzinowicz**. New York: Free Press, 1974, in John E. Conklin, **Criminology**, 4th ed., New York: Macmillan Publishing Company, 1992.

Karl O. Christiansen. "A Preliminary Study of Criminality among Twins, in Sarnoff A. Mednick and Karl O. Christiansen, eds., **Biosocial Bases of Criminal Behavior**. New York: Gardner Press, 1977, in John E. Conklin, **Criminology**, 4th ed., New York: Macmillan Publishing Company, 1992.

Richard Cloward and Lloyd Ohlin. **Delinquency and Opportunity: A Theory of Delinquent Gangs**. NY: The Free Press. 1960.

Elliott Currie. **Reckoning: Drugs, the Cities, and the American Future**. New York: Hill and Wang, 1993).

Emile Durkheim. **Suicide**, Trans. John A. Spaulding and George Simpson. Glencoe, Il: Free Press. 1951.

Emile Durkheim. **The Rules of the Sociological Method,** Trans. Sarah A. Solovay and John H. Mueller. NY: Free Press. 1938.

Richard G. Fox. "The XYY Offender: A Modern Myth?" **Journal of Criminal Law, Criminology, and Police Science**, 62(1971): 59-73.

Don C. Gibbons. **Society, Crime, and Criminal Behavior**, 6th ed. Englewood Cliffs, N.J.:(Prentice-Hall, Inc., 1992).

Travis Hirschi. **Causes of Delinquency**. (Berkeley: University of California Press, 1969).

Travis Hirschi. "The Family," in James Q. Wilson and Joan Petersilia, eds., **Crime: Twenty eight Leading Experts look at the most Pressing Problem of Our Time**. San Francisco: ICS Press. 1995.

George W. Knox, James G. Houston, John A. Laskey, Thomas F. McCurrie, Edward D. Tromanhauser, and David L. Laske. **Gangs and Guns**. (Chicago: National Gang Crime Research Center, 1994).

George W. Knox, Edward D. Tromanhauser, James G. Houston, Brad Martin, Robert E. Morris, Thomas F. McCurrie, John L. Laskey, Dorothy Papachristos, Judith Feinberg, and Charla Waxman. **The Economics of Gang Life**. (Chicago: National Gang Crime Research Center, 1995).

Robert K. Merton. "Social Structure and Anomie." **American Sociological Review**. 3(October, 1938). Pp. 672-682.

Saleem A. Shah and Loren H. Roth. "Biological and Psychophysiological Factors in Criminality," in Daniel E. Glaser, ed., **Handbook of Criminology** (Chicago: Rand McNally, 1974).

Edwin H. Sutherland. "The Development of the Concept of Differential Association." Ohio Valley Sociologist. 15:May, 1942. Pp. 34.

Edwin H. Sutherland and Donald R. Cressy. **Principles of Criminology**, 7th ed. Philidelphia: J. B. Lippencott Company.

Ian Taylor, Paul Walton, and Jock Young. **The New Criminology: For a Social Theory of Deviance**. London: Routledge and Kegan Paul. 1973.

George B. Vold and Thomas J. Bernard. **Theoretical Criminology**, 3rd. ed. (N.Y.: Oxford University Press, 1986).

Samuel Yochelson and Stanton E. Samenow. **The Criminal Personality: A Profile for Change**, Vols. 1 and 2. New York: Jason Aronson, 1976, 1977.

Chapter 7

Juvenile Delinquency

Introduction

Juvenile delinquency is not a new phenomenon as there has always been deviance by young people. What is new, since the Civil War, is the definition of juvenile delinquency as a separate issue from adult criminality. Prior to the end of the nineteenth century, children were treated much like adults. They were arrested for crimes, placed in jail if necessary, and tried in adult courts under an adversary system. If found guilty, at best they were apt to be sent to Houses of Refuge which were prisons for children and at worst, were confined in prisons with adult criminals. We must remember that in the period leading up to 1900, American cities were overcrowded, unhealthy places where being orphaned was most common. Therefore, a child often turned to criminality simply to survive, if he did not run off to the frontier where criminality was still an option.

Juvenile Delinquency as a Separate Issue

We have already discussed why people become involved in criminal behavior and the reader is referred to chapter six. Whether children became involved in criminal behavior due to a character defect or because of flaws in their environment was of no great concern to nineteenth century reformers. They were concerned that children were subjected to an unnecessary degree of harshness in the judicial process and wished to see that treatment mitigated. As a result, the House of Refuge was established in 1824 in New York. It was designed to accept criminal and vagrant children and while most reformers pointed out that it was constructed for humanitarian reasons, one scholar states it was constructed to control the delinquency of lower class youth (Fox, 1970).

Soon Houses of Refuge were built in many locations throughout the United States. Ultimately, they turned out to be abominable places where stronger, more sophisticated boys exploited younger, weaker boys and where the filth and treatment by their adult supervisors was just as bad as adult prisons. In reaction, many alternatives were devised to keep children out of the Houses of Refuge. One such proposal was suggested by a group of reformers in Chicago. They persuaded the State Board of Charities to ask the Chicago Bar Association to draft a juvenile court bill and send it to the state legislature. It passed on the last day of the session in 1899 (Thornton, Jr., and Voigt, 1992).

The idea caught on and gradually spread throughout the country and by 1904 ten states had a juvenile court and by 1909 twenty states had adopted the idea. By 1923 every state had a juvenile court except Maine and Wyoming (Thornton, Jr. and Voigt, 1992). The philosophy of the juvenile court, then and now, was to shield the child from the harshness of the adult court and to provide treatment and care to children who had run afoul of the law. The notion of such an approach was marinated in the idea of the era that, as a Christian one was obligated to care for those who were less fortunate and to see that children had an opportunity to grow without the undue influences of alcohol and gambling, and with the care and love of parents or concerned adults.

The juvenile court is unique for it operates under the doctrine of parens patriae. Parens patriae means that the government operates as substitute parents for children and other persons who are under a legal disability. For the first time the approach to crime was focused on the future, rather than simply punish the individual for their misdeeds. The idea of probation as a legitimate sentence was devised as a means to deal with the child in the community, under the supervision of a responsible adult who was to supervise and counsel the child. The task was believed to be so noble that the thought of paying someone to be a juvenile probation officer was too vulgar and would attract the wrong sort of person.

Juvenile Delinquency and the Status Offender

Juvenile delinquency is a very broad term and can be defined as any crime committed by a juvenile under the age of 17 or 18, depending upon the state, and which would be a crime if committed by an adult. Juvenile delinquency, however, can be divided into two categories: criminal offenses and status offenses. Criminal offenses are crimes such as burglary, assault, robbery and so on. Status offenses are different. A status offense is any crime committed by a child which would not be a crime if committed by an adult. Examples include: runaway, truancy, promiscuity, drinking, and incorrigibility.

The control of the behavior of children has always been considered consistent with the doctrine of parens patriae and is deemed necessary to protect the interests of the child. However, it wasn't until the 1960's that the abuses of status offenders were brought to light by social reformers. Until then, status offenders were treated much like criminal offenders and critics thought that such treatment caused status offenders to veer towards involvement in criminal conduct. As a result, states enacted a separate category for this type of child variously called: CHINS (Child in Need of Services), PINS (Persons in Need of Services), and so on.

The purpose of the reforms were to shield the child from the stigma of delinquency and to refer to them as troubled youth. Still, even as troubled youth, the distinction was, and still is to a degree, usually blurred. They are arrested by the same police officers, brought before the same magistrate or juvenile referee in the same juvenile court, assigned to the same probation officer, and often detained in the same detention center (usually in a non-secure section) as are juvenile criminal offenders.

In the 1970's the Office of Juvenile Justice and Delinquency Prevention made it a top priority to remove status offenders from jails and other secure lock-ups. That attempt has been largely successful. By any yardstick it makes no sense to lock a status offender in jail or a detention center. It is frustrating, however, to have limited options when dealing with runaways, for example, but it does force authorities to look elsewhere for the real problem, which usually exists. Such problems include sexual and physical abuse and other problems in the home that should be dealt with.

Critics of justice system intervention in the conduct of status offenders point out that status offenders should not be brought before the court and constitutes a broadening of the criminal justice system net and once ensnared in the net it is difficult for the child to become disentangled. However, if we believe that failure to attend school, drugs, and waywardness in general are good for children, then the critics are right. If, on the other hand, we believe that parents, no matter how inept, should be assisted and given the support necessary to raise their children, then we would be abdicating our responsibility by ignoring the outright pleas of the parents and the silent pleas of children in need.

The Scope of Delinquency

We should be troubled by the number of arrests of young people under the age of eighteen. In the decade 1987 to 1996 the arrests of youth under the age of 18 increased 35.4%, that is from 1,398,050 arrests in 1987 to 1,892,312 arrests in 1996. During the same period arrests for those over 18 increased by 12.6%, that is from 7,176,682 in 1987 to 8,082,632 in 1996 (Maguire and Pastore, 1998). Table 7.1 illustrates the numbers and offenses of juveniles and adults arrested for 1987 and 1996.

We can see from Table 7.1 that arrests for youth in nearly all categories are up from 1987. The exceptions are forcible rape, burglary, sex offenses, and Driving Under the Influence (DUI). We have discussed the problems with crime statistics in Chapter 1, but even if the data are flawed to an extent, the rise in juvenile crime gives us reason to be alarmed. However, as pointed out earlier, the nation is not descending into a state of chaos and our youth are not, in general, any worse than previous generations. Close examination of the arrests for youth reveals that 73.8% percent of all arrests for youth 17 years of age and younger in 1997 occurred in only eighteen states which are mostly characterized by large urban populations such as California and Texas. Therefore 32 states share the remaining 26.2 percent of all juvenile arrests. Table 7.2 depicts reported arrests of juveniles.

As we discussed in chapter 1, much crime occurs in just a few areas of the nation and the same is true of juvenile crime. Clearly, we must not view the sensationalized stories we read and hear of in the media as representative of our nation's youth. The growth of the juvenile population does not bear out the fear of a juvenile crime wave. According to the U.S. Census, the 10-19 age group population grew from 34,992,000 to 37,705,000 in the period 1987 to 1996. An increase of less than three million youth. It seems clear enough that the "juvenile crime problem" is not evenly distributed across the nation. What juvenile crime that does exist should concern all citizens and policy makers for a long time to come, especially in the nineteen states that are responsible for three quarters of juvenile arrests. A later discussion will cover possible answers to juvenile crime, but we now turn to a question that concerns us all; who is responsible for the bulk of violent juvenile crime.

The Chronic and Violent Juvenile Offender

Much of what we know about the chronic offender is due to the work of Marvin Wolfgang and his associates. In 1972 Wolfgang, Figlio, and Sellin published a report that has had a profound affect on our notions of delinquency. They tracked a group of 9,945 boys born in Philadelphia in 1945. Using official records they noted contacts with police and juvenile court until their 18th birthday. They believed that by noting the onset of delinquency and how it progressed they would be able "to relate these phenomena to certain personal or social characteristics of the delinquents and to make appropriate comparisons" (Wolfgang, Figlio, and Sellin, 1972).

Of the 9,945 boys, 3,475 had some police contact and the remainder had no police contact. They learned that of the 3,475 boys with police contact, they were responsible for 10,214 crimes. Race was found to be the most significant predictor of police contact. They also found that school related variables were significantly related to delinquency in that a greater proportion of delinquents attended public schools rather than parochial schools. Nondelinquents had a greater probability of receiving more education than delinquents (11.24 years of schooling compared to 9.96 years of schooling) and this relationship was consistent across racial lines with whites receiving more schooling than minorities.

More importantly, the "discovery" of the chronic offender has greater significance for public policy. The data indicated that a little more than one-half (54%) of the sample were repeat offenders and the remaining 46% were one-time offenders. They further categorized the chronic offenders as **nonchronic recidivists** and **chronic recidivists**. The nonchronic recidivists consisted of 1,235 boys who had been arrested more than once, but less than five times. This group made up 35.6% of all delinquents, but the **chronic recidivists** consisted of 627 boys arrested five or more times and accounted for 18% of all delinquents and represented only 6% of the total sample of 9,945 boys.

The 6% (627 boys) were responsible for 51.9% of all offenses (5,305). According to Wolfgang, et al, an even more significant finding was their involvement in serious offenses. That is, they were involved in 71% of the homicides, 73% of the rapes, 82% of the robberies, and 69% of the aggravated assaults. Contrary to conventional wisdom, arrest and juvenile court did not deter further delinquent conduct. In fact, it appears that the more severe the disposition of the court, the more likely the youth would be involved in repeated delinquent behavior. They concluded that the juvenile system did little to control or eliminate the behavior of the chronic recidivist.

Wolfgang and his associates were interested in how behavior changed over the years and if their findings would hold for a later population group. They selected a second birth cohort born in 1958 and followed them until maturity. There were 28,338 youths, 13,811 males and 14,527 females in the cohort (Tracy and Figlio, 1982). They discovered that the chronic delinquents comprised 7.5% of the total sample (compared to 6.3% of the earlier cohort) and that the chronic delinquents were responsible for a disproportionate number of offenses including serious offenses. The findings of Wolfgang, et al., were subsequently upheld by a number of other studies.

Violence and the Chronic Offender

James Alan Fox, former Dean of the School of Criminal Justice at Northeastern University is one of the foremost authorities on the subject of violent crime. He is not optimistic about the future of a segment of our juvenile population. Fox and Pierce (1994) point out that while homicide by adults age 25 and older is declining, the rate for 18-24 year olds increased 62% between 1986-1991. In the 14-17 age bracket, murder increased by 124% in the same period. Others have called our attention to the precariousness of the existence of young, black males and Fox and Pierce, as well, point out that while that group constitutes 1% of the total U.S. population, they constitute 14% of the victims of homicide and 19% of the perpetrators

The cause for Fox and Pierce's pessimism stems from several factors, much of it from the availability of drugs and guns. Perhaps even more important is a change in the attitude of young people. According to Fox and Pierce, there has been a reduction in moral responsibility on the part of both youth and adults that may be attributed in part to the abundance of violence seen on television and in the movies. It is not that young people are guilty of being copy cats, but rather over time they have been desensitized by the constant bombardment of violence on television and movies. In addition, "Television docudramas glorify criminals, transforming insignificant and obscure nobodies into national celebrities" (Fox and Pierce, 1994).

Research on the subject is mixed. However, if we accept the positive affect of **Sesame Street** and Barney as a vehicle for the instruction of children through the medium of television, we cannot ignore the same principle when it comes to the ability of television to negatively affect children during prime time viewing. In 1972 the Surgeon General commissioned a report that "found a preliminary and tentative indication of a causal relationship" (Milavsky, no date). Subsequently, the National Institute of Mental Health (NIMH) in 1982 reviewed studies completed in the period after the release of the 1972 report. It was even more emphatic in its conclusion that television causes violence, but the report was severely criticized by the National Academy of Sciences because it dealt with mild forms of aggression among children and not criminal behavior (Milavsky).

Fox and Pierce call our attention to another contributing factor- the entry of women into the work force. As the need for two income earners has increased, women have entered the work force both of necessity and due to the liberation of women and their search for fulfillment outside of the home. In addition, men have not taken on a greater a share of household responsibility in raising children. This has resulted in a number of consequences: (1) children are left to their own devices and, as a consequence, watch a lot of murders and other violence on television, (2) families are not as connected to the community as previous generations through membership in the PTA or Scouts, for example, (3) volunteerism of mothers in other organizations has suffered and in general women

Table 7.1 – Arrests by Age and Offense 1987 and 1996

Offense Charged	Total All Ages			Under 18 years of age			18 years of age and older		
	1987	1996	Percent change	1987	1996	Percent change	1987	1996	Percent change
Total	8,574,732	9,974,944	16.3	1,398,050	1,892,312	35.4	7,176,682	8,082,632	12.6
Murder and non-negligent manslaughter	13,966	13,446	-3.7	1,355	2,039	50.5	12,611	11,407	-9.5
Forcible Rape	24,850	21,752	-12.5	3,782	3,680	-2.7	21,068	18,072	-14.2
Robbery	102,316	113,089	10.5	23,229	36,569	57.4	79,087	76,520	-3.2
Aggravated assault	241,498	345,644	43.1	29,705	50,560	70.2	211,793	295,084	39.3
Burglary	288,483	236,266	-18.1	98,707	87,233	-11.6	189,776	149,033	-21.5
Larceny-theft	960,888	993,209	3.4	295,785	336,774	13.9	665,103	656,435	-1.3
Motor vehicle theft	118,058	120,989	2.6	46,143	50,212	8.8	71,915	70,777	-1.6
Arson	11,747	12,291	4.6	4,823	6,553	35.9	6,924	5,738	-17.1
Violent Crime	382,630	493,931	29.1	58,071	92,848	59.9	324,559	401,083	23.6
Property Crime	1,379,176	1,362,755	-1.2	445,458	480,772	7.9	933,718	881,983	-5.5
Crime Index Total	1,761,806	1,856,686	5.4	503,529	573,620	13.9	1,258,277	1,283,066	2.0

Table 7.1 – Arrests by Age and Offense 1987 and 1996 (Continued)

Offense Charged	Total All Ages			Under 18 years of age			18 years of age and older		
	1987	1996	Percent change	1987	1996	Percent change	1987	1996	Percent change
Other assaults	536,527	873,030	62.7	77,415	154,762	99.9	459,112	718,268	56.4
Forgery & counterfeiting	60,987	79,477	30.3	5,500	5,644	2.6	55,487	73,833	33.1
Fraud	226,009	285,131	26.2	17,227	18,187	5.6	208,782	266,944	27.9
Embezzlement	8,684	10,252	18.1	745	862	15.7	7,939	9,390	18.3
Stolen property; buying, receiving, possessing	98,190	99,302	1.1	24,764	26,773	8.1	73,426	72,529	-1.2
Vandalism	179,704	212,045	18.0	73,826	93,139	26.2	105,878	118,906	12.3
Weapons: carrying, Possessing, etc.	133,580	147,202	10.2	21,049	35,670	69.5	112,531	111,532	-0.9
Prostitution & comm. Vice	85,588	76,754	-10.3	1,779	1,048	-41.1	83,909	75,706	-9.7
Sex offenses[1]	67,289	64,386	-4.3	10,636	11,493	8.1	56,653	52,893	-6.6
Drug abuse violations	654,426	1,030,888	57.5	61,358	142,922	132.9	593,068	887,966	49.7
Gambling	19,558	16,040	-18.0	677	2,121	213.3	18,881	13,919	-26.3
Offenses against the family & children	36,530	80,571	120.6	2,063	4,400	113.3	34,467	76,171	121.0
Driving under the influence	1,111,391	887,181	-20.2	15,627	11,318	-27.6	1,05,764	875,863	-20.1
Liquor laws	389,570	436,193	12.0	103,068	97,967	-4.9	286,502	338,226	18.1
Drunkeness	602,428	480,261	-20.3	17,558	15,637	-10.9	584,870	464,624	-20.6
Disorderly conduct	480,196	554,081	15.4	72,598	139,781	92.5	407,598	414,300	1.6
Vagrancy	30,763	20,303	-34.0	2,160	2,553	18.2	28,603	17,750	-37.9
All other offenses (except traffic)	1,922,653	2,504,296	30.3	217,618	293,550	34.9	1,705,035	2,210,746	29.7
Suspicion (not included in totals)	6,110	3,768	-38.3	2,149	1,440	-33.0	3,961	2,328	-41.2
Curfew & loitering law violations	62,316	132,747	113.0	62,316	132,747	113.0	X	X	X
Runaways	106,537	128,118	20.3	106,537	128,118	20.3	X	X	X

[1] Except forcible rape and prostitution

Source: Kathleen Maguire and Ann K, Pastore, eds., Sourcebook of Criminal Justice Statistics, 1997. U. S. Department of Justice Bureau of Justice Statistics, Washington, DC: USPGO, 1998

Table 7.2 – Reported Arrests of Youths 17 Years and Younger, 1998

Rank	State	ALPHA ORDER Arrests	% of USA	Rank	State	RANK ORDER Arrests	% of USA
32	Alabama	18,234	0.9	1	California	273,012	13.9
45	Alaska	3,554	0.2	2	Texas	223,039	11.3
7	Arizona	63,287	3.2	3	Wisconsin	112,549	5.7
31	Arkansas	20,047	1.0	4	New Jersey	81,101	4.1
1	California	273,012	13.9	5	Ohio	66,672	3.4
18	Colorado	39,653	2.0	6	Minnesota	63,937	3.2
23	Connecticut	31,059	1.6	7	Arizona	63,287	3.2
44	Delaware	4,499	0.2	8	New York	63,225	3.2
NA	Florida	NA	NA	9	Illinois	62,501	3.2
25	Georgia	25,675	1.3	10	Virginia	58,401	3.0
33	Hawaii	16,840	0.9	11	Maryland	57,865	2.9
27	Idaho	22,517	1.1	12	North Carolina	57,727	2.9
9	Illinois	62,501	3.2	13	Michigan	52,635	2.7
20	Indiana	37,183	1.9	14	Louisiana	49,150	2.5
29	Iowa	21,046	1.1	15	Pennsylvania	48,499	2.5
NA	Kansas	NA	NA	16	Washington	47,499	2.4
42	Kentucky	7,918	0.4	17	Oregon	42,274	2.1
14	Louisiana	49,150	2.5	18	Colorado	39,653	2.0
37	Maine	12,223	0.6	19	Missouri	38,932	2.0
11	Maryland	57,865	2.9	20	Indiana	37,183	1.9
28	Massachusetts	22,513	1.1	21	Oklahoma	32,279	1.6
13	Michigan	52,635	2.7	22	Utah	31,206	1.6
6	Minnesota	63,937	3.2	23	Connecticut	31,059	1.6
36	Mississippi	12,387	0.6	24	South Carolina	30,226	1.5
19	Missouri	38,932	2.0	25	Georgia	25,675	1.3
46	Montana	3,011	0.2	26	Tennessee	23,851	1.2
30	Nebraska	20,051	1.0	27	Idaho	22,517	1.1
35	Nevada	13,674	0.7	28	Massachusetts	22,513	1.1
NA	New Hampshire	NA	NA	29	Iowa	21,046	1.1
4	New Jersey	81,101	4.1	30	Nebraska	20,051	1.0
34	New Mexico	15,504	0.8	31	Arkansas	20,047	1.0
8	New York	63,225	3.2	32	Alabama	18,234	0.9
12	North Carolina	57,727	2.9	33	Hawaii	16,840	0.9

Table 7.2 – Reported Arrests of Youths 17 Years and Younger, 1998 (Continued)

		ALPHA ORDER				RANK ORDER	
Rank	State	Arrests	% of USA	Rank	State	Arrests	% of USA
40	North Dakota	8,643	0.4	34	New Mexico	15,054	0.8
5	Ohio	66,672	3.4	35	Nevada	13,674	0.7
21	Oklahoma	32,279	1.6	36	Mississippi	12,387	0.6
17	Oregon	22,274	2.1	37	Maine	12,223	0.6
15	Pennsylvania	48,499	2.5	38	Rhode Island	8,633	0.4
38	Rhode Island	8,633	0.4	39	Wyoming	8,664	0.4
24	South Carolina	30,226	1.5	40	North Dakota	8,643	0.4
41	South Dakota	8,204	0.4	41	South Dakota	8,204	0.4
26	Tennessee	23,851	1.2	42	Kentucky	7,918	0.4
2	Texas	223,039	11.3	43	West Virginia	7,608	0.4
22	Utah	31,206	1.6	44	Delaware	4,499	0.2
NA	Vermont	NA	NA	45	Alaska	3,554	0.2
10	Virginia	58,401	3.0	46	Montana	3,011	0.2
16	Washington	47,499	2.4	NA	Florida	NA	NA
43	West Virginia	7,608	0.4	NA	Kansas	NA	NA
3	Wisconsin	112,549	5.7	NA	New Hampshire	NA	NA
39	Wyoming	8,664	0.4	NA	Vermont	NA	NA
NA	District of Columbia	NA	NA	NA	District of Columbia	NA	NA

Source: *Crime State Rankings*, 1998. Lawrence, KS:Morgan Quinto Press, 1998.

are not around as much to supervise their children as well as other children, (4) too many homes are disrupted by divorce or economic stress and too many children emerge from childhood undersocialized and undersupervised.

The above points are not made in order to blame women for juvenile delinquency in the United States. Quite the contrary, women have gone to work in such numbers for at least three reasons; (1) to preserve their standard of living, (2) to keep the family together, and (3) to maintain the illusion that the family has a chance to achieve *the American Dream*. The above points illustrate quite clearly that crime and delinquency are not problems that can be separated from social and economic issues and any attempt to solve the problem of crime and delinquency must consider all facets of the American experience over the past forty years.

To remark that the United States has undergone great economic and social change in the past two decades is to understate the point. What impact have these changes had on delinquency? Can they be altered? How have youth reacted to these issues psychologically and socially? We now turn to a discussion of gangs as a substitute for family and as a vehicle to overcome despair and hopelessness.

> *Proposition #13: Juvenile delinquency is the result of a number*
> *of social and economic forces that must be addressed if we are*
> *to successfully do anything about juvenile crime.*

Gangs

The apparent disintegration of our inner cities and the violence that accompanies that disintegration has scorched the soul of America and led to a sense of impotence among our citizens. It has engendered fear of the streets, as well as anger and frustration with our elected officials. At times we seem powerless to do anything about deteriorating cities and street gangs. Many of our citizens and elected officials are in a state of denial about gangs and have not recognized, or refuse to recognize, law enforcement and social problems associated with the presence of street gangs. It is difficult to estimate the amount of delinquent behavior related to gangs, but there is no denying that street gangs have become a fact of life for many cities and smaller communities.

Pernicious Ignorance

During the early 1980's we re-discovered street gangs. We learned of their activities in the inner city and shook our heads in dismay as we read or heard television reports of frightening gang activity in areas that seemed to be far removed from our daily lives. Our inclination was to deny their existence or to believe they had no impact on our immediate life.

How wrong we were. A 1994 survey of Police Chiefs and Sheriffs (Knox, et al. 1994) reveals that street gangs are more than an inner city problem. They estimated that nearly one in six crimes committed were gang related. This includes murders, robberies, sexual crimes, drug offenses and petty theft. Gangs have penetrated many cities and towns that previously thought they were isolated and safe from their predations.

Why did this phenomenon explode upon our consciousness with the impact of a nuclear bomb? To begin, we ignored the link between family and a steady paycheck for the primary breadwinner. The loss of opportunity for primary breadwinners to hold meaningful jobs has been sneered at or dismissed by "knowledgeable" business and financial executives whose lives are untouched by the despair and hopelessness brought on by prolonged unemployment, underemployment, and downsizing. To them the bottom line is what counts. During the 1980's when the tax structure and economic conditions fueled the merger and acquisitions frenzy, many companies were looted and the employees discarded like yesterday's Wall Street Journal. Today, companies with a healthy bottom line are laying off employees, it seems, just to impress the Barons of Wall Street. During the 1990s, while new jobs were created, medical care and a wage that is apace with the purchasing power of wages in the 1970s are few and far between for working America. Again at the beginning of the new century, economists are projecting a downturn in the economy and many plants have notified employees that production will be cut or entire shifts eliminated.

Nowhere has the tragedy of job loss been acted out more disastrously than in the inner cities and to a lesser extent in nearly every town and city in America. Pamala Irving Jackson (1991) sheds light on the consequences of our lack of will to do something about gangs. After reviewing unemployment figures, crime statistics, gang crime statistics, and other demographic variables in all cities in the United States with a population over 25,000, she concludes that loss of jobs and the social dislocation caused by the transition of the American economy has harmed us far beyond what we thought could have been possible. Jackson asserts that the result has been a rise in street gangs. It is her contention that gangs serve a useful social purpose by providing acceptance, recognition, and a sense of belonging. It used to be that these were the things one gained from one's family or from one's employment or union. However when there are no meaningful job prospects, a multitude of single parent families, irresponsible parents, a glorification of violence, a supply of weapons, and a plentiful supply of cheap crack cocaine for use and resale, we should hardly be surprised at the consequences.

Our knee-jerk reaction has been to hire more police, build more prisons, and to send the gangster off to prison for longer periods of time. Few of us doubt the need for police, for evil people exist among us and we need protection. Few of us would quarrel with the existence of prisons; an orderly society must separate criminals from law-abiding citizens. However, we are compelled to ask, how many people must we lock up before such tactics begin to offer a return? Today, according to the Bureau of Justice Statistics, we have over 1.2 million people in prisons. By the end of 2000 we will probably have 2 million people in prisons and jails. Add to this another 3 million people on probation and parole and we are talking about a large chunk of the American population. Where does it end?

Gangs are an Endemic Problem

According to media accounts and many scholars, our nation is in trouble. We are assailed with daily accounts of violent gang activity and with the speculation that our nation's youth, particularly our African-American youth, are a lost generation. An article in Newsweek (1993) is illustrative of media accounts: "Law enforcement and public-health officials describe a virtual 'epidemic' of youth violence in the last five years, spreading from the inner cities to the suburbs." Indeed, youth crime, violence and gang activity are two sides of the same coin. According to The 1992 Law Enforcement Survey (Knox, et al.), Police Chiefs around the nation estimated that over 14% of total crime in their jurisdiction was caused by gang activity. County Sheriffs estimated that over 11% of all crime was the result of gang activity. In addition, 89% of Police Chiefs and over 78% of County Sheriffs throughout the nation stated that youth gangs were a problem in their jurisdictions. In addition to violent crimes they cite drug sales, burglary, robbery, drive-by shootings and car theft as the more troublesome activities of youth gangs (Knox, et al, 1992).

A more recent (1994) estimate of street gang activity is put forward by the St. Louis Police Department Intelligence Division (Gang Section). They estimated that between 240,000 and 400,000 gang members in up to 9,000 gangs are active in the United States. The average age is 16-17 years of age with some members up to age 26 and older. The report points out that systems for reporting gang-related crime is grossly inadequate, but still we can glean some useful estimates of crime from existing systems.

There appears to be not one, but two gang problems in America. One is the problem that we read about in the media and of which we are all fearful: random violence. For example, we do not know who, or how many of the young people in the movie theater with us, are armed and ready to use weapons against others in retaliation for a real or imagined insult, thereby endangering us if we are caught in the resultant crossfire. According to the Center for Disease Control (CDC) one in five high school youth carry a weapon at least once a month for self-protection or use in a fight (1991). The second problem is that our elected officials at the state and federal level seem to be unwilling, or unable, to address the real issues that have brought about the formation of gangs. Instead they attack the symptoms and ignore more fundamental and basic reasons for the spread of gangs.

It is not too late to attack the problem, but our list of options are growing smaller. It has now become frighteningly apparent that gangs are not confined to the inner city but have spread to smaller towns across America and that they follow a weakness in the social fabric composed of the socially and economically disadvantaged. Thus, perhaps we have passed beyond an "epidemic" to what we must call the endemic problem of gangs.

Until now, what energy federal, state, and local policy makers have devoted to gangs has been repressive in nature and has not led to the development of a long term perspective in the fight against gangs and crime. Some jurisdictions have awakened to the need for strategic planning and The 1992 Law Enforcement Survey reveals that as the threat of gangs increase, so too does the likelihood that the police or sheriffs department will have a strategic plan to deal with the problem (Knox, et. al.). Still, these strategic plans are for the police and rarely do they include not only plans for suppression, but also plans for the economic, social, medical and educational needs of the community.

It should be clear by now that quick-fix approaches to crime and gangs are ineffective, as are repressive measures alone. Our prisons are full, probation caseloads are unmanageable, and valuable resources have been diverted away from programs that benefit the general good such as parks, education, medical care, and transportation. Unfortunately the "quick fix" mentality dominates crime policy generally, and methods for dealing with crime are merely a reflection of broader policy failure.

Homeboys, Guns, and Mobility

Why young people join gangs may be a puzzle for some, but there are some well thought out explanations. Knox (1991) neatly summarizes the thoughts of various scholars on why young people join gangs. Thrasher (1936) called our attention to a lack of controls, a permissive environment and the presence of criminals who have high status in the community as factors that promote gang activity. Whyte (1943), as did Thrasher, saw gangs arising from the continuous association of members over a long period of time. Cohen (1955) focused upon social class and pointed to the frustration of lower class boys in their search for status in a world favoring middle class boys.

Bloch and Niederhoffer (1958) recognized the importance of family and called our attention to the role gangs play as family substitutes, providing such things as support and recognition, which are not found in the existing social structure. Cloward and Ohlin (1959) stress the lack of opportunities in the legitimate opportunity structure and the corresponding presence of opportunities in the illegitimate opportunity structure. They point out that when there is no opportunity to be found legitimately, youth will turn to the illegitimate opportunity structure. Klein (1968) asserts that external realities such as poverty, poor job opportunities, and dysfunctional families, to name just three, drive young people together in a meager effort to make life more endurable.

Yablonsky states that young people join gangs for protection and a sense of belonging (Houston, 1993). Jackson calls our attention to the vacuum created by a lack of employment, and suggests that youth join a gang in order to fill a need for self esteem and a sense of belonging. In a survey of police gang specialists (Knox, et al. 1992) the respondents report that in their opinion youth join gangs out of a need for self-esteem, a need for a sense of belonging, as well as in response to pressure from friends and acquaintances. Also cited as moderately important are a need for protection, family influence, and the ability to commit illegal acts for financial gain. One officer stated that white youths in his jurisdiction join gangs as an activity. This may be a particularly disturbing observation in that, as he observes, many of these youths are from intact families and have not suffered the privation common to many inner city youths.

Whatever the reasons for the youthful propensity to join gangs, it may well be that gangs as we know them today are the end result of technological advances, economic change and social neglect. For example, the automobile has proven to be a mixed blessing. The automobile provides unparalleled mobility but at the same time gave birth to a variety of modern social problems including the ability of criminals and gangsters to easily move around in pursuit of drugs, loot, or to commit drive-by shootings.

We can arguably trace the modern gang to the mid 1950's when the Federal Aid Highway Transportation Act was passed by the United States Congress. The intent of the sponsors of the legislation was to develop a highway system capable of moving supplies and military resources around the nation in the event of a national emergency. Perhaps the most unanticipated consequence of the interstate highway system is that it enabled the middle class to drive out of the city a comfortable distance, build a home and commute to work. The result was the flight of the middle class from the central city and with them a stable tax base. Simultaneously, a demographic shift was occurring among rural residents, both black and white. Due to technological and social changes, farming became less labor intensive and people began to be pushed off the farm and were lured to the cities by the promise of jobs. The available housing served the poor immigrants, and many were able to secure adequate employment. For over a decade cities were able to maintain services and an adequate tax base. Then in the 1970's jobs began to leave the central cities and with them an erosion of the tax base began to occur. Thus, the cities were unable to keep up with the demand for services, resulting in a downward spiral to decay.

As the migration of rural workers and southern African -Americans to northern American cities progressed, initially work was to be found in the city. However, as jobs began to flow out of the northern cities to the suburbs, the sunbelt and to foreign countries there also occurred a slow decline in the standard of living of those left behind. Unable to find employment, unable keep up with the demand for greater skills, and unable to travel to the suburbs for employment, many inner city workers began to take on an air of desperation and hopelessness.

With the declining standard of living also went a declining tax base and the services normally paid for by a prosperous tax base.

The extent of the damage done to urban life is illustrated by noting that in 1970 26% of our national income was derived from manufacturing; in 1987 that percentage had fallen to 20%. During the period 1970-1987 the number of manufacturing jobs in the United States remained relatively constant, that is there was a net loss of approximately 100,000 jobs; a drop from 19 million jobs in 1970 to 18.9 million jobs in 1987. However, during that time many jobs were relocated from the inner city to the suburbs and to the sun-belt. During the same time period, 1970-1987, expenditures for new plants and equipment fell from 60% to 54% (1987 Census of Manufactures).

Most economists and politicians will point out that there was a net increase of service sector jobs during this time. That is true, but many inner city inhabitants were ill-prepared to take these jobs as well. There appears to be a paradox here in that during this time (roughly 1970-1980) the individual income from manufacturing increased by three times. The paradox fades when one considers who was left out of the prosperity of the 1970's and 80's: inner city residents who are mostly minority.

With declining prospects for employment, declining funds available for training, and no incentives to keep employers near the available labor pool, the result was a chronically high unemployment rate for healthy males, a spiraling crime rate, and gangs. The process was repeated all over the nation to one extent or another. As employers left the cities and towns either by relocation or because of downsizing, a vacuum was created that was filled to a large extent by gangs. This is the point at which Pamela Irving Jackson steps in and correctly identifies the lack of employment prospects as a contributing factor in the reemergence of gangs.

The prosperity of the 90s seems to have contributed to a decline in the growth rate of gangs, or a least a slowing of the rate of growth. However, they have not gone away as gangs follow the fault line of poverty and hopelessness that runs throughout American society. As a consequence, we see gangs appearing in somewhat unexpected places. For example, a recent survey in Western Michigan reveals that in the Kalamazoo and Ottawa County Juvenile Detention Centers, more than 60% of youth surveyed claim to be a member of a gang. This is noteworthy due to the prosperity and very conservative nature of the area.

The failure to adequately confront the proliferation of guns in today's society has also had a profound impact on how gang members do business. Formerly, disputes were handled with fists, knives, clubs, zip guns, and occasionally a "real "gun. Today we read daily accounts of guns used in drive-by shootings, to even the odds during a petty argument, and as a means to settle disputes over turf. Thus the automobile and the gun are powerful tools used by gang members to intimidate competitors, enforce discipline, and to expand their influence. Over half of the respondents to the **1992 Law Enforcement Survey** revealed that youth gangs in their jurisdictions were the perpetrators of drive-by shootings (Knox, et al.).

Since 1980 crack cocaine has emerged as a cheap and profitable source of money for street gangs, and we seem powerless to stem the flow of drugs of any kind into the country (Currie, 1993). As legitimate employment possibilities declined, entrepreneurs stepped into the void and offered relatively high paying jobs to those willing to take the risk. We should not be surprised that young people in the inner city want the same access to *the American Dream* as do other youth, and that they are willing to innovate in order to obtain that dream. Gangs have supplied the organization and willing workers have provided the labor to supply crack and other drugs to willing customers in an innovative approach to *the American Dream.*

> *Proposition # 14: Youth join a gang to meet a need that is not being met in the home environment. Thus efforts to meet the needs of the family will decrease gang membership.*

A Gang Typology

One misconception is that street gangs are confined to the mostly black or Hispanic inner city. It is true that minorities make up the bulk of gang membership, but the reasons are related to poverty and the inability of many minority members to become fully integrated into mainstream America. However, to think that all gangs are minority or that white youth do not join gangs is not true. That fact was brutally brought to light in May, 1993 in Davenport, Iowa when four white boys, purporting to belong to the Vice Lords, a well known black Chicago Street gang, murdered a high school senior for the keys to her car (Terry, 1994). Cooper (1994) also found that white, middle-class children were joining gangs as an activity and because they identified with black gang members. In addition the St. Louis Police Department has documented the appearance of street gangs in more affluent areas of their city (1994).

In one research project by the National Gang Crime Research Center, 29.1% of the respondents stated that their gang is racially integrated (Knox, et al.). Subsequent research has documented that white youth join street gangs for the same reasons as minority youth. Clearly, variables are at work in American society that must dealt with.

The definition of a gang is somewhat elusive, but most authorities agree that in order to avoid identifying members of the high school football team or a college fraternity as a gang, the following components must be present in a definition of a gang: (1) a group of two or more; (2) the group members must be in regular contact and identify with each other and identify themselves as a gang, organization, or organization; (3) group members must subscribe to a code of conduct and use certain colors, signs, and signals for identification; and (4) activities must revolve around illegal behavior. Obviously, the key component is the presence of illegal activities.

Street gangs break down into two basic groups, People (which includes the west coast Blood gangs) and Folks (which includes the west coast Crips gangs). Loyalty is prized very highly and both "nations" have a clannish form of identification including certain forms of jewelry, costume, and insignia. For example, Folk gang members all wear or indicate membership by wearing their identifiers on the right side such a cap tilted to the right. People gang members wear their identifiers to the left. Clearly we are not including white gangs such as the Aryan Brotherhood, the KKK, Biker Gangs, or other security threat groups who do not fit into this typology.

Knox, et al. (1994) found that basically there are no ideological differences between People and Folks. A few minor differences did show up: folk gang members reported that their gang was racially mixed (70.4% compared to 59.7% of Peoples gang members), more folks reported shoot-outs with police, and fewer folks are deterred by the threat of a natural life sentence for committing a gun crime.

There are literally thousands of gangs across the nation. Some are designed more for social reasons, others exist primarily for the pursuit of violence, and others affect a corporate approach to the distribution of drugs. (See Curry and Decker, 1998, for a good discussion of gangs and their organization). Figure 7.3 is a partial list of gangs according to People or Folks allegiance. This list reflects primarily a Chicago orientation and illustrates the migration of the gangs from Chicago out to the rest of the mid-west.

Gangs and the American Dream

The American Dream is a part of our mythology and is a concept that captures the essence of the American spirit. It is a belief that if one just works hard enough, he or she will overcome any obstacle and achieve material success. In turn success will provide public testimony of one's worth as an individual. *The American Dream* is promoted by our culture, our politicians, and our legends and

Figure 7.3

People and Folks
(a partial listing)

Peoples Gangs	Folks Gangs
Bloods	Crips
Four Corner Hustlers	Almighty Ambrose
Black p Stone Nation	Brothers of theStruggle
Conservative Vice Lords	Black Disciples
Familia Stones	Black Gangster Nation
Honky Head	Black Souls
Insane Vice Lords	Gangster Disciples
Latin Counts	F.B.I.
Latin Kings	Harrison Gents
Loco Boys	Insane Spanish Cobras
Peoples Gangs	Folks Gangs
Mickey Cobras	Simon City Royals
Traveling Vice Lords	Maniac Royals
Twin City Boys	Satans Disciples
Unknown Vice Lords	Two six Nation
Vice Lords	Young Latin Organization
Northsiders	Black Activitist Disciples
Insane two-twos	Winged Disciples
	Washington Park Disciples
	Sons and Daughters of the
	Divine Temple of the Universal Star Inc.
	Insane Gangster Disciples
	15th Street Disciples
	89th Street Disciples
	Young Voters of Illinois Inc.

lore all hold the rags to riches ideal up for emulation and adoration. We are encouraged to work hard and compete for material success. Just because one lives in the inner city does not mean that they do not, or should not, have access to the *American Dream*. Gangs may be in some ways a manifestation of a desire for a piece of the American Dream.

Jennifer L. Hochschild (1995) found that blacks and whites both believe in *the American Dream*. In one survey of Californians, 70% of blacks and 80% of whites agree that "trying to get ahead is very important in '"making someone a true American.'" However, in her view, whites and blacks see "a barrier, if not an enemy, when they look at each other," in that many blacks see themselves as being denied a place at the table and whites see blacks as making excessive demands.

In her research, she found that the percentage of blacks who perceived they had a shot at *the American Dream* had actually declined. In 1954 a survey question asked of blacks "Life will be better for you...in the next few years than it is now." Sixty-four percent (64%) agreed with this statement. In 1989 a similar question was asked, "My opportunities for promotion are high." Thirty-four percent (34%) agreed with this statement. Similarly, in 1991 the question was asked, "In the next five years, how likely are you to be promoted?" Forty-three percent (43%) stated likely or very likely. Thus, in her view if blacks and whites continue to hold on to their views, a society based on belief in *the American Dream* is in jeopardy.

A unique look at crime in American Society is found in **Crime and the American Dream** (Messner and Rosenfeld, 1996). It is an excellent book that recasts an American aphorism in terms of opportunity and how we access that opportunity. According to the authors, *the American Dream* has been responsible for much that is good in American society: technological innovation, economic expansion, social mobility, and so on. However, it is also responsible for much on the dark side of the American psyche: it drives people apart, weakens a sense of community, and instills a drive to succeed at any cost.

Messner and Rosenfeld call another point to mind; that is the spirit of capitalism and its birth. *The American Dream* has its institutional underpinnings in the economy. A capitalist economy presumes an attraction to monetary rewards as a result of achievement and property-owners are profit oriented and eager to invest. The resultant competition demands that firms keep up with a changing market and workers must keep up with changing skill requirements. As a consequence, "a capitalist economy cultivates a competitive, innovative spirit" (Messner and Rosenfeld, 1996).

Capitalism in America is different from that found in the rest of the world. In America capitalism has an "exaggerated emphasis on monetary success and the unrestrained receptivity to innovation" (Messner and Rosenfeld, 1996). The goal of success overwhelms other goals and becomes the only measurement of achievement. This, according to Messner and Rosenfeld, tilts the balance of power towards the economy.

Capitalism in America developed free of preexisting institutions, as was not the case in other societies. As a result American society was profoundly shaped by the requirements of capitalist economic development. Thus, a purity of form emerged in America that is unknown in other societies in which capitalism was imposed on social institutions whose roots and traditions go back several hundred years at least.

The result is a culture that both stimulates crime and fosters weak social control because of the dominance of the economy. The stimulation of crime derives largely from the content of *the American Dream*. That is, according to Messner and Rosenfeld, a strong, relentless pressure for everyone to succeed is defined in terms of monetary goals. This pressure fosters a willingness to substitute efficient but illegal means in the pursuit of success. At the same time, they argue, *the American Dream* does not contain within it strong injunctions against substituting more effective, illegitimate means for less effective, legitimate means in the pursuit of monetary success. Quite the contrary, the message is to succeed at any cost.

One reason the prosocial messages are not given credence at times is that certain tendencies in favor of the economy overwhelm the institutional balance of power. As a consequence, family, schools, churches and synagogues and other institutional influences are devalued and play a subservient role to the economy. As a consequence, it becomes harder and harder for the controlling institutions in American society to do what they are supposed to do: control youthful impulses, socialize the young, and act as a leveling influence throughout society.

As Messner and Rosenfeld (1996) point out:

> Impotent families and schools are severely handicapped in their efforts to promote allegiance to social rules, including legal prohibitions. In the absence of strong socializing influences from

these non-economic institutions, the cultural message that comes
through with greatest force is the one most compatible with the logic
of the economy: the competitive, individualistic,
and materialistic message of the American Dream.

Young people who pursue a piece of the *American Dream*, who do not
have the benefit of strong, loving parents, and who are enjoined to pursue the
same goals as everyone else often come up against barriers that prevent their
achievement of legitimate goals. One of the major barriers is poverty. Street gangs
appear to thrive wherever poverty and normlessness exist, thus any discussion of
gangs and crime is not complete without a concomitant discussion of poverty.
The presence of poverty is not a necessary precondition for the existence of crime,
but poverty does establish the conditions that breed crime (Gibbons, 1992). The
viability of a strong democracy is dependent on a large middle class and in the past
two decades the growth of the middle class has slowed. Many working class
families are finding that the purchasing power continues to slip (Sweeney, 1997).

In 1991 35.7 million Americans, or roughly 14% of the population, lived
under conditions of poverty. By 1998, that figure had dropped slightly to 34.5
million people or 12.5%. What is not measured, however, is the number of people
trapped in a cycle of too much month and not enough money.

Our nation's cities have undergone a transformation caused by the erosion
of their tax base in the last 25 years, but add to that transformation the fact that
many of our citizens who live in the inner cities and smaller towns appear to be
trapped by endemic poverty, hopelessness and despair. From 1973 to the early
1990s poverty increased dramatically (Devine and Wright, 1993). Poverty had
steadily decreased until 1973 when it began to track upward. Specifically they
found that:

* Nearly a third of black households (29.7%) have been poor in more than
  half of the nineteen years studied, while only 4.5% of white households
  have experienced ten or more years of impoverishment.

* Attesting to the feminization of poverty thesis, female-headed
  households are more than five times as likely to have experienced five
  or more years of poverty and better than seven times as likely to have
  experienced ten or more years of poverty than male-headed households.

* Only one in eight households (12.4%) headed by black females have not
  had a single year in poverty. The corresponding figure for households
  headed by white females, black males, and white males are 44.4%,
  43.9%, and 79.6% respectively. Similarly, half of the black female-
  headed households were poor in ten or more years, while 21.6% of black

male-headed households, and only 1.8% of white male-headed households experienced this degree of impoverishment.

While poverty continues to grip the lives of many of our fellow citizens, many minorities have been able to take advantage of opportunities and through education and hard work moved out of dead end lives into lives characterized by affluence and comfort. Those minority members who have taken advantage of opportunity and moved out of the inner city have done so leaving behind fewer legitimate opportunities and fewer positive role models for those left behind to emulate. The result has been a higher degree of alienation and rebelliousness among those who see few opportunities.

The flight of upwardly mobile minorities left a vacuum waiting to be filled and gangs moved into the vacuum and provided a vehicle for those aspiring to better things (Jackson, 1991). During the 1980's this drama began to be played out in smaller towns and cities throughout the United States and the loss of opportunity suffered by minorities since the early 1970's also began to be felt by the white, working class in ever larger numbers.

The American Dream lived on in spite of endemic poverty and the loss of legitimate opportunity through manufacturing jobs. Those who use the phrase freely should take heart because in spite of rhetoric to the contrary, inner city residents and their small town brethren still subscribe to *The American Dream*. The twist is in the mode of adaptation to a dysfunctional opportunity structure. Drugs, weapons, extortion, fees, and purchase or start of small businesses with illegitimate profits are all instruments used by gangs to achieve *The American Dream*.

The Gang Life

The National Gang Crime Research Center has conducted a number of projects including **The Economics of Gang Life** Knox, et al., (1995). The findings of this project sheds light on a number of issues of gang economics and *the American Dream*:

* The gang appears to function much like a union guild.

* Gangs operate a wide variety of cash business enterprises.

* Gang members pay dues which flow upward to the leadership.

* Organizationally sophisticated gangs have a number of economic functions.

* Gangs serve a welfare function in that they provide welfare payments for members who are in jail.

A questionnaire was administered to a sample of jail inmates, gang intervention programs, reform school inmates, and children in a juvenile detention center in a number of states across the nation. The results are somewhat startling and illustrate that *the American Dream* is alive and well in American cities.

Gang members believe in the same culturally acceptable goals as the rest of society. The survey asked gang members to agree or disagree with the statement "I believe in such things as education, having a nice home, and supporting my family." Over ninety-three percent (93.6%) agreed with this statement.

Collecting protection money on behalf of the gang. Approximately one-fifth of the gang members surveyed (21.2%) stated they had collected protection money on behalf of their gang. Additional information on how much money the respondent collected in protection money during the last year was available for N=155 respondents. The 155 respondents report collecting from a low of $1.50 to a high of $12,000. The mean amount of protection money collected was $8,696.

Parents of gang members are usually described as being employed. Respondents were asked "Which best describes your father: has a regular job or has no regular job. Most of the gang members (70.8%, N=635) described their father as having a regular job. However, nearly one-third (29.2%) described their father as not having a regular job.

In the same fashion the survey also asked the respondent to describe their mother. Most gang members (72.7%) described their mother as having a regular job. On the other hand, a little over one-fourth described their mother as not having a regular job.

Family structure. Respondents were asked to describe their family of origin. Among gang members the largest group (42.1%) state that they come from an intact family, that is a family characterized by mother, father, and siblings. Nearly sixteen percent (15.9%) state they come from a family characterized by a mother, step-father, and siblings, 3.4% state they came from a family characterized by a step-mother, father and siblings. However, one-third of gang members state they come from a family composed of mother and siblings. Only 2% indicated a father and siblings.

The parent(s) of most gang members held or hold full time employment according to gang members who responded to the questionnaire. This holds true whether or not the gang member is from a single parent family or an intact family.

Number of close friends/Associates who are gang members. Acceptance of criminal behavior and the learning of specific skills is conducted in intimate relationships and as a consequence the researchers thought that it was important to determine the number of close friends who are gang members. The survey asked "How many of your close friends and associates are gang members?" Possible responses were: zero, one, two, three, four, five or more. The vast majority (76.9%) indicated they had five or more close friends and associates who are gang members.

Age when first entered a gang. The range of responses indicating the age when the respondent entered a gang was broad (1 year of age to age 35) but the mean age was 12.9 years

Reasons for joining a gang. The survey asked "What one reason comes closest to describing why you first joined any gang?" One fourth (24.6%) claim they joined a gang to "make money." The largest response (37.9%) indicated they "just grew up in it." Other responses include: to be with friends (14.7%), because a family member was in the gang (9.7%), and for protection (2.7%).

Operation of legitimate businesses. The operation of legitimate businesses is important in that at the least it provides cover for the laundering of illegitimate profits. The question was asked, "Does the gang you belong to have any legitimate businesses?" Just under one-half (47.5%) indicated that their gang does have legitimate businesses.

Older gang members manage the gangs. The stereotypical view held by most Americans of street gangs is that they are loosely knit organizations that are managed by and for young people for a variety of purposes, including for social purposes and for criminal activities. The survey asked, "Does your gang have adult leaders who have been in the gang for many years?" Eighty-seven percent (87.8%) of the respondents answered yes, their gang has adult leaders who have been in the gang for many years. Thus, a reasonable conclusion is that these are not youth gangs.

Working as a "runner" in a retail drug operation. If one has accepted culturally accepted goals and legitimate opportunities are closed, the innovative person will seek out those opportunities in the illegitimate opportunity structure that meets his or her needs. The survey asked "Have you ever worked as a runner in a retail drug sales operation?" Nearly one-half (43.8%) of the respondents stated they had worked as a runner. A follow-up question on income asked "How much money do you get to keep on the average?" The results ranged from a low of $50.00 to a high of $25,000 with the mean at $1,631.

Committing crimes of financial gain with the gang. The survey asked "Have you ever committed a crime for financial gain with your gang?" Over one-half (61.3%) stated they had committed a crime for financial gain with their gang. Specifically, 75.2% sold drugs, 34.9% committed burglary, 48% robbery, 41.5% car theft, 16.4% arson, 28.9% shoplifting, and 48.6% transported guns, drugs, or a wanted person.

Views on work. A strong work ethic is important for individual success in the contemporary U.S. The survey asked, "Which sentence best describes your thoughts on work?" Most gang members (74.3%) responded that "work is good and necessary." Eight percent (8.8%) state "My mother/father worked their tails off and didn't get a thing for it," 7.9% replied "I had a job once and didn't like it," and 9% stated "there's no sense working for the man because he doesn't appreciate it."

The survey also attempted to determine if gang members had been exposed to role models who did have a regular job and were admired by the individual. The fact is, a little over three-fourths (78.2%) of responding gang members stated they do know working people they look up to and admire.

Views on racial oppression and poverty. Two questions attempted to get at the attitude of gang members in regard to poverty. About one fourth of the gang members (27.7%) agreed with the statement "Being poor is mostly a racial thing." Nearly a fourth (23.7%) also agreed with the statement "I am poor mostly because of my skin color." An interesting caveat is that some white gang members complained about this item in the survey as being "offensive" to them, particularly those who identified themselves as skinheads, neo-nazis, and members of the Aryan Nation/Brotherhood.

Family economic backgrounds of gang members. A series of questions were included in the survey instrument that examines the economic conditions in which the respondents live. Over half (62.7%) of the gang members who responded stated that their family "sometimes used food stamps." Half (55.8%) stated their family "sometimes received public aid or welfare checks." Nearly half (47.8%) replied "their family had to take odd jobs just to get by." A third (33.4%) said their family "sometimes received food baskets from churches, etc. Over one-fourth said their family "sometimes lived in a public housing project." Two-fifths (40.5%) said their family "sometimes had lights, gas, and telephone cut off because the bills could not be paid." Over one-third (35.6%) stated "sometimes there was very little if any food in the house." On the other hand in a rather bizarre revelation, over half (61.5%) stated they "sometimes got a regular weekly allowance for spending money."

Regular employment and losing a job. Two-thirds (68.8%) of the professed gang members stated they had held a legitimate job at one time and over one-fourth said they had been fired from any legitimate job.

Gangs serve a welfare function. The survey asked if the gang served needy members. Three-fourths (77.7%) stated that their gang does help needy gang members.

Extortion of protection money from small businesses. The survey asked "Have you ever engaged in shakedowns of small businesses?" More than one-fourth (27.5%) stated they had done so. A follow-up question sought to determine which types of target preferences gang members had. Among those who claimed to extort from small businesses: 41.7% would choose white businesses, 44.6% would choose black businesses, 30.2% would choose Asian businesses, 32.5% would choose Arab businesses, and 31.5% would choose Hispanic/Latino businesses.

The economic study of gangs is valuable for several reasons. Padilla (1992) points out that there is a group of young men and women who have renounced the general culture and who

> have lost faith in the capacity of the society to work on their behalf. Because of this perception of society, many of these young people have organized and created counter-cultural structures that they believe are capable of delivering the kinds of emotional support and material goods the larger society promises but does not make available to youngsters like themselves.

One such structure is the gang (see Padilla, 1992 and Jackson,1991). Gangs provide not only a unit with which to identify, a place for acceptance, and a family substitute, but also an chance for economic opportunity (see Jackson, 1991; Knox, et al, 1992; Vigil, 1993; Knox, 1995).

Padilla (1992) illustrates the perception of "Diamond" gang members who "point out the poignant paradox between having culturally defined goals and ineffective but socially legitimate means for achieving them... the contradiction lies in the absence of avenues and resources necessary for securing the rewards that society most values and which it purports to offer its members." So it is with the majority of gang members interviewed for the present project.

A positive attitude toward opportunity is important if one is to achieve a measure of success in later life. Merton points out that a dysfunctional opportunity structure promotes innovation (Merton, 1957, see also Cloward and Ohlin, 1960) and gangs have moved into the vacuum created by the loss of manufacturing jobs in many cities as a vehicle for innovation (Jackson, 1991). Table 7.3 illustrates the relationship between parents employment and employment of gang members.

The data from the study by the National Gang Crime Research Center points out that *the American Dream* is alive and well. The majority of respondents report that work is good and necessary. Indeed, work provides a purpose and rhythm to our lives that is irreplaceable. It helps to structure our time and provides a feeling of worthwhileness. Thus, if young people do not have a regular job or if they feel shut out of legitimate opportunities, they can structure their time and earn a good income by pursuing opportunities in the illegitimate opportunity structure.

Findings from the above study illustrate that gang members believe in the same things as everyone else in American society. In addition, they are first rate consumers and entrepreneurs. A number of businesses have been started on profits from gang activities and those businesses contribute to the overall economic blood of the community (Knox, et al., 1995).

Poverty appears to play a part in gang membership as illustrated by the data. Nearly two-thirds of the respondents state that they have lived in public housing and had received welfare in one form or another. When coupled with the fact that of those reporting who felt shut out of legitimate opportunity (58.5%) (58.5%) and whose mother had ever been arrested, we have an explosive

Table 7.3
Employment and Opportunity

	Father has a Regular Job Percent Yes	Mother has a Regular Job Percent Yes	Gang Member Felt Shut Out Percent Yes
I believe in such things as education, having a nice home and supporting my family			
False	58.0%	53.8%	73.8%
True	71.8%	73.9%	47.8%
	p=.02	p<.001	p<.001
Which best describes your father?			
Has a regular job	n.a.		71.6%
Has no regular job	n.a		61.0%
			P=.003
Have you ever held a part-time job?			
No	63.9%	67.6%	n.a.
Yes	74.0%	75.7%	n.a.
Which best describes the type of family you come from?			
Mother, father, and sibling	78.9%	n.s.	n.s.
Single other and siblings	57.5%	n.s.	n.s.
Which sentence best describes your thoughts on work?			
Work is good and necessary	74.1%	75.0%	45.0%
There's no sens in working for the man because he doesn't appreciate it.	50.7%	61.3%	55.0%
I am poor mostly because of my skin color.			
False	72.8%	n.s.	43.9%
True	63.1%	n.s.	63.0%
My family			
Sometimes used food stamps	66.4%	67.1%	n.s.
Never used food stamps	78.2%	83.3%	n.s.
Sometimes received public aid or welfare checks	65.0%	65.4%	n.s.
Never received public air or welfare checks	78.1%	82.8%	n.s.
	p<.02	p<.001	
Sometimes lives in a public housing project	66.6%	68.7%	n.s.
Never lived in a public housing project	73.3%	75.2%	n.s.
	p=.05	p=.04	

Table 7.3
Employment and Opportunity
(Continued)

	Father has a Regular Job Percent Yes	Mother has a Regular Job Percent Yes	Gang Member Felt Shut Out Percent Yes
Has father ever been arrested?			
No	77.8%	n.s.	n.s.
Yes	60.6%		
	p<.001		
Has mother ever been arrested?			
No	74.8%	75.7%	46.1%
Yes	52.0%	58.2%	58.5%
	p<.001	p<.001	p=.004

mixture. There also appears to be a significant relationship between the employment status of parents on a variety of factors that affect the lives of gang members. Thus, it may be that family acts as an important buffer between the young person and continued gang membership. What is not entirely clear is what type of program can bolster these effects and what can juvenile courts, social service agencies, and the private sector do to be of assistance. However, evidence is coming to light that there are approaches and programs that can work in separating individual gang members from gang activity (Palmer, 1994 and Conly, 1993). Clearly, more research is needed if communities are going to successfully combat the allure of gangs.

Gangs have certain signs, colors, and indicators that parents ought to be aware of in order to attempt to deal with a child who has a fascination with gangs. Appendix A illustrates some of the better known signs and if they are spotted in your neighborhood it should be taken as a warning that there is a gang presence. If one sign is crossed out and another sign appears over it, it should be taken as a warning that two rival gangs are present and violence is apt to occur in the near future.

Appendix A also contains a partial listing of mid-west gangs and explains west coast gangs. Mid-west and west coast gangs have migrated to smaller cities and towns and one research project found that 89 percent of Police Chiefs in a nation-wide survey agreed that gangs are a problem in their jurisdiction (Knox, et al., 1992). In another study, Jerome Skolnick, found that the Bloods and Crips of the west coast had migrated as far as Kansas City by 1989 (Skolnick, 1989). Parents can look for the noted drawings on school books and other possessions of a child and an awareness of the type of clothing worn or preferred by a child can be an indicator of a gang "wannabe," associate, or member. If a parent is aware of a child becoming involved with a gang, he or she should contact a local social service agency, juvenile court, or the police juvenile division for advice.

*Proposition #15: If we can unleash legitimate
economic opportunity in selected areas of our
nation, we will see a decrease in gang membership.*

The Juvenile Court

As pointed out earlier the first juvenile court was started in Cook county in 1899. The principles of the Court are basically the same as they were nearly 100 years ago: to protect the child from the harshness of the adversary system and to provide treatment and guidance to wayward youth. To be sure, American culture and events have overwhelmed the capacity of the juvenile court to fully accomplish that mission and many legislatures are moving to make it easier to try juveniles in adult court for more serious crimes. However, this discussion is restricted to the handling of children in juvenile court.

Referral

Before a child can be brought into juvenile court he or she must be referred. That is a formal complaint must be made by an adult and the adult must sign a petition. The referral can come from a police officer, teacher, parent, or anyone else who has firsthand knowledge that a crime has been, or may have been committed by the child in question. If a police officer has made the referral and signed a petition, it is accompanied by an arrest report and other supporting documents. The referral is then sent on by an established mechanism to the juvenile court where an intake officer will take it up. The Intake Officer must give the child and parents at least 24 hour notice of an initial hearing and notice of the charges, in writing.

Initial/Detention Hearing

This hearing is the initial contact between the court and the child and parent(s). The hearing begins with the Officer advising the child and parents of his or her constitutional rights. The child is then made aware of the charges against him or her and they are given a chance to explain or to speak on their own behalf. The hearing is informal and the child's best interests are at heart. After the Intake Officer has determined that an offense has occurred further decisions must be made. At this point, the hearing becomes a detention hearing. Often a matter is settled informally by referral to a community agency such as a child guidance clinic or, in less serious matters, the child and parents may agree to a period of informal probation.

The Intake Officer must determine whether or not the child is a danger to himself or to the community. Unlike adults, the court can hold a child if he or she is deemed to be a threat to himself. If the child is released, pending a Formal Hearing, he or she must be released to a responsible adult, which can be a problem at times.

Adjudicatory Hearing

If the child's case is not handled informally, he or she will be given notice of an Adjudicatory Hearing. Since the case of **In Re Gault** in 1967, the juvenile court has undergone a great many changes. The child must be accorded the same rights as adults, particularly:

1). sufficient notice of a hearing and which specifies the charges against the child,
2). the child has a right to counsel and if the child cannot afford an attorney, one will be appointed,

3). the child holds the privilege against self-incrimination,

4). the child has the right to confront witnesses and to cross-examine witnesses.

The child also has the right to a jury trial which will vary in size by the state. In short, children have the same rights as adults.

Today the adjudicatory hearing is more formal than it was prior to the Gault decision. The judge begins the hearing by advising the child of his or her rights and the charges against him or her and the judge again asks the child how he or she pleads. The prosecutor begins by presenting the case and witnesses are called, cross examined by the defense attorney, and so on. Closing arguments will be made and the judge will either order the child held in detention or released to the custody of parent(s) or guardian pending the completion of a pre-disposition report.

Disposition Hearing

The Disposition Hearing will be held a few weeks after the Adjudicatory Hearing because the judge will order the probation department to complete a pre-disposition report prior to the Disposition Hearing. Once released, the child will be assigned to a probation officer for a pre-disposition investigation. In an earlier chapter we discussed the presentence investigation for adults. The pre-hearing investigation is the same, except for a child. The probation officer will gather the facts and make a recommendation to the Judge who will determine the sanction to be applied.

With the pre-disposition hearing report in hand, the judge will ask the child, his attorney, and often the parent(s) to stand before him or her to hear the disposition. Many factors come into play in making the disposition: age of the child, seriousness of the offense, prior record, school achievement, and so on. The options before the judge vary depending upon the location. All jurisdictions can: place the child on probation or continue the child on probation, send him or her to state reform school, or send the child to a private residential facility. Beyond that, the options begin to narrow depending upon the progressiveness of the jurisdiction, available money, and local attitudes and values.

It is informative here to briefly comment on the waiver of juveniles to adult court. This practice is the traditional safety valve that permits serious or chronic offenders to be transferred after a hearing in juvenile court. However, since late 1970s the "get tough" attitude regarding juvenile offenders has resulted in reforms aimed at ensuring accountability on the part of juveniles and the vilification of the juvenile court. In the last decade almost every state has modified its laws relating to juvenile court reform and in nearly every instance the direction of reforms has been in the direction of shifting away from the rehabilitation model to the punishment model (Frazier, Bishop, and Lanza-Kaduce, 1999). The Florida experience has revealed that while large numbers of youth have been transferred to adult court, the impact has been negligible. In fact, in some instances it has been found that juveniles sent to adult court serve less time in prison than if they had remained in juvenile court and been placed in a secure juvenile facility. Thus, the lesson seems to be that legislators continue to want to appear tough on crime and fail to think through the consequences of their legislation.

Summary

Juvenile delinquency is a serious problem and it may get worse if we as a nation fail to address problems that contribute to its growth. The reasons for delinquency are many and varied. What is apparent is the value of the family as a buffer to delinquency and as the most important agent in preventing children from becoming delinquent. We can divide delinquents into criminal or status offenders. Status offenders are those children who have committed an offense, which if committed by an adult, would not be a crime. Such offenses as truancy, runaway, and incorrigibility are examples of status offenses.

The juvenile court arose out of a desire to shield the child from the harshness of the adversary system and adult prisons. It began in 1899 in Cook County, Illinois and by 1923 every state except Maine and Wyoming had a juvenile court. If a child is referred to the juvenile court, he or she must have a petition signed by an adult and the first step is the initial hearing. After that the child will go through an intake process, the detention hearing, the adjudicatory hearing, and a disposition hearing. If he or she is placed on probation, a probation officer will be assigned to supervise the child and to oversee his or her treatment program.

Gangs have become a national scandal. No discussion of delinquency would be complete with out an examination of gangs. Street gangs exist in nearly every city in the United States and are now a visible presence in many small towns. Gangs can be divided into People and Folks factions and they are ideologically the same. Differences between the two are mostly concerned with colors, signs, and allegiances.

The Juvenile Court was initially conceived as a means to shield the juvenile from the harshness of the adult court. Many critics today do not believe that the juvenile court is meeting the needs of society and is too lenient. However, the problem is not one of a lenient juvenile court, it is a problem of too few resources devoted to the juvenile system.

Bibliography

Herbert Bloch and Arthur Niederhoffer. **The Gang: A Study in Adolescent Behavior**. (New York: Philosophical Press, 1958).

Richard D. Cloward and Lloyd E. Ohlin. **Delinquency and Opportunity**. (New York: The Free Press, 1960).

Albert K. Cohen. **Delinquent Boys: The Culture of the Gang**. (Glencoe, Il: The Free Press, 1955).

Catherine H. Conly. **Street Gangs: Current Knowledge and Strategies**. (Washington, D.C.: National Institute of Justice, 1983). Prepared by Abt Associates under contract #OJP-89-C-009.

Marc Cooper. "Reality Check." **Spin**. 10:4 (July, 1994).

Elliot Currie. **Reckoning: Drugs, the Cities, and the American Future**. (New York: Hill an Wang, 1993).

G. David Curry and Scott H. Decker. **Confronting Gangs: Crime and Community**. Los Angeles, CA: Roxbury Publishing Company. 1998.

Joel A. Devine and James D. Wright. **The Greatest of Evils: Urban Poverty and the American Underclass**. (New York: Aldine De Gruyter, 1993).

James Alan Fox and Glenn Pierce. "American Killers are Getting Younger" from **USA Today Magazine**, January, 1994, pp. 24-26, in **Criminal Justice 95/96**, 19th ed. John J. Sullivan and Joseph L. Victor. Guilford, CN: Duchkin Publishing Group, 1995.

S. J. Fox. 1970. "Juvenile Justice Reform: An Historical Perspective." **Stanford Law Review**. 22: pp. 1187-1239.

Frazier, Charles E., Donna M. Bishop, and Lonn Lanza-Kaduce. "Get-Tough Juvenile Justice Reforms: The Florida Experience," **The Annals of the American Academy of Political and Social Science**. V 564 (July 1999). 167-184.

Don C. Gibbons. **Society, Crime, and Criminal Behavior**, 6th ed. (Englewood Cliffs, NJ: Prentice Hall, 1992).

Jennifer L. Hochschild. **Facing up to the American Dream: Race, Class, and the Soul of the Nation**. Princeton, NJ: Princeton University Press, 1995.

James Houston. "The Violent Gang and Beyond: In Interview with Lewis Yablonsky" **The Gang Journal**. 1:2 (1993) pp. 59-67.

Mary Jensen and Phil Yerington. **Gangs: Shooting from the Hip**. (Longmont, CO: Sopris West) (forthcoming).

Malcom Klein. **The Ladino Hills Project** (Final Report). (Washington, D. C.: Office of Juvenile Delinquency and Youth Development, 1968).

George W. Knox. **An Introduction to Gangs** (New Revised Edition). (Bristol, IN: Wyndham Hall Press, 1994).

George W. Knox, James G. Houston, John A. Laskey, Thomas F. McCurrie, Edward D. Tromanhauser, and David L. Laske. **Gangs and Guns**. (Chicago: National Gang Crime Research Center, 1994).

George W. Knox, Thomas F. McCurrie, James G. Houston, Edward D. Tromanhauser, and John A. Laskey. **The 1994 Illinois Law Enforcement Survey: A Report on Gang Migration and Other Gang Problems in Illinois Today**. (Chicago: National Gang Crime Research Center, 1994).

George W. Knox, Edward D. Tromanhauser, Pamela Irving Jackson, Darn Niklas, James G. Houston, Paul Koch, James R. Sutten, and Dick Ward. **The 1992 Law Enforcement Survey.** (Chicago: National Gang Crime Research Center, 1992).

George W. Knox, Edward D. Tromanhauser, James G. Houston, Brad Martin, Robert E. Morris, Thomas F. McCurrie, John L. Laskey, Dorothy Papachristos, Judith Feinberg, and Charla Waxman. **The Economics of Gang Life**. (Chicago: National Gang Crime Research Center, 1995).

Pamela Irving Jackson. "Crime, Youth Gangs, and Urban Transition: The Social Dislocations of Postindustrial Economic Development." **Justice Quarterly**. 8:3 (1991) pp. 379-397.

Robert K. Merton. Social Theory and Social Structure, rev. ed. (New York: Free Press, 1957).

Steven F. Messner and Richard Rosenfeld. **Crime and the American Dream** 2nd ed. (Belmont, CA: Wadsworth Publishing Company, 1996).

J. Ronald Milavsky. **TV and Violence**. Crime File Study Guide. U.S. Washington, D.C.: Department of Justice (no Date Given).
Felix M. Padilla. **The Gang as an American Enterprise**. (New Brunswick, NJ: Rutgers University Press, 1992).

Ted Palmer. **A Profile of Correctional Effectiveness and New Directions for Research**. (Albany, NY: University of New York Press, 1994).

222

Jerome H. Skolnick. **Gang Organization and Migration.** Research undertaken for the Department of Justice, State of California, 1989.

John Sweeney and David Kusnet. **America Needs a Raise: Fighting for Economic Security and Social Justice**. NY: Houghton Mifflin Company. 1997.

Don Terry. "Killed by Her Friends in an All-White Gang," **New York Times**, May 18, 1994.

William E. Thornton, Jr. and Lydia Voigt. **Delinquency and Justice**, 3rd ed. (New York: McGraw-Hill, Inc, 1992).

Frederick Thrasher. **The Gang.** (Chicago: University of Chicago Press, 1936).

Paul Tracy and Robert Figlio. "Chronic Recidivism in the 1958 Birth Cohort," Paper presented at the American Society of Criminology meeting, Toronto, Canada, October, 1982, in Larry J. Siegal and Joseph J. Senna. **Juvenile Delinquency: Theory, Practice, and Law**, 2nd ed. (St. Paul, MN: West Publishing Co., 1985).

U.S. Bureau of the Census. **1987 Census of Manufacturers**. (Washington, D.C.: U.S. Government Printing Office, 1987).
Diego Vigil. "The Established Gang," in **Gangs: The Origins and Impact of contemporary Youth Gangs in the United States,** Scott Cummings and Daniel J. Monti, eds. (Albany, NY: State University of New York Press, 1993).

William Foote White. **Street Corner Society: The Social Structure of an Italian Slum** 3rd ed. (Chicago: University of Chicago Press, 1943).

Marvin Wolfgang, Robert Figlio, and Thorsten Sellin. **Delinquency in a Birth Cohort**. (Chicago: University of Chicago Press, 1972).
1972

Chapter 8

Citizen Involvement and the Future

Introduction

In the long run if we are to do anything about crime we must do it ourselves. It seems odd that we no longer think the best way to ward off evil spirits is to dance around a bonfire, yet we continue to dance at the alter of repression and negativity. We no longer build hospitals for tuberculosis patients, yet we continue to build prisons for thousands of people who have no business being in prison and who only leave prison more sophisticated and angry. The truth is that if we are going to successfully win our war against crime we need to do more than simply attack the symptoms and dance around the fire. It will require a long-term effort by committed citizens and politicians. The question is, do we have the stamina to do so.

We must continue to mount effective law enforcement activities that are aimed at getting violent offenders off the street. Today, the glorification of violence, the availability of guns, an abundance of youthful males with no positive role models to follow and with no hope for the future, all contribute to a growing community problem. There are a number of evil, pathological people who will continue to victimize us and they must be removed from our midst and placed where they can do no harm to law abiding citizens. On the other hand, there are violators who need guidance more than prison, a job rather than prison industries, and social structure rather than barbed wire.

In the long run, any effort to successfully win against crime must begin at home in a number of ways. We must begin by taking back our families. Once we do that we will take back our streets. This, however, is the toughest task of all. Over the past thirty years we have allowed the informal control mechanisms of shame, ridicule, and ostracism to fall by the way side and the hormones and selfishness of baby boomers have allowed 100,000 years of social evolution to be nearly undone. The family is the cornerstone of any civilization and any behavior that contributes to family disintegration must be changed. Over the past thirty years, the liberalization of attitudes towards divorce and illegitimacy, as well as the acceptance of welfare by able-bodied people have seriously impacted the family. An alarming divorce rate, an over-abundance of teen pregnancies, and children growing up without the benefit of two legitimate parents to discipline and love the child has contributed to delinquency, the growth of gangs, and the escalation of juvenile violence.

There is a place for government in this task. State and federal government can develop policies and programs that are friendly to the family and that assists them without tearing away the values of hard work, acquiring an education or trade, and loyalty to one's employer. Such programs require consensus across all levels of society. Before proceeding, it may be instructive to review the legislative and policy process. Armed with such knowledge, the average citizen is better equipped to recognize empty statements, the falsehoods of ideology, platitudes, and outright lies by those running for political office. If citizens understand the policy process, they are better equipped to demand constructive, effective policies and programs from their legislators. Many of the lessons articulated below are drawn from federal experiences, but the same concepts apply to the state and local level.

Federal Legislative Initiatives and Crime

While the federal response to youth crime and crime in general has been meager, there have been attempts to confront the problem posed by crime, at least in terms of suppression and incarceration. It has been more than thirty years since the **1968 Omnibus Crime Control and Safe Streets Act** was enacted. It has taken more than ten years to get the U.S. Congress to agree on a new crime bill (signed into law by President Clinton in December, 1994). Subsequent to signing of the Crime Bill, Congress attempted to change the "liberal" portions of the bill in order to make it "tougher on crime." Whether or not one feels that the 1994 Crime Bill is too easy on crime or not, the fact remains that Congress may have been working too hard on the wrong issues and it may well be that the best anti-crime and anti-delinquency legislation is that which takes a broader view of society. In the history of juvenile justice legislation, suppression is a recent phenomenon and prior to 1994 legislation was oriented to programs and treatment. Federal legislative efforts to respond to delinquency are neatly summarized by Cavenagh and Teasley (1992).

As early as 1953 the Senate Judiciary Committee held hearings on the problem of juvenile delinquency. Subsequently, President Eisenhower called for legislation to assist the states in fighting youth crime. However, it was not until 1961 that Congress passed the **Juvenile Delinquency and Youth Offenses Control Act of 1961** (P.L. 87-274), which authorized HEW to administer a grant program aimed at developing techniques to control delinquency and to train personnel to control or prevent juvenile delinquency.

In 1968 two acts were passed in regard to juvenile delinquency and crime: **The Juvenile Delinquency Prevention and Control Act** (P.L. 91-445) and **The Omnibus Crime Control and Safe Streets Act** (P.L. 91-351). **The Juvenile Delinquency Prevention and Control Act** replaced the 1961 act and authorized HEW to provide assistance to the states and local governments for improvement of their juvenile justice programs and the coordination of services in their areas. **The Omnibus Crime Control and Safe Streets Act** allowed the use of block grant money by the states for the prevention and control of juvenile delinquency.

A comprehensive approach to juvenile delinquency remained elusive until the **Juvenile Justice and Delinquency Prevention Act of 1974** (P.L. 93-415) was passed by Congress. Titles I and II established the Office of Juvenile Justice and Delinquency Prevention (OJJDP) within the Department of Justice and was given the responsibility to administer block and discretionary grants for the purpose of improving the juvenile justice system and for the prevention of juvenile delinquency. Title III delegates to the DOJ's Office of Juvenile Justice and Juvenile Justice and Delinquency Prevention and HHS's Administration on Children, Youth, and Families the primary responsibility for the administration of current programs aimed at the prevention and control of delinquency and youth gangs. In 1987 the OJJDP authorized the National Youth Gang Suppression and Intervention Program. It is a four stage process that includes: an assessment of the gang problem, a model program development for preventing the rise of youth gangs, a review of the literature on gangs, and a national survey of youth gangs.

In 1988 the **Anti-Drug Abuse Act of 1988** (P.L. 100-690) addressed the gang problem. It established grant programs through the OJJDP for prevention and treatment relating to juvenile gangs, drug abuse and trafficking, and within the

Administration on Children, Youth, and Families for drug abuse education and prevention relating to youth gangs.

1994 Saw passage of the Crime Bill and in 1997 Congress passed the **Violent and Repeat Juvenile Offenders Act**. The purpose of this act ostensibly is to (1) reform juvenile law so that the paramount concerns of the juvenile justice system are providing for the safety of the public and holding juvenile wrongdoers accountable for their actions, while providing the wrongdoers a genuine opportunity for self reform; (2) to revise the procedures in Federal Court that are applicable to the prosecution of juvenile offenders; (3) to address specifically the problem of violent crime and controlled substance offenses committed by youth gangs; and (4) to encourage and promote, consistent with the ideals of federalism, adoption of policies by the states to ensure that the victims of crimes of violence committed by juveniles receive the same level of justice as do victims of violent crimes that are committed by adults.

The reality of the 1997 Act is that it has become easier to waive juveniles to adult court, a number of offenses have been federalized, and funding for federal assistance for prevention programs were either severely criticized or cut entirely. The reader is urged to see Appendix 1 at the end of the chapter for a more complete picture of crime legislation.

With a few exceptions, the effective policy changes that have occurred since 1989 to fight crime have been initiated by agencies within government. For example, in January 1992 Attorney General Barr and FBI Director Sessions announced the assignment of 300 FBI agents to aid in the efforts against gang-related crime. The "Safe Streets" program is meant to develop joint efforts between federal, state, and local law enforcement to combat violent crime in general and gang related crime in particular (FBI Media Release, 1992). In addition, the Bureau of Alcohol, Tobacco and Firearms (ATF) was given the task of establishing a gang intelligence center. The Center is not supposed to be a data based system, but rather a system that allows the inquirer to be put in touch with the law enforcement agency that has the requested information (Cavanagh and Teasley, 1992).

Clearly, Congress has attempted to meet the need of communities as they struggle with the issue of delinquency and crime. However, those efforts are the result of partisan politics and attempts by Congress to be all things to all people. Policy initiatives by the FBI and other law enforcement agencies have resulted in more effective programs to deal with crime than Congressional efforts. In order to understand the problem faced by policy makers, we need to gain an understanding of the policy and legislative process.

Crime vs. the Closed Agenda

The term "policy" is a much misunderstood word. For example, a Police Chief may state that his department has a policy on gangs, and the mayor may tell the press that the city has a policy to aid single parent families. To be truthful, most people confuse procedures with policy. A policy provides broad, philosophical guidelines, and procedures specify how to implement the policy and the steps necessary for the attainment of stated or inferred objectives.

Public policy is much more comprehensive, encompassing politics, scientific research, and analysis. Thus, policy is more than execution of procedures. Definitions of the public policy approach are numerous. Heclo defines policy as ". . . a course of action intended to accomplish some end" (1972). Eulau and Prewitt define policy as a "standing decision characterized by behavioral consistency and repetitiveness on the part of both those who make it [policy] and those who abide by it" (1973). Yet another definition of policy is "a standing plan that furnishes broad, general guidelines for channeling management thinking toward taking action consistent with reaching organizational objectives" (Certo, 1986). The above definitions, while not all-encompassing, capture the essence of policy from both a macro and a micro level. However, they shed little light on how the United States has arrived at the point where gangs battle each other and the police for control of our inner cities, our prison population and our probation caseloads are unmanageable, and we are unable to agree upon a course of action.

The scope of government action seems to expand or contract based upon changes in attitudes and the impact of events. Some people think the government ought to back off, others think government ought to continue what it is doing and still others think the government ought to increase its scope of action. Hence, the range of what is legitimate for government action steadily expanded (Wilson, 1992), at least until the 104th Congress took office. The process can be referred to as "disjointed incrementalism." In meeting the need to overcome social ills, the process ". . . is also better described as moving away from social ills rather than as moving toward a known and relatively stable goal" (Braybrook and Lindblom, 1963).

The actions of Congress and preferences of members of Congress and the state legislatures leads me to propose a list of "realities" (inspired by Charles O. Jones, 1977) that must be reckoned with when considering any kind of crime legislation.

Events and social issues are interpreted by different people in different ways.

People have varying degrees of access to government.

Not all crime is acted upon by government.

Most crime problems are not solved by government.

Policy makers hesitate to face a real decision.

Government emphasizes remedies, not solutions to problems.

Most decisions involving crime are based upon feelings rather than information.

Crime legislation is based upon symbolic consensus of what to do, rather than a real objective, analytical attack on the problem.

Public problems and demands are constantly being refined and redefined. The public is directionless leaving the issue open to the influence of special interests who are concerned only with their self-interests and not the elimination of crime.

Much legislation is discussed and passed without the problem being adequately defined.

These "realities" suggest a closed decision-making system that is often unresponsive to public need with the policy maker often- times in the position of defining what that need is. In the case of crime, poor people are the most victimized group. Since they have no access to government, or at least very little, little attention was paid initially to the problem of crime. As incidents of reported crime became more widespread in the media and as more and more members of the middle-class began to see their interests threatened, members of Congress and the State Legislatures began to take notice.

The key lies in getting the problem to government. A policy problem exists if there is a situation in which there is dissatisfaction on the part of people for whom some sort of relief or redress is sought. Thus, such matters as crime, smog, automobile safety, and health may become policy problems if there is enough dissatisfaction on the part of a public. During the last two decades crime and gangs were increasingly brought to the attention of the public by the media, and while crime no longer tops the list of concerns to the public, there is still the attitude among members of the general public that demands instant action on issues of crime.

Anderson (1990) points out that there are two kinds of agenda: systemic agenda and institutional agenda. The systemic agenda is basically discursive and consists of issues that are commonly perceived by members of the political community as meriting public attention. An institutional agenda consists of those problems to which "legislators and public officials feel obligated to give serious and active attention" (1990). Crime falls into the arena of institutional agenda, but there is a problem. When calling an issue to the attention of government, the segment of the population that is underrepresented is unlikely to get their issue on the agenda. Thus, the poor, families on welfare of one sort or another, parents of gang members, and others who are victimized to one extent or another will have their pleas fall on deaf ears and must rely upon others to define the problem for them and devise a solution. Thus, it is up to concerned, influential members of the community to assure that the issue of crime is kept on the institutional agenda.

Admission to an institutional agenda is controlled by a "gatekeeper" such as legislative leaders who decide what is important and also what is potentially solvable. Thus, those issues that are deemed unsolvable or apt to use up scarce legislative time are kept off the agenda. On occasion, a particular legislator will take the lead in adopting an issue for a variety of reasons, and force it on the agenda. In regard to crime and gangs, over the past five years the reader will note from Appendix 8.1 that several pieces of legislation have been proposed over the past decade, but nearly all have died in committee. In addition, most are repressive in nature and proposed little other than to increase sanctions against criminal activity. Clearly, the way to get the issue of crime and acceptable solutions to government is by organized and persuasive action by grass roots groups interested in the welfare of the community.

A Framework for the Analysis of Crime Policy

Charles O. Jones (1977) suggests a workable framework for the analysis of policy that contains five dimensions: formulation, legitimation. appropriation, implementation, and evaluation. Armed with this knowledge, the average taxpayer may better understand the relative impotence of government in dealing with the problem of crime. The role of power, personal prejudices, and the propensity of the legislators to protect the interests of special groups who have access to government are clearly evident.

In any discussion of legislation and policy it is important to use a framework because it provides a ready frame of reference in which to view successes and failures. We take a snapshot so to speak and analyze the content at that moment, hoping to derive knowledge, draw conclusions, and plot our direction for further policy action. Direction is important, and unless we gain our bearings from a map of sorts, significant parts of the process might be missed, or one might miss opportunities or stumble upon unexpected problems. Thus a road map provides us with the ability to deal with issues that are not covered by social science theory and when combined with practical experience, allows us to analyze policy and suggest ways to improve the process and the probability of success.

A case in point is the creation of the Law Enforcement Assistance Administration (LEAA) in 1968 and its directive to assist law enforcement agencies in their pursuit of crime reduction. The LEAA was responsible for the administration of the federal Block Grant Program which funneled funds to local agencies. Under LEAA guidance State Planning Agencies (SPA's) were established to prepare plans for the coordination and pooling of activities within each state criminal justice system. The assumption was that the SPA would rationally and fairly distribute funds throughout the state. This seems to be much the thinking of present day congressmen in their push for "local" control of crime fighting funds provided by the 1994 Omnibus Crime bill. The reality was that state plans were reduced to drudgery and the SPA's were overloaded with representatives of the police, resulting in state plans becoming nothing more than hardware wish lists for chiefs of police (Task Force, 1976).

Thus, the problem of over-representation of law enforcement in the implementation of the LEAA objectives was the result of special interest groups gaining the ear of policy makers and the media creating a crisis mentality. Formulation was also influenced by legislators not defining the problem properly and proceeding from faulty assumptions. Likewise, one of the problems in the formulation of the 1994 Omnibus Crime bill was faulty definition of the problem and special interest groups gaining the ear of federal legislators.

Formulation

The average citizen who wants to get involved in governmental action usually storms ahead without much thought to how one attains action on a given issue. Legislation and policy are entities that have a process and if one knows the process, there is a considerably increased chance of success. Formulation, the first of the five dimensions proposed by Jones (1977), means the creation of a formula or a solution to a problem. What has happened has happened. Crime is a reality and very little of a long term nature has been done to meet the problem.

The formulation phase is the first step in acting on a problem and the phase in which means are proposed to resolve the problem. It involves recognizing the problem, or opportunity, and then dealing with several ill-defined and inappropriate solutions. It also includes determining risks and costs, as well as the benefits associated with each solution. Finally, it includes selection of a solution. This is the most political phase of the process and is subject to a great deal of negotiation and compromise. Non-decisions are always possible and even preferable in cases where legislators or policy makers determine that the risks outweigh the benefits, particularly if the problem is an especially vexing one such as gun control.

Jones (1977) proposes several guidelines to assist us in reviewing the formulation stage of policy development:

* Formulation does not need to be limited to one group of actors.
  In fact there may be two or more groups with competing proposals.

* Formulation may proceed without a clear definition of the problem
  or without the formulators having much contact with the target
  group(s).

* Formulation and reformulation may occur over a long time without
  sufficient support for any one proposal.

* For those who lose in the formulation process, there are often several appeal points along the way.

* The process is never neutral.

Agencies also develop and implement policy. They will often identify a need and formulate and implement a policy on specific issues that are believed to fall within the particular agencies' areas of responsibility. For example, the FBI's recent Safe Streets Program is an example of agency policy by which they have moved some resources from espionage to the suppression of gangs. This reallocation of resources has been a welcome addition to the sometimes meager resources at the disposal of local gang units.

Congressmen or Senators involved in the legislative process rely upon an information network made up of legislative actors, i.e., staff, the Congressional Research Office, and groups outside of government with access to government and who influence policy decisions. Other groups outside of government who influence policy decisions relative to crime include the National Rifle Association, MADD, the International Association of Chiefs of Police, and the American Correctional Association. The American Society of Criminology has recently attempted to influence policy by providing knowledgeable experts for congressional testimony, but it appears that, in many instances, empirical knowledge only interferes with preconceived notions of crime causation and control.

In government creative formulation is rare. There have been instances of creative formulation, and perhaps the best known and the most innovative instance in criminal justice is the Omnibus Crime Control Bill and Safe Streets Act of 1968. However, even that piece of legislation was clouded by events of the time. The Act was passed in the wake of the assassinations of President Kennedy, Martin Luther King, and Senator Robert Kennedy. Against the background of riots in the major cities, campus disturbances against the Vietnam War, and civil rights demonstrations, the Republicans were calling for anti-crime legislation, and law and order were becoming buzz words of the political right.

The Newark, New Jersey, disorders ended on the day the original House bill was reported out by the Judiciary Committee. A bloody riot in Detroit in which 43 persons were killed brought on a curfew that was lifted the day debate in the House began. The House accepted the Senate version of the bill the day after the assassination of Robert Kennedy in Los Angeles...(Task Force, 41).

Thus, it is unclear whether Congress was voting against lawlessness or for safe streets or to improve the criminal justice system (Task Force, 1976). Nevertheless, the Act had several features that were innovative and attempted to fight crime in unique ways such as calling for standardization and planning as well as providing educational opportunities for those employed in, or planning a career in, law enforcement or corrections. Many of these innovations were included in the recent 1994 Crime Bill.

The formulation phase of policy making is the only phase where the policy maker must look forward and backward at the same time. He or she must look forward to the implementation phase in order to assure that the program specified in the legislation is viable. It is also important that the formulator look backward in order to judge future needs and for a reference point to guide ones self when negotiating the shoals of special interests.

As social systems increase in complexity, more and more externalities arise that can pose serious problems for the policy formulator (Brewer and deLeon, 1983). Externalities can take the form of economic factors such as unemployment and recessions. They also take the form of changing values and demographic shifts. In the case of crime and the public's concern with crime, the media play an important role in determining what shall be brought to the government for placement on the agenda. The notoriety of issues and the role of the media are important in the legitimation of an issue and whether or not the problem is placed on the agenda. Widely publicized events that allow the media to label a problem a "crisis" often spur a demand for action. The involvement of gangs in the drug trade and the resultant violence and related problems caused by abusers to obtain funds for the purchase of drugs also play into the hands of reporters and often result in a crisis mentality.

Another example includes the federalization of car jacking. Subsequent to the brutal murder of a young mother in Maryland by two young thugs, Congress took up car-jacking, which is essentially a local concern and made it a federal crime. Thus, they were able to demonstrate that they were serious about getting tough on crime. In short, the media's ability to create impressions (often distant from the truth) is related to the rule of thumb "if it bleeds, it leads." In turn, this leads to assumptions on the part of the public, which in turn leads to demands by the public for action on the "problem."

There are two forms of legitimation. The first, which will be called legitimacy, authorizes the basic political processes to solve the problem at hand.

The second, which we will call legitimation, includes the specific processes by which government programs are authorized (Jones, 1977). Legitimacy is important in that it involves the authority, consent, and obligation of the government to solve a problem. Legitimacy is important in legislation purporting to deal with crime because it may be viewed as meeting the needs of only a small segment of the public. We cannot ignore the importance of legitimacy in any instance of legislation, for to do so in any analysis would be to ignore the relevance of Congress and other legislators in the fight against crime.

Legitimation is important in that it is necessary in order to approve specific proposals. That is, within specific decision-making processes one person, or one group has the last word. Each person or group will be aware of the established means for officials of the various publics to perceive each decision and how it will be acceptable to the various significant publics (Jones, 1977). The legislature is commonly accepted as representing the people, thus conferring legitimation on approved programs. But other interests sometimes prevail: bureaucrats, lobbyists, and state and local officials for example. The president, or the Governor in the instance of state legislation, also plays a role in legitimation in that his, or her, approval is necessary before a bill can become law.

In 1968 legitimation of the Omnibus Crime Control Bill and Safe Streets Act occurred before formulation in some respects, but on the other hand it nearly suffered a pocket veto because President Johnson did not like the "potentially dangerous" wiretapping section which he believed "might intrude on the right to privacy of ordinary citizens." As a consequence he held off until the last day to sign the bill into law (Task Force).

The diversity of publics that Congress attempts to address has resulted in what Theodore Lowi believes is a paradox (1979). In 1968 the conditions that existed in our nation's cities and on many campuses forced many legislators to conclude that a stronger approach to crime had to be devised. Many voices contributed to the debate on the approach to be taken. However, Attorney General Clark alienated many members of Congress by his view of needed reforms in the criminal justice system. Many officials at the state level were fearful that LEAA money would be controlled by "local people" who did not bow to state house concerns. As a result, the Cahill Amendment was added to the legislation to prevent local individuals, over whom the governor had no control, from gaining access to distribution of LEAA funds. Finally, Congress added some anti-riot provisions to the bill that allowed top priority in grant requests for riot control equipment to be funded through the Justice Department even before the bill was passed and without going through the state planning agency.

To illustrate further the politics of legitimation, Theodore Lowi (1979) points out that in an effort to respond to everyone and their demands and the almost total democratization of the Constitution, there has arisen a paradox. Not only has there been a rise in public distrust with every addition of a federal program, but "it is as if each new program or program expansion [has] been an admission of prior governmental inadequacy or failure without itself being able to make any significant contributions to order and well being" (1979). And so it is in regard to crime.

The failure of the federal government to act on street crime and youth gangs is evidence that legislators are aware that previous economic policies, various crime control bills , and sundry social programs have failed and that to act in any manner other than symbolically is an admission of failure and insensitivity toward the systemic causes of crime. And yet, government keeps adding more and more of the same policies to the waste basket of failed legislation. Government today is not equipped to say no to any interest. Whether the tried and tested policy succeeds or fails is irrelevant. The failure of government to say no has led to a government that cannot succeed at anything. Therefore, it must say yes to all, hoping that some of its policies will work. It is up to responsible, informed citizens to point out that they are aware of their inability to act and to point the way with sound ideas and informed ideas on programs that will work in their particular jurisdiction.

Legislative Response: Real or Symbolic?

The manner in which incumbents treat problem issues is important for their re-election. It is important for the incumbent to at least appear to be interested in national and local issues even though he or she can do nothing about them. The issue of abortion is illustrative of symbolic interest in an issue. Many would-be Representatives and U.S. Senators have included a plank in their platform promising action that would further either pro-choice or right-to-life interests when they know it is an issue that cannot and should not be settled at the federal level or likely to be resolved in the near future.

In addition to the symbolic efforts at lawmaking, Senators and Congressional Representatives serve on a variety of Senate and House

Committees and thus serve a valuable purpose in the management of Congressional and national affairs. However, the system has evolved to the point that it is important for a Senator or Representative to serve on the "right" committee in order to be better able to get his or her proposed legislation into committee, approved by that committee and back to the floor for action. Thus the importance of coalition or majority building.

Majority building in the U.S. Congress is difficult because the legislative process in the United States Congress is one of the most difficult in the world, and legislators perform policy roles other than as legitimators (Jones, 1977). We also need to consider the fact that legislators may need to construct several coalitions in order to get proposed legislation approved. As a consequence there are several points along the way for proposed legislation to be struck down.

Since 1981, eighteen pieces of legislation have been proposed that were intended to address the issue of crime or street gangs. There are several items on the list that hint at coalition building. For example, two Senators each propose a bill to fight crime in some way. One will vote for the others crime bill and the other will vote for the second Senator's bill on another matter. All proposals in Appendix 8.1 have been proposed since 1988 and with six exceptions, all died in committee. A critical review of Appendix 8.1 reveals coalition building in action and perhaps illustrates agreements for various legislators to serve as co-sponsors for legislation while at the same time going on record as being tough on crime or gangs and the like.

In examining the committee membership of the legislators who proposed crime and gang legislation since 1988, it becomes clear that they either had other priorities or did not put together the necessary coalition to get their proposed legislation approved. In all fairness, nearly everyone recognizes that members of Congress are busy people and must balance competing demands. A further examination of committee membership through the 105rd Congress reveals that sincere efforts of legislators has been rather spotty. Interestingly, of members of the House of Representatives who proposed legislation up to the present Congress, none serve on committees to which the legislation was referred.

The reactive nature of the U.S. Congress can be seen in the types of legislation proposed in both Houses of Congress. Thirteen out of the twenty pieces of proposed legislation are suppressive in nature, calling for measures ranging from more police to expanded use of the death penalty. In addition, there are repeated calls for amending the use of Habeas corpus and the exclusionary rule.

Clearly, law enforcement needs adequate tools and resources to get the job done, but failure to recognize that systemic issues remain unresolved is just short of incomprehensible. For example, the 1988 re-authorization of the Juvenile Justice and Delinquency Prevention Act of 1974 funds $25 million each year for grants to be let by the U.S. Department of Justice. Considering the magnitude of the problem, it amounts to a drop in the bucket.

Within the last decade, federal assistance for local law enforcement has realized some support. Five omnibus crime control bills were passed during the last decade and a half (Cavanagh, 1993):

> The Comprehensive Crime Control Act of 1984 (P.L. 98-473) revised the federal sentencing system and bail and forfeiture procedures.
>
> The Anti-Drug Abuse Act of 1986 (P.L. 99-570).
>
> The Anti-Drug-Abuse Act of 1988 (P.L. 100-690) included enhanced penalties for drug- related crimes and provided funding for State and local drug enforcement .
>
> The Crime Control Act of 1990 (P.L. 101-647) authorized $900 million for the Federal Drug Control Grant Program, codified a Victim's Bill of Rights within the Federal justice system, and expanded coverage under the Public Safety Officer's Death Benefits Program.

The 1994 Crime Bill is the latest attempt to confront crime. On January 21, 1993, Senator Hatch introduced an omnibus bill (S.8) on behalf of the Republicans. A Democratic measure was also introduced and the Congressional process went to work. Finally, the 1994 Crime Bill was passed by both houses of Congress and signed into law by President Clinton on September 13, 1994. Provisions of the bill include:

* Funding for 100,000 new police officers

* Fifteen high crime cities will share $895 million for intensive community services which will serve as models for new crime-prevention programs.

* Money for at-risk youth programs at school and after school. This provision includes the mid-night basketball program.

* $1.6 Billion for Local Partnership Act grants aimed toward areas with high unemployment and poverty rates. Communities will be encouraged to use the money for job training, education, and drug treatment.

* First-time non-violent drug offenders will be allowed to serve less than the minimum 5-year term .

* Drug-addicted defendants will be allowed to be diverted into state treatment programs and $383 million allocated for drug treatment.

The 104th Congress attempted to change the 1994 Omnibus Crime Bill and many members criticized it as soft on crime. They pointed out that "They passed a $30 billion bill that will fight crime with weakened justice provisions, federally dictated midnight basketball, arts and crafts." That statement hardly dignifies the efforts of corrections workers and dedicated social workers across the nation. Arts and crafts have never been passed off as a program to rehabilitate offenders. It may have been used in the past to occupy the time of elementary age children who are at risk, but are at risk children to be thrown away?

We have already discussed the fact that keeping a man or woman in prison may incapacitate that individual for a period of time, but when he or she is released, the path back to prison is easy enough to find even if the individual had access to intervention programs. Therefore, it makes good management sense to make the most of a situation in which we attempt to maximize opportunities to keep people out of prison. Once they are in prison, it is wise to do what we can to keep interested and motivated inmates from coming back to prison.

The United States Congress and the 50 state legislatures have been neglectful in two ways. First, they have focused upon repressive measures and largely ignored measures that approach crime control with a more fundamental logic. Secondly, and perhaps most importantly, Congress and the various state legislatures have ignored systemic issues that have given impetus to crime and the conditions that nurture the hopelessness and sense of despair that are at the root of much street crime. Several authors (see for example, Currie, 1993; Huff, 1991, 1993; Jackson, 1992) imply that good crime control legislation may be that which takes a two pronged approach: use of police and sound law enforcement principles, and measures that offer a future with hope and the possibility of meaningful employment.

The policy formulation process in the U.S. Congress and the state legislatures are flawed for two reasons. First, those who define the problem do not often have first hand experience with the problem of crime and rely upon other members of the legislative network for information who themselves may have no experience with crime. Secondly, in drafting solutions to the problem of crime, the thoughts of police officers and lawyers appear to be considered almost to the exclusion of others who may have valuable input for the formulators. Those with valuable input should include academics such as economists, criminologists, sociologists, educators and social workers. In addition, representatives of business, industry and organized labor should be included. The solution should reflect that the problem of crime is not a problem with only one face. Rather it is multi-faceted with many implications for the future.

It is not that Congress or the legislature has neglected the issue of crime; they have addressed those issues. It is not that our elected representatives have been sitting on their hands and doing nothing. The problem is that they have been quite busy doing the wrong things and looking for solutions in the wrong places. The formulation of policy in regard to crime has flowed from a need to suppress rather than an understanding that our present crime problem exists for reasons that are more clearly understood when one views the economic and social events of the last thirty years. In fact, Gary LaFree (1998) points out that crime in the United States since WWII is the result of a drastic changes in social institutions that promoted conformity of behavior.

The focus on repressive measures must be rethought. There have been a number of programs begun via grants let by the National Institute of Justice and the Office of Juvenile Justice and Delinquency Prevention. There are examples of private and local efforts to fight crime all over the nation. Perhaps a number of them hold promise in turning young people away from crime. However, while all contributions count, it will take much more than a few grants or a few thoughtful and concerned people to meet the challenge.

Certainly we need to address the needs of law enforcement and we need to prosecute violent criminals to the fullest extent of the law. However, Congress can address other more meaningful issues that will ultimately push citizens into the middle class and allow them to have a stake in the future of their community and nation. Many families left behind by the economic revolution of the 1970's and 80's are ill-equipped to make the necessary changes to fit into the new economy. Many public school jurisdictions, whose resources are meager at best, experience an unacceptably high dropout rate. For young people with a high school education, there are now fewer opportunities to pursue because of a lack of training or entry level jobs that lead to employment that will sustain a family.

Employment rates and involvement in crime are tenuously linked at best (Freeman, 1983). However, employment may serve as a buffer to continued involvement in crime and, perhaps more importantly, involvement in senseless violent crime. For example, Whyte (1981) notes that as gang youth age they begin to think of family and marriage. In the past gangs made space for the member to hold a job and maintain a family. The opportunity existed for the member to secure employment and pursue other interests outside of the gang, resulting perhaps in a measure of social stability and the presence of acceptable role models for lower class youth.

In order for Congress to effectively have an impact on the problem of street crime, they must put partisan politics behind them and work together. They must be unafraid to say no to certain interest groups and be prepared to act in the best interests of the nation and our citizens whose lives are at risk physically, socially, and economically. In the formulation of crime policy and legislation our elected representatives must shed their normal timidity and exhibit a degree of boldness.

When the U. S. Congress and the state legislatures determine that it is time to act decisively upon the problem of street crime, they must get help in defining the problem. As was learned from the example of the LEAA, the over-representation of law enforcement on the various State Planning Agencies resulted in a bias toward police hardware and programs. The issue of crime is too important and multi-dimensional to allow us to conceive of the problem only in terms of suppression. Congress must solicit the advice of experts in fields other than law enforcement and a blue ribbon commission should be established to examine solutions, much like the President's Commission on Law Enforcement and the Administration of Justice created by President Lyndon Johnson. The recommendations of the Commission must be given credence in Congressional deliberations and legislative initiatives.

On to the Future

The following areas must be given priority in any U.S. Congressional legislation or state legislation purporting to deal with crime:

Law enforcement activities - Passage of the 1994 Omnibus Crime Control bill was a positive step towards the future. However, as with much crime legislation, few congressional members acted upon fact. Rather, ideology guided the discussion and political infighting and deliberate misinformation contributed to a confused public. All in all Congress is to be commended for their efforts and the responsibility has now shifted to the states. The Crime Bill allows individual states to use allocated money for diversion programs and other efforts to keep law breakers out of prison. Therefore, the individual states must make an effort to determine what works and does not work.

Enhancing economic opportunity - Clearly no issue is more important than the opportunity for all citizens to obtain meaningful work and to have a chance to achieve a piece of *the American Dream*. Work is important for it gives meaning to life. It provides a rhythm to one's existence that is necessary if one is to feel worthwhile. There is no evidence to support the notion that holding a job will prevent someone with a character defect from committing a crime. Quite the contrary, there are many persons in prison who committed their crime while holding full-time employment.

What is important is that jobs must be available for young people to step into when they decide to enter the labor force. For many areas of our country, that option is remote at best. Thus, as young men and women age and begin to think of family and marriage, they must have the opportunity to secure employment and support a family.

A large and stable middle class is the key to our way of life. If young people do not believe that they have a stake in their community, they will not contribute to it's growth. In spite of the prosperity of the past decade the middle class has been barely unable to keep up with the previous years purchasing power been shrinking and the working class and middle class are frightened. It is imperative that we do all we can to preserve the middle class and give a hand to those trying to move into the middle class in order that they have a stake in our democracy.

We can begin that process by devoting adequate funds to the task of training youth for a place in the work force. No other country in the industrialized world devotes so little spending for employment and training. During the 1980's public spending for job training dropped to 0.6 per cent of our gross national product and that has not changed in the past decade (Currie, 1993, see also for example, Huff 1990, and Jackson, 1992). The link between employment and crime is tenuous, but in regard to youth having an idea of their place in society and some hope for the future, employment plays a large part. Partnerships between education, government, private enterprise, and organized labor can provide not only the money, but also the opportunity for youth to begin work careers under the watchful tutelage of journeymen tradesmen and other employees.

The government should not be an employer of last resort. The economy of the United States is strong enough to provide jobs for all our citizens. However, Job Corp is an excellent example of a program that enhances opportunities for at-risk youth. Few employers want to take time with young people who are short on social skills and have no clue as to proper etiquette in the work place, let alone few or no work skills as currency in the job market. One can make a good argument that training opportunities are much cheaper than prison and perhaps money spent on the youth will preclude money spent on trying to mend the adult.

Currently there are over 41,500 beds available at 110 sites throughout the United States. Job Corps students receive life skills training, social skills training, academic training and vocational training to enhance their employability and probability of access to legitimate opportunities after graduation. At present it costs a little more than $22,000 per year to train each student, less than an average year in prison. Recent Job Corp research indicates that 70% of discharged youth are employed within six months of discharge. Clearly, Job Corp is a bargain considering that prison inmates spend years in prison and a stint with Job Corp is for a few months. With the availability of closed military bases, the opportunity exists to turn several more of them into training bases for willing, motivated youth, rather than prisons.

Encourage the Heart. For too long we have been exposed to the negative rhetoric of politicians and the media. We have been bombarded with the impression and opinion that Americans live in a dangerous and threatening environment, we hear that we are overtaxed, overburdened, and that our culture is nearly overwhelmed. Conveniently overlooked is the fact that we as a people are generous, hard working, capable, trusting, and willing to give a person a break. It is time that our elected officials begin to tell the truth about the scope and extent of crime in America. It is time for elected officials and the media to play up the positive qualities of the American people and begin to lead instead of following special interest groups and personal aggrandizement or pursuing only the bottom line.

Build the Family. Finally, if we are to be successful in our efforts to stem the growth of crime, we must strengthen the family. However, there are two sides to this equation. If the juvenile court is obligated to assist parents during difficult times with children, then parents must accept accountability for the behavior of their children. Many states have statutes on the books that allow the judge to fine, jail or otherwise sanction lazy or careless parents for the delinquent behavior of children. These statutes can be utilized more fully and, if so, we may see fewer unsupervised children on the streets in the evening and perhaps an increase in school attendance.

Today too many children live in single parent families, live under the poverty line, and have too few positive role models to emulate. We are guilty of putting children behind our own selfish wants and throwing such abstracts as duty and obligation out the window. It is important that young people have responsible adults around to supervise activities and to administer loving discipline when needed.

In this regard, our spiritual communities have hardly been leaders. Churches, synagogues, and mosques can be most effective in our challenge to take back our streets and families and prayer alone will not work. Prayer, leadership, and decisive action at the neighborhood level will, however, accomplish much. Instead of great sums of money given to overseas missionary work, money should be given to local missionaries that work with youth and families in the neighborhoods. Programs that address parenting, marital relationships, divorce, and the needs of latch-key children should be conducted in the evenings and on weekends in unused religious facilities. Such programs not only glorify God, they also uplift the family and present unlimited opportunities for community ministry. However, even if divorces stopped immediately and all children were to be born into an intact family starting tomorrow we would not see measurable results for some time. Therefore we must be ready to pursue a goal of decreased crime sometime in the future, hopefully for our children and grandchildren.

Become Involved in Your Community. Many people want to be involved more in their community, but feel that they lack the time. Look at it another way. If we are not involved, what are the consequences. There are citizen involvement groups everywhere: PTO, Scouts, Big Brother/Big Sister, church or synagogue, sports leagues for children, police reserve units, Neighborhood Watch programs, and so on. The list is nearly endless. We must begin to put community first instead of ourselves.

Finally this chapter has provided a framework for citizen involvement in the formulation and reformulation of crime policy and legislation. This text has provided the tools necessary for the identification of lies and misstatements on the part of people seeking election to public office. If candidates running for office cannot represent the truth in seeking an office, can we trust them to effectively carry out the responsibilities of the office if elected? If they spend an inordinate amount of time attacking each other on ideological grounds instead of attacking issues of real importance to the family, can we trust them to honestly pursue honest solutions?

A Final Word

We are not in danger of being over run by barbarians at the gate. Nevertheless, there are young people at risk in our society that deserve a chance at success and there are adults who prey upon the weak, the gullible, and the vulnerable. We will never eradicate crime for it appears to be an integral part of the human condition. However, we can pursue action that looks to the future and is positive in nature rather than pessimistic and regressive.

None of the suggestions offered in this book offer a quick fix. Any effort to control crime must be sustained over a long period of time and we need to be prepared for failures in the short term. However, it is time to question our present course of action. If the federal and state governments fail to pursue policies that are favorable to families, sustained employment on the part of those at the bottom of the economic heap, and provide proper incentives to business to locate in areas that need jobs and discourage the loss of smokestack type of jobs, all the suppression and rehabilitation programs in the world will not get us out of this fix.

Not all of our younger citizens want to go to college, but they do want a future. That future must include training geared to the demands of the 21st century, the opportunity to obtain meaningful employment, and employers who have the incentive to invest in the future by building plants, updating old equipment, maintaining loyalty to employees and pursuing an aggressive research and development program. We do not live in a vacuum unconcerned with what is happening in other parts of our community or country. Likewise, policies are not implemented in a vacuum. When we consider implementing one policy, we must consider the impact on other existing policies and the unanticipated consequences of change.

The public demands that action be taken now to build a future that is relatively safe. We need to avoid the urge for a quick fix and look to the long term in order to effectively fight crime. Elected officials must seize the moment and get to work on that future.

Ten Ways to Decrease Crime

There are ways we can assure that the crime rate will continue to decline. I propose the following top ten list as a guide to families and concerned citizens. They are not new ideas, but deserve mentioning because they get at the heart of what is important to the future of America. In reverse order:

10. Support police efforts to implement community policing.

9. Support community programs that keep unsophisticated and first time offenders out of prison and in rehabilitation programs. This includes drug users.

8. Support efforts to bring family sustaining jobs to your area. Insist on cooperation between government, industry, labor, and financial institutions.

7. Encourage involvement of children in positive school and community activities. This includes a focus on completion of home work and pursuit of excellence in school.

6. Be aware of what is going on in your community and hold elected officials accountable. Do not rely exclusively on the media for information about what is going on.

5. Be generous with encouragement and praise of children.

4. Support public education as it is an investment for the future.

3. Be fair and consistent in discipline of children.

2. Do not be afraid to say no to children, including teenagers.

1. Parents must set a good example of responsible citizenship including effective supervision of children, especially Jr. High and High School age children.

Notes

1. These "realities" are inspired by Charles O. Jones list of "initial Realities," in <u>An Introduction to the Study of Public Policy</u>, 2nd. ed.. (North Scituate, Mass.: Duxbury Press, 1977).

Bibliography

James E. Anderson. **Public Policymaking: An Introduction.** (Boston: Houghton Mifflin Company, 1990).

Garry D. Brewer and Peter deLeon. **Foundations of Policy Analysis.** (Pacific Grove, Ca.: Brooks/Cole Publishing Company, 1983).

Bureau of the Census. **1987 Census of Manufactures.** (Washington, D.C.: U.S. Government Printing Office, 1987).

Suzanne Cavanagh. **Crime Control: The Federal Response.** (Washington, D. C.: Congressional Research Service, Updated, April 29, 1993).

Suzanne Cavanagh and David Teasley. **Youth Gangs: An Overview.** (Washington, D.C.: Congressional Research Service, June 9, 1992)

Center for Disease Control. "Weapon-Carrying Among High School Students, 1990." **Morbidity and Mortality Weekly Report,** October 11, 1991.

Samuel C. Certo. **Principles of Modern Management,** 3rd ed.. (Dubuque, Iowa: Wm. C. Brown, Publishers, 1986). pp. 147.

Heinz Eulau and Kenneth Prewitt, **Labyrinths of Democracy.** (Indianapolis: Bobbs-Merrill, 1973) in Charles O. Jones. An Introduction to the Study of **Public Policy,** 2nd ed..(North Scituate, Mass.: Duxbury Press, 1977). p. 5.

Richard B. Freeman. "Crime and Unemployment," in James Q. Wilson. **Crime and Public Policy.** (San Francisco: ICS Press, 1983). pp. 89-106.

H. Hugh Heclo. "Review Article: Policy Analysis." **British Journal of Political Science.** Vol. 2 (January 1972). pp. 84-85.

Pamela Irving Jackson. "Crime, Youth Gangs, and Urban Transition: The Social Dislocations of Postindustrial Economic Development." **Justice Quarterly.** 8:3 (1991) pp. 379-397.

Charles O. Jones. **An Introduction to the Study of Public Policy,** 2nd ed.. (North Scituate, Mass.: Duxbury Press, 1977).

George W. Knox. **An Introduction to Gangs.** (Berrien Springs, MI.: Vande Vere Publishing Ltd. 1991).

Gary LaFree. **Losing Legitimacy: Street Crime and the Decline of Social Institutions in America.** Boulder, CO: Westview Press. 1998.

Theodore J. Lowi. **The End of Liberalism: The Second Republic of the United States,** 2nd. ed.. (New York: W.W. Norton and Company, 1979).

Twentieth Century Fund Task Force on the Law Enforcement Assistance Administration. **Law Enforcement: The Federal Role.** (New York: McGraw Hill Book Company, 1976).

James Q. Wilson. **American Government.** (Lexington, Mass.: D.C. Heath and Company, 1992).

Appendix 8.1

A Partial list of
Crime/Gang Legislation Proposed Since 1988

Sponsor	Title/Abstract	Action
Rep. Coats	A Bill to establish a clearinghouse of juvenile justice in the Office of Juvenile Justice and Delinquency Prevention.	10/20/88 Referred to House Sub-Committee on Human Resources and was included as part of Public Law 102-132.
Rep. Coats	A bill to provide a financial incentive to States to provide services to, and intensive supervision of, juveniles who are released after having been found to have committed acts in violation of State law that would have been crimes under such law if committed	10/20/88 Referred to House Sub-Committee on Human. Resources.Died in committee.
Sen. Bradley	A bill to amend the Juvenile Justice and Delinquency Prevention Act of 1974 to establish and support prevention and treatment programs relating to juvenile gangs	Read twice and referred to the Judiciary. Included into Public Law 102-132.
Sen. Nunn	A bill to provide for an omnibus Federal, State, and local effort against substance abuse, to provide for a cabinet-level position to centralize and streamline Federal activities with respect to both drug supply and drug demand. To expand Federal support to ensure a long term commitment of resources and personnel for substance abuse education, treatment, and rehabilitation efforts.	H.R.5210 passed in Senate.
Rep. J. Lewis	A bill to establish programs to strengthen America's families and for other special purposes.	Referred to Sub-Committee on Social Security, where it died.

Sen. Coats	A bill to establish programs to strengthen America's families, and other purposes.	5/18/89 Read twice and referred to the Committee on Finance. Died.
Sen Wirth	AMDT: To develop a coordinated policy in conjunction with State and local govn'ts to counteract youth gang involvement in distribution, sale and use of illegal drugs.	Died Committee.
Sen Kerry	AMDT: To improve the ability of States and localities impacted by narcotics related crime to monitor, track, and prosecute major narcotics offenders, money launderers, and youth gangs involved in narcotics trafficking and money laundering operations.	Died in Committee.
Rep. Torres	A bill to amend title 18, USC, to provide penalties for participation in street gangs and to provide additional penalties for felonies in furtherance of the activities of such gangs.	Died in Committee.
Sen Spector	A bill to implement a Federal crime control and Law Enforcement program and to assist states in crime control and L/E efforts	4/18/89 Referred to the Committee on the Judiciary where it died.
Rep. Goodling	A bill to extend authorizations of appropriations for certain youth programs under the Anti-Drug Abuse Act of 1988.	Died in Committee.
Rep. Martinez	Public Law 102-132 (10/18/91) A bill to authorize appropriations for drug abuse education and prevention programs relating to youth gangs and to runaway and homeless youth.	Floor action occurred.
Sen. Biden	A bill to establish a juvenile justice anti-gang program.	Died in Committee.
Rep. Michel	Restore an enforceable federal death penalty, curb abuse of Habeas Corpus, reform the exclusionary rule, combat violence involving firearms, protect witnesses, to address the problem of gang and serious juvenile offenders, and to curb child abuse.	Died in Committee.
Rep. Serrano	A bill to provide assistance to local educational agencies for the prevention and reduction of violent crime in elementary and secondary schools.	Died in Committee.

Rep. Kildee	Amend the Juvenile Justice and Delinquency Prevention Act of 1974 to provide assistance to achieve gang free schools and communities.	Died in Committee.
Rep. Schroeder	A bill to grant employees family and temporary medical leave, to treat the costs of the Head Start program and other programs for children as emergency funding requirements, to provide aid to parents in providing the best possible learning environment for children, to promote investments in child welfare and family preservation, to reduce violence and improve the safety of children and their families.	Died in Committee.
Rep. Waters	A bill to establish a program to provide grants to improve the quality and availability of compre -hensive education, health, and social services for at-risk youth and their families.	Died in Committee.
Sen. Diconcini	A bill to enhance the federal governments ability to eliminate violent crime committed by outlaw street and motorcycle gangs.	Died in Committee.
Sen. Biden	A bill to control and reduce violent crime	Floor action occurred.
Sen. Thurmond	A bill to restore an enforceable federal death penalty, to curb the abuse of habeas corpus, to reform the exclusionary rule, to combat criminal violence involving firearms, to protect witnesses and other participants in the criminal justice system from violence and intimidation, to address the problem of gangs and serious juvenile offenders, to combat terrorism, to combat sexual violence and child abuse, to provide for drug testing of offenders in the criminal justice process, to secure the right of victims and defendants to equal justice without regard to race or color, to enhance the rights of crime victims.	Floor action occurred.
Sen. Diconcini	A bill to enhance the Federal governments authority and ability to eliminate violent crime committed by outlaw gangs.	Died in Committee.
Sen. Simon	A bill to authorize grants to state, local, and private entities for programs to prevent youth from becoming involved in gangs.	Died in Committee.
Sen. Lautenberg	A bill to encourage the development of mentoring programs that link children in high crime areas with L/E Officers and other responsible adults.	Died in Committee.

Sen. Kennedy	AMDT: amend public health act to establish a program to provide grants to improve quality and availability of comprehensive education, health, and social services for at-risk youth and their families.	
Sen. Seymore	A bill to control and prevent criminal gang activity and violence.	Died in Committee.
Sen. Bradley	To establish sports mentoring and coaching programs in which athletes serve as role models for youth and to teach that athletics provide a positive alternative to drug and gang involvement.	Died in Committee.
Rep. Waters	A bill to provide grants to cities to establish teen resource and education centers to provide education, employment, recreation, social, and cultural awareness assistance to at-risk youth and their families.	Died in
Rep. C. Cox	A Bill to amend the Internal Revenue Code of 1986 to provide for the designation of turbo enterprise zones to assist areas of high unemployment and severe blight.	Died in Committee.
Rep. Schumer	Handgun Waiting Period. Known as the **Brady bill** requires gun buyers to wait five business days before purchasing a handgun.	HR 1025 passed 11/10/93 Senate cleared 11/24/93 signed by President 11/30/93
Sen. Biden	Omnibus Anti-Crime Bill. A bi-partisan $22.3 billion Senate bill would boost money for prison construction, expand death penalty, to dozens of new federal crimes, provide money 100,000 additional police officers, create an anti-crime "trust-fund" to fight crime House approved HR3355 on 8-26-94.	Senate amended and passed HR 3355 11/19/94. Signed into law by President Clinton, 12/94,
Sen. Abraham	Violent Juvenile and Repeat Offender Act. A bill to reduce violent juvenile crime, promote accountability by rehabilitation of juvenile criminals, punish and deter violent gang crime, and for other purposes	5/20/1999-- Passed Senate, Amended.

Gang Identifiers

Graffiti. A strong indication that gangs are forming, or have formed, in your area is the presence of certain kinds of graffiti found on the side of buildings, fences, sidewalks, street signs, bridges, anywhere a flat surface presents itself for the use of a can of spray paint. Initially, the graffiti will be found in less visible places in order to test the tolerance of the public. If no adverse reaction occurs, then the gangsters will be come more bold. When the graffiti is found on the front of buildings and in highly visible places, it is a sign that the gang, or gangs, are signifying to the public at large that it has particular control of that neighborhood. According to every gang expert, this is why it is important to remove or cover graffiti as soon as it becomes visible. It is important for community members to keep the upper hand and not allow gangs to set the tome of a neighborhood.

Many people see graffiti as a childish prank, but gang members see graffiti as a sort of newspaper. It announces territory, gang leaders, and to "put down" opposing gangs. Occasionally, graffiti is used to eulogize gang members killed in fights with police or opposing gangs.

If a community member observes graffiti in the community, and this graffiti is crossed out, it is an indication that more than one gang is active in that area. It is also an indication that the two gangs are ready to fight and often violence will follow. Most parents are interested in what to look for as indications of gang involvement. We must be mindful that often impressionable Jr. high school and high school age children will imitate that which they see around them such as wearing of certain team jackets or other "colors," but largely they are wholesome youth simply wanting to fit in. Still, the following may be indications of possible involvement in gang activities. [*]

1. Buying (or wanting you to buy) and excessive amount of Blues, Reds, Blacks, or Browns for their wardrobe.
2. Wearing their slacks or pants sagging down "too low" on their hips.
3. Wearing a lot of Gold and or silver jewelry. You need to ask how they obtained it.
4. Willing to get, have or wear only certain types and colors of shoes or shoe laces.
5. Using "Gang Slang" in their conversations with you or with others.
6. Withdrawing from family members and not wanting to be around the family (at least more than is usual for an adolescent).
7. Having troubles at school, such as: dropping grade point average, fighting, suspensions, skipping, carrying weapons at school, getting home late.
8. Associating with "undesirables," especially those wearing too much of the same "colors."

9. Not willing to tell you where, with whom, or what they will be doing when out of the house.
10. Not willing for you to meet their friends or give you information about them.
11. Staying out later than usual and breaking curfew frequently.
12. Desiring "too much" privacy, almost secretive.
13. Developing a "major attitude" with you, teachers, or others in authority. Can be physically aggressive or threatening.
14. Starting to use drugs, alcohol, tobacco, and/or having drug paraphernalia.
15. Using "hand signs" to friends.
16. Receiving and /or having money and material goods without your permission and cannot adequately explain where he or she obtained them.
17. Carrying or talking about weapons, beepers, cell phones, or drugs.
18. Getting tattoos on hands or arms (usually) that are gang symbols some of which are to follow.
19. Writing gang graffiti on school books, clothing and other places.
20. Saying he or she has been *Initiated, Blessed Into*, or *Is in a* gang. Also includes the child who wants to be in a gang or hangs around with other children who say they are in a gang.
21. Getting caught by police, and perhaps charged, with other youth in "Gang related activities."
22. Other people tell you that your child is involved with other youth who are in a gang.

If a parent finds out two or three or more of these identifies your child could be headed for trouble. Corrective action is important and help can be found by calling the police or juvenile court.

To follow are some examples of gang graffiti. They indicate mid-west gangs and their off-shoots to a large extent. West coast gangs such as the Crips and Bloods do not engage so heavily in graffiti. they do mark territory by the use of the set name followed by either Bloods or Crips, i.e. **4th Street Crips**, or **14th Street Bloods.** The term set refers to a particular group that run together and identify with the same gang, sort of a clique within a gang.

GLOSSARY OF TERMS

Adjudacatory Hearing. The trial in which the child is allowed to answer charges against him or her. The Disposition Hearing is held a few weeks later, in some cases the judge will go into the Disposition Hearing immediately after the Adjudacatory Hearing. Most often the Disposition Hearing is held after the Probation Department has had time to compete a pre-Hearing Report.

Arraignment. A hearing in which the identity of a defendant is established, he or she is informed of their rights, and the defendant is allowed to enter a plea of guilty or not guilty.

Anomie. A term coined by Emile Durkheim, a French sociologist meaning a state of normlessness.

Bail. Conditional release into the community pending a court hearing. The defendant must put up a sum of money to assure his or her appearance in court on an appointed date.

Community Policing. More of a philosophy than an approach which states that the police and members of the community can effectively maintain safety and security together.

Community Service. The opportunity for an offender to perform service in the community either as an alternative to a jail sentence or in conjunction with a jail sentence or probation.

Conditions of Probation. Rules of conduct imposed by the court when an individual is placed on probation. Violation of any of the rules is called a technical violation and may cause the probation to be revoked and the individual sent to prison for service of sentence.

Differential Association. A theory of criminal behavior conceived by Edwin Sutherland stating that criminal behavior is learned just like any other behavior through social interaction.

Discretion. The freedom to make decisions on the job. Criminal justice officials such as police and correctional officers have a good deal of discretion.

Deterrence. The theory that swift and harsh punishment will cause future potential law breakers from committing a crime.

Diversion. Any program that divert the offender away from the criminal justice system. It can occur at several points in the process, but usually before sentencing. Programs include: substance abuse, mental health programs, marital counseling, and so on.

Electronic Monitoring. Technology that allows an offender to submit to the wearing of an ankle or wrist bracelet that is tied in with a telephone terminal that constantly monitors the location of the offender.

Felony. A criminal offense punishable by more than one year in prison.

Gang. A group of individuals that get together regularly, identify with each other, affect common identifiers, and engage in criminal activity.

Goals/Means Disjunction. A term coined by Robert K. Merton pointing out that while we all are told to pursue certain socially acceptable goals, not everyone has the same access to the means to achieve those goals.

Grand Jury. A body of persons selected according to law and convened for the purpose of investigating whether or not sufficient evidence exists to require an individual to be brought to trial. Also convened to investigate criminal activity in general, the conduct of public agencies, and public officials.

Home Confinement. An alternative to jail or prison in which the offender is allowed to remain at home subject to certain restrictions and often monitored by electronic means.

Initial Hearing. The first appearance of a juvenile before a Referee to determine if a crime did occur, to make the child and parents aware of the charges against him or her, and to determine if the child should be held in detention pending a formal hearing or released to the care of parents.

Intensive Probation. A form of probation with increased contact between the probationer and probation officer. Often includes some form of electronic monitoring and increased drug surveillance through urinalysis.

Juvenile Court. A class of courts having original jurisdiction over persons statutorily defined as juveniles. Has jurisdiction over, neglected and delinquent children. First appeared in 1899 in Cook County, Illinois.

Juvenile Delinquency. Any crime committed by a person under the age of 17 or 18, depending upon state law.

Labeling. A school of thought pointing out that behavior exists along a continuum and that abnormal behavior is a product of those who witness the behavior. Further, being labeled restricts the social roles of the labeled individual and he or she will continue the behavior for a lack of acceptable alternatives.

Law and Order. A political euphemism for controlling the rabble and street crime without investigating environmental or white collar crime.

Minneapolis Domestic Violence Experiment. A program conducted in Minneapolis in which it was found that automatic arrest of perpetrators of domestic violence caused a significant decline in subsequent behaviors.

Misdemeanor. An offense punishable by less than one year, usually in a local facility such as the County Jail.

National Crime Victimization Survey (NCVS). Conducted by the Bureau of Census and samples the general population seeking information directly from victims of crime. Published annually.

Neighborhood Watch. A program established with the police in which residents act as extra eyes and ears for the police.

New Generation Jail. Jail design that calls for prisoners to be held in pods of 15-20 in which the officer(s) are in the pods with the prisoners and can be proactive in their supervision of the prisoners.

Pains of Imprisonment. Five deprivations associated with the inmate subculture in prison; deprivation of liberty, deprivation of goods and services, deprivation of heterosexual relationships, deprivation of autonomy, and deprivation of security.

Parole. The conditional release of a prisoner from prison subject to certain conditions and rules.

Policy. A standing plan that furnishes broad, general guidelines for channeling management thinking toward taking action consistent with reaching organizational objectives.

Preliminary Hearing. A proceeding before a judge in which the following must be decided: did a crime occur, did the crime occur in the jurisdiction of the court, and is there reasonable cause to believe the defendant committed the crime.

Presentence Investigation (Prehearing investigation in the case of juveniles). An investigation conducted by a probation agency at the order of a court. The report is used by the sentencing judge to assist him or her in determining sentence. The PSI is also valuable to prison or reform school authorities in making case management decisions in the institution.

Probation. Conditional freedom allowed an offender sentenced to a term in prison. The sentence is set aside and the individual is placed on probation subject to certain conditions.

Recognizance. From the Latin, to call to mind. A pledge by a defendant to refrain from certain behaviors and to appear at an appointed time and place.

Referral. In juvenile matters, the sending on of a complaint against a juvenile alleging delinquent behavior.

Rehabilitation. A correctional philosophy stating that inmates can be reformed through a number of programs designed to prepare them for re-entry into the community as law abiding citizens.

Restitution Center. Residential facility for small number of inmates (25-75 or more) who are placed in the facility for purposes of service of sentence. Inmates are allowed to enter the community for purposes of work or community service. Usually must reimburse victims or court for costs or fines.

Social Control Theory. A theory of criminal behavior coined by Travis Hirshi stating that juveniles become free to commit delinquent acts when their ties to the conventional social order are severed.

Status Offense. A crime committed by a juvenile that when committed by an adult would not be a crime, e.g., truancy.

Symbolic Assailant. In police work a form of perceptual short hand in which persons who use gestures, language and attire that the police have come to recognize as a prelude to violence.

Uniform Crime Report (UCR). Published annually by the FBI containing all reported crime and some analysis of the data.

Work Release Center. Residential facility for small number of inmates (25-150) who are allowed to enter the community each day for purposes of work or to seek work. Inmates subject to strict rules to control behavior and location to as great extent as possible. Restricted to inmates within 30-120 days of release from prison or jail. Usually reimburses holding authority for part of costs of room and board.

XYY Chromosome. A chromosome anomaly found in every 400-500 live male births. Researchers have concluded that it is linked to some abnormalities in the male population. The sample is too small to explain crime.

Author Index

Subject Index

CRIMINOLOGY STUDIES